PR. OF EFFECTIVE PRAYER

Wentworth Pike

PO Box 1047
129 Mobilization Dr.
Waynesboro, GA 30830, U.S.A.
Tel.: (706) 554-1594
E-mail: gabriel@omlit.om.org

Copyright 2002 by Wentworth Pike

First printing, 1983
Seventh printing, 2002

ISBN: 1-884543-65-0

Cover design: Paul Lewis

Impreso en Colombia
Printed in Colombia

This book is dedicated to Doloris,
my beloved wife and prayer partner,
who is still teaching me to trust the leading of the Spirit in our
hearts rather than the reasonings of my head
when we bring our petitions before the throne of grace.

A PERSONAL MESSAGE FROM the AUTHOR
ABOUT THIS
21ST CENTURY EDITION

Isn't God good? This edition of ***Principles of Effective Prayer*** is one of the great answers to prayer He has given to my wife Doloris and me. Let me tell you how He has guided its development into an easy-to-read book and is using it for His glory.

Years ago, perhaps 35, Lee turned from the papers he was grading for me and said, "Mr. Pike, I wish you would start a course on prayer". Just like that, right out of the blue!

"A what?" I asked.

"An elective course on prayer", he replied. "Oh, I know we study the whole Bible in Bible college, but I mean a workshop-type course. We have lectures all week, but we students have problems concerning prayer and we need to have someone to lead us into God's Word to dig out answers. What we need is not just a professor's theological ideas and not just our own notions - we need to come to grips with our problems and find out what God says about prayer." (At least, these comments are as near as I can remember Lee's words.)

"A course on prayer? I have never heard of such a thing", I spluttered. I was teaching too many subjects besides chairing a department, narrating a radio program, and doing all the other things I was involved in. In fact, I was so busy that I did not have time to pray like I knew I should, let alone teach a course on prayer. No, I was not the man for it. Furthermore, how could a teacher grade students on their prayer life? I suggested Lee take his request to the administration. Perhaps they could assign it to a veteran missionary - a *real* prayer warrior.

About fifteen years later, Alban Douglas and I were coming home from teaching Friday night extension courses in the city 85 miles away. It was the first time all week that we could relax. We exchanged stories of the Lord's blessings, how He had answered prayer for Alban and Anne in the Orient and for Doloris and me in Alaska. For some reason, I mentioned Lee's request. Alban was a veteran missionary with loads of experience. *He* was the one that should teach a course on prayer if anyone should.

"Wentworth, that boy was right", he declared. "We do need a course like that. And furthermore, you are the man for it. You should get busy right away, do your research and submit a course description to the Curriculum Review Committee."

That's how it all started. I had known when I started preaching as a youth that prayer was the absolute essential for a Spirit-anointed ministry and had made some sort of commitment. But I had never learned to say "No" to lesser things. Finally, the Lord impressed powerfully on my mind the silent words, If you are not the man for it, its time you changed. Many good books on prayer were in the Bible-college library. Some were devotional, some were biographical, some deep teaching about certain aspects of prayer. But I could not find one that covered the topics I wanted for a course on prayer. So I developed a syllabus and study questions that would send students to the Bible and to some of the biographies of prayer warriors and other library books.

The college did not have room in the curriculum, so we started a Sunday school class. I asked for a room to seat 30 people. That way if as many as 12 to 15 signed up, we could divide into two small discussion groups. The first Sunday, *160 people enrolled*! Community friends, college students, missionaries on Home Assignment. And more wanted in, so I taught it to 135 second semester. By then the college was asking for it as a regular elective course. The class averaged 60 students first semester of each year. The group discussions contributed to revisions of the syllabus every time it was taught.

After a few years, the Principal of the Bible College approached me. "Do you have that prayer syllabus about where you want it?" he asked.

"I don't know. The class is a workshop, so it is never exactly the same twice. I make revisions for every new class."

"Well, see whether you can settle on something you can live with for a while so we can print it as a textbook instead of a syllabus."

That is how ***Principles of Effective Prayer*** came into being. It is very informal. I just share out of my heart; I say I and me when that's what I mean. Prayer is a very personal matter!

Since the syllabus was to be published as a book, Doloris and I prayed, "Lord, if You can be glorified through it and it will bless people, please use it more widely than just this one course." He heard. He answered. And He continues to answer. Although small groups and classes far and wide use it, most comments come from individuals who have been blessed by it.

Prairie Bible College printed it first. Action International Ministries (ACTION) printed it for national pastors; evangelists and Christian workers in the Philippines translated it into Spanish for South America. Canadian Revival Fellowship sold it on their conference book tables. Through the 90's people in our seminars in Canada, the USA and Mexico purchased them. In 2000-2001, SIM International published 15,000 for their Pastors Book Sets in India, 3000 for Ghana and 700 for Sudan. I have not tried to keep any record, but a conservative estimate is that at least 50,000 are in print. I have no idea how many editions there have been.

That's why I call this the 21st Century Edition. Gabriel Publishing is producing it for Christian bookstores in North America as well as many outlets around the world, and the countries ACTION is entering in Africa.

No one takes any royalties from it. Proceeds go to ACTION's Project BookShare to publish more for national pastors and Christian workers in poverty-stricken areas of the Third World. We have to go to the atlas to look up some of the places we get letters from! (Please do not write to me for books. Check with your local bookstore or Gabriel Resources.)

See what I mean? Isn't God good? He just loves to answer prayer!

Oh, I almost forgot. Gabriel is also publishing *Worldwide Journeys in Prayer* at the same time as this edition - 101 of my favorite stories about prayer from many nations. Most are about ordinary folks like you and me - teachers and toddlers, families and farmers, housewives and hooligans, missionaries and street kids like the folks you might meet in your neighborhood, your church or the other side of the world.

I hope the Lord uses both of these books, *Principles of Effective Prayer* and *Worldwide Journeys in Prayer*, to bless you and many others. I know He will because that's what Doloris and I have asked Him to do. He has and he is and He will for His glory (that's what its all about!).

Wentworth Pike
October, 2001

TABLE OF CONTENTS

INTRODUCTION

PRAYER is the MOST . . .
WONDERFUL PRIVILEGE
SACRED DUTY
PRECIOUS RIGHT
SIMPLE ACTIVITY
POWERFUL WEAPON
MYSTERIOUS BLESSING
. . . God has given to His children!

Since God is infinite and true prayer is God's work, it is infinitely effective.

WHY do you want to learn more about effective praying?

CURIOSITY?

I would not discourage you. Rather, I pray that your curiosity will lead you into a study which God can use to whet your appetite for a productive prayer life.

TO FIND OUT HOW TO PERSUADE GOD TO DO WHAT YOU WANT HIM TO DO FOR YOU?

Have you become frustrated (as I have at times) and felt like not praying anymore when God has not given what you asked for? Don't feel unspiritual about that. Some of God's stalwarts of the faith have gone through such times. Let's acknowledge our frustrations and then sit at Jesus' feet and learn. After all, maybe...

PRAYER
is NOT
a sanctified Aladdin's lamp to rub
when you want something very much!

To give credit to the scores of authors from whom I have gleaned valuable insights would be impossible. However, the notes at the end of the book will identify some who have influenced me most. I recommend their books to you.

Discussion Questions are to be found at the end of each chapter, and Teaching Suggestions appear at the end of the book.

Although the book is designed as a textbook for groups. Its style is devotional, and it is hoped that it will prove to be equally helpful for personal study. It has grown out of the needs of a Bible college class. The material in this book has been shared with groups in North America, Africa, and Europe. May God be pleased to apply these truths to your life, too.

Any time we want to stop and pray about something, let's do it.

Any time while reading this book.

Any time in your class on Prayer.

We can include the Lord in our conversation any time.

Dear Father,
Please teach us to pray effectively. Use this book to lead many into a life and ministry of effective, God-glorifying prayer.

In Jesus' name,
Wentworth Pike

1

WHAT IS PRAYER?

"Prayer is a mystery!"[1] Our understanding is constantly challenged with new insights, and our comprehension will never penetrate all the mystery in this life. Prayer is not a library science, in spite of hundreds of books on the subject, but a "lab" science, learned in the laboratory of the secret place. It yields its secrets, not to the scientific investigation of the intellectual, but to the childlike in faith. Principles of effective prayer can be taught through a book and in a classroom, but effective prayer must be learned through a do-it-yourself program.

Books on how to swim, how to ski, and how to fly an airplane have much in common with books on how to pray. Their only value lies in application.

Yet, principles and precepts, promises and practices of prayer abound in the Old Testament and the New. It is doubtful whether any other subject is treated more extensively. Like a mighty river, teaching about prayer flows from Genesis to Revelation. No matter how often we dip our pail of faith into the stream to draw from its life-giving waters, there will always be an abundance of truth yet available.

"Can prayer be learned?" asks Samuel Chadwick. He reminds us that "the disciples of Jesus asked to be taught to pray.... There is no way to learn but by praying. No reasoning philosophy of prayer ever taught a soul to pray.... Though a man should have all knowledge about prayer, and though he understand all mysteries about prayer, unless he prays he will never learn to pray. Those who became mighty in prayer, learned to pray."[2]

Authors frequently enumerate different types of prayer. Some list four types, some five. What categories shall we expound: petition, intercession, confession, thanksgiving, praise, adoration? Among the excellent tracts for Christians written by Elmer V. Thompson is one entitled "Prayer in Four Words," which is based on four terms in 1 Timothy 2:1 — *supplications, prayers, intercession, and giving of thanks.* Mr. Thompson sees in these terms the suggestion "that prayer may advance from a lesser to a greater intensity and power."[3]

Our purpose in this chapter, however, is not to limit categories, but to expand our thoughts regarding prayer and to motivate involvement in a variety of effective prayer ministries.

PRAYER IS ASKING

A student asked, "Why do you talk about *asking* God for things? I think of prayer as fellowship with God — a way of life, not *asking!*"

"Because Jesus recommended it so highly," I replied.

We cannot improve on Jesus' attitude toward prayer. His statements were pointed and clear.

"Ask and it will be given to you; seek and you will find; knock and the door will be opened to you" (Matt. 7:7). "If you believe, you will receive whatever you ask for in prayer" (Matt. 21:22).

Asking God for blessings for ourselves is called PETITION. Elmer Thompson indicates that "supplications" might also be rendered "petitions." "Petitions in the Bible sense," he declares, "signifies the earnest presentation before God in Jesus' name of specific heart-felt needs. This is real prayer. It counteracts the Apostle James' criticism, 'Ye receive not because ye ask not.' It conforms to our Lord's direction, 'Ask and ye shall receive.' However, it is the simplest expression, the most elementary form of honest prayer."[4]

Practical praying for "our daily bread" is not unspiritual. It honors God for us to ask Him for whatever we need. It demonstrates our faith that He and He alone can provide for that need. Jesus taught that asking in His name is to His Father's glory. "And I will do whatever you ask in My name, so that the Son may bring glory to the Father. You may ask Me for anything in My name, and I will do it" (John 14:13,14).

If asking brings glory to our Heavenly Father, then asking often and asking largely brings much glory to His name.

Dr. Helen Roseveare of the Worldwide Evangelization Crusade tells of a mother in Zaire who died in childbirth leaving a tiny premature baby and a two-year-old daughter. When Dr. Roseveare was having prayers with the orphan children under her care at the mission compound, she mentioned the baby and how difficult it was going to be to keep it alive. She requested prayer for a hot-water bottle, because the only one on the station had burst that day and one was desperately needed. She also mentioned the little girl who was crying because her mommy had died.

> "Now prayer is this: A man ... insistently claiming that Satan shall yield before Jesus' victory, step by step, life after life."
> — S.D. Gordon

Nammy, a ten-year-old girl, prayed, "Please God, send us a hot-water bottle. It'll be no good tomorrow, God, the baby'll be dead. Please send it this afternoon." Then she added, "And while you're about it, God, would You send a doll for the little girl so that she'll know You really love her."

The doctor then had grave misgivings. How could God possibly answer such requests? In the many months she had been there she had never received a parcel other than pharmaceuticals which she had ordered. And no one would ever think of sending a hot-water bottle to the *equator*!

That afternoon a 22-pound parcel was delivered which had been en route from a Sunday school class in England for five months. Dr. Roseveare and her orphan kiddies opened it together. Among the vests, bandages, soap, and mixed fruits, there was a brand-new hot water bottle.

Nammy made a dash for the box as she said, "If God sent the bottle, He must have sent the doll." Pulling it from the bottom of the box, she looked up at the doctor with bright eyes, "Please, Mommy, may I go over with you to the maternity to give this doll to the little girl so she'll know that Jesus really loves her?"[5]

Five months before the little children asked, God had started the answer on the way so it would arrive at just the right time. "Before they call I will answer; while they are still speaking I will hear" (Isa. 65:24).

R. Earl Allen relates an account of Sir Walter Raleigh. Queen Elizabeth demanded, "Raleigh, when will you leave off begging?"

"When your Majesty leaves off giving," came Raleigh's quick reply. His request was granted.[6]

The Apostle Paul related God's glory to our asking: "Now to him who is able to do immeasurably more than all we ask or imagine, according to His power that is at work within us, to Him be glory in the church and in Christ Jesus throughout all generations, for ever and ever! Amen" (Eph. 3:20,21).

If we do not have wisdom to know what to ask, we should ask for wisdom (Jas. 1:5) in faith without doubting (verse 6). And if we lack faith, the answer is still to ASK, like the father of the demon-possessed boy. The distraught father cried, "I do believe; help me overcome my unbelief!" (Mark 9:24).

"This is the assurance we have in approaching God: that if we ask anything according to His will, He hears us. And if we know that He hears us — whatever we ask — we know that we have what we asked of Him" (1 John 5:14,15).

Asking God for blessings for others is called INTERCESSION.

"However, we must remember that we often pray for others in our petitions," Elmer Thompson reminds us. "The difference is that intercessory prayer for others goes deeper. Intercession means praying for others as if we were the person for whom we pray. In other words, praying with the concern and the words that those for whom we pray ought to be presenting to God. In its deepest sense, therefore, intercession carries the force of mediating or bringing into application the grace of God on behalf of others."[7]

Since intercession will be discussed in more detail later, we shall limit ourselves to this brief introduction here.

PRAYER IS COMMUNION

What is prayer? Wayne R. Spear's broad definition, "human speech addressed to God,"[8] hardly satisfies, because it could include a person's raving, ranting, and cursing against God. No, the "Unknown Christian's" definition, "communion with God, intercourse with God — talking with (not only to) God"[9] is better. This idea of "conversing with God"[10] is basic to our understanding of prayer.

A lot of people have the idea of asking for something in prayer who never progress to communion with God. Some turn prayer wheels or place their written requests in water wheels so the current can turn them and send up a prayer on each rotation. Some say memorized formulae while counting beads. Others read prayers from a book. We should not assume that communion with God is the generally held concept of prayer.

A newspaper article in Nigeria addressed to faithful Muslim worshippers concerned the fast of Ramadan. "Toothbrushing is highly recommended," stated the Alhaji, who serves as Imam of the Nigerian Air Force Training Command in Kaduna. "A Salaat or a holy recital or any prayer said after toothbrushing and mouth-cleansing is 77 times greater in reward than the same act with an unbrushed mouth."[11] Obviously, the thought here is not of communion with God, who loves to answer prayer, but of obtaining reward for performance of a ritual.

Real communion with God is not recital of ritual. It is relationship, friendship, affinity of spirit, and sharing of thoughts and feelings. It is knowing and understanding. It is harmony between kindred spirits and communication. It is expression of love, usually (but not always) in words. It is a glorious privilege afforded those who have been reconciled to Him. It can become a moment-by-moment way of life rather than a mere act performed. It should.

Of Peter and John it is recorded that even their persecutors "took note that these men had been with Jesus" (Acts 4:13), although Jesus was no longer physically present on earth. John tells us that our fellowship with each other is rooted in fellowship "with the Father and with His Son, Jesus Christ" (1 John 1:3).

When the Lord Jesus went out early in the morning to pray or spent whole nights in prayer, surely He did not spend all of those precious moments asking for things. Actually, He did not seem to be much interested in *things* other than the things of nature. There is no evidence that He ever owned anything more than His necessary clothing. John 17 shows that His one desire in prayer was for the glory of His Father. I'm sure that praise, thanksgiving, and adoration contributed to His regular communion with His Father. John 17 is also permeated with information and argumentation upon which is based Jesus' plea for His disciples and for all believers.

Dr. George Sweeting, President of Moody Bible Institute, has written:

> Prayer is a dialogue. "How rare it is," said Fenelon, "to find a soul quiet enough to hear God speak." Prayer is our talking to God and having Him talk to us. It is spending time in communion with our Heavenly Father.[12]

Dr. Sweeting illustrates his point with the story of D.L. Moody's five-year-old son, who interrupted his father in his study while Moody was busy writing.

"What do you want, son?" asked Moody rather gruffly.

"Nothing, Daddy," the boy replied. "I just wanted to be where you are."

J. Oswald Sanders stressed the same truth by quoting Thomas Goodwin, who said, "I have known men who came to God for nothing else but just to come to Him, they so loved Him. They scorned to soil Him and themselves with any other errand than just purely to be alone with Him in His presence."[13]

> Oh, the pure delight of a single hour
> That before Thy throne I spend,
> When I kneel in prayer, and with
> Thee my God,
> I commune as friend with friend!
> — Fanny Crosby, 1820-1915

Have you ever noticed how the twenty-third Psalm changes right in the middle? The first three verses use the pronoun "He" for God as they declare His all-sufficiency as the good Shepherd, but the last half of the poem uses "You" (or "Thou") to address Him personally and intimately. Maybe the following story will clarify the point I'm trying to make.

> *The primary office of prayer is communion with God. To have Him is to have all ...to aim at anything less than God Himself is to miss the mark."*
> — Li. Huegel

A very small girl was traveling with her mother by train. A gregarious child, she quickly made friends with others in the coach. One lady lifted the wee lass up into the seat beside her.

"Where did you get that pretty yellow dress?" asked the lady.

"My Mommy made it," was the reply.

"And where did you get those lovely blue eyes?" continued her new friend.

"I take after my Mommy."

And so the conversation went. With every answer the little one showed her deep love for her mother. She talked about her constantly.

But suddenly the train plunged into a dark tunnel. At once, the little girl jumped down, ran across the aisle, and climbed into her mother's lap. Entwining her baby arms about her mother's neck, she whispered into her ear, "I love you, Mommy."

There are times when talking *about* the Lord is inadequate. We need the closeness of His presence. What a grievous error it would be to wait until we are in the "valley of the shadow" to seek Him out.

PRAYER IS ADORATION

How right they are to adore You!
... I delight to sit in His shade.
... My Lover is mine and I am His
(Song. Sol. 1:4b;2:3b,16a).

The late Dr. A.C. Snead, former Foreign Secretary of the Christian and Missionary Alliance, shared with me the thoughts on which he had been meditating one evening. He said, "I've been sitting here this evening thinking about prayer. It seems to me that prayer is something like the Tabernacle in the wilderness. Oh, the analogy isn't perfect, but I've enjoyed just letting my mind run to and fro on the possibilities."

Then he compared prayer to the Outer Court, the Holy Place, and the Holy of Holies. "We would call the Outer Court 'Petition'. That's most of our praying: the 'Now I lay me down to sleep' prayer of infancy, the pastoral prayer for government leaders and the sick on Sunday morning, the blessing on the food at meals — most of our praying. It is good — nothing wrong with it — real prayer. But I am afraid that the vast majority of Christians never get any further."

Then Dr. Snead compared the Holy Place to the priestly praying of intercession. New Testament believers are all priests called to a ministry of identifying with the needs of others and standing in the gap between them and God.

> "To pray is nothing more involved than to let Jesus into our needs."
> —O. Nallesby

Finally, the old prayer warrior identified the Holy of Holies, not only as a place of intercession, but as a place of adoration, where one person is shut in alone with God, apart from all the cares and business of the world, not to ask for anything for himself, but simply adoring God and enjoying the blessing of His Presence.

I was so occupied with these thoughts that I almost missed his next pensive remarks: "Then I wondered, 'Have I ever been there?' I think I have — just a few times — but it was too wonderful for me. I couldn't stand it. Soon I was back into the Holy Place and on back into the Outer Court, the places where most of my praying takes place."

Some authors on the subject of prayer suggest that adoration is the starting place. That's good. Let us start with praise and thanksgiving. But somehow I felt that Dr. Snead was sharing something deeper than anything we can rush into out of the crowds and the business of the day. He was speaking about seeking the Lord's face, sitting at His feet, being occupied with Himself alone.

> Lord, I have shut the door,
> Here do I bow;
> Speak, for my soul attent
> Turns to Thee now.
> —William M. Runyan[14]

PRAYER IS THE MINISTRY OF THE TRINITY

"Prayer is God the Holy Spirit talking to God the Father in the name of God the Son, and the believer's heart is the prayer room," said Dr. Samuel Zwemer. Here is profundity in poetry. Prayer originates with God, proceeds from God to God in the character, work, and authority of God. So where does that leave me? Ah, it takes me at once to the place of both power and humility. For God in love has chosen my heart as His prayer room.

What a humbling truth: prayer is all God's work!

What an ennobling truth: the triune God chooses to perform His work through the heart of finite man!

"In the same way, the Spirit helps us in our weakness. We do not know what we ought to pray, but the Spirit Himself intercedes for us with groans that words cannot express. And He who searches our hearts knows the mind of the Spirit, because the Spirit intercedes for the saints in accordance with God's will" (Rom. 8:26,27).

CONCLUSION

We cannot answer the question posed by this lesson without saying that prayer is warfare, but that is a lesson in itself and so will have to wait.

There are many more definitions, explanations, and illustrations of what prayer is — all worthy of meditation in an effort to begin exploring the vast horizons of prayer, yet all inadequate to fully comprehend the subject.

Watchman Nee said it well: "Prayer is the most wonderful act in the spiritual realm as well as a most mysterious affair."[15]

Study and Discussion Questions

1. Tell what you like about each of the following statements about prayer.
    a. "Prayer is a mystery."
    b. "Though a man should have all knowledge about prayer... unless he prays he will never learn to pray."
    c. Asking "Is the most elementary form of honest prayer."
    d. "Intercession means praying for others as if we were the person for whom we pray."
    e. "Prayer is communion with God."
    f. "Prayer is a dialogue."
    g. "There are times when... we need the closeness of His presence."
    h. "Prayer is adoration."
    i. Prayer is "seeking the Lord's face, sitting at His feet, being occupied with Himself alone."
    j. "Prayer is God the Holy Spirit talking to God the Father in the name of God the Son, and the believer's heart is the prayer room."

2. Give three reasons why we ask God for the things we need.

3. Choose any **one** of the following passages of Scripture (Bible prayers) and list the requests you find in it. Discuss whether these were requests for material and physical needs or requests for spiritual needs.
    Ephesians 3:14-21; Colossians 1:9-12; Matthew 6:9-13

4. Discuss Dr. Snead's meditation about prayer — starting with petition, proceeding to intercession, and climaxing with adoration. Do you prefer starting with **adoration**? Explain how one pattern might be ideal on some occasions but the other might be more practical at other times.

5. Why is Dr. Zwemer's definition of prayer a **humbling** thought? In what way is it an **ennobling** thought — one that lifts the person praying to the highest spiritual plane?

2

A WAY OF ACCESS TO THE THRONE

The very first principle of effective prayer is:
**We must be RIGHTLY RELATED TO GOD
for our prayers to be** *effective.*

Can *everyone* pray with assurance that God will hear and answer?
NO!

Does that surprise you? Many people think that anyone can pray at any time or place and God will be pleased and will listen. But principles of prayer, to be effective, must be derived, not from what people think, but from God's own Word. And the Bible declares to a great many people: "even if you offer many prayers, I will not listen" (Isa. 1:15b).

Can *anyone* pray with assurance that God will hear and answer?
YES!

There is a way in which "whosoever will may come." There is a credential which qualifies any true seeker to come before God's throne of grace and make known his petitions with the absolute assurance of being heard and answered.

The only prayer an unsaved person has assurance of God's hearing is a prayer of humble repentance. A self-righteous attitude disqualifies, but a sincere cry for mercy puts one on "praying ground."

> Two men went up to the temple to pray, one a Pharisee and the other a tax collector. The Pharisee stood up and prayed about himself; "God, I thank You that I am not like all other men — robbers, evildoers, adulterers — or even like this tax collector.

> I fast twice a week and give a tenth of all I get." But the tax collector stood at a distance. He would not even look up to heaven, but beat his breast and said, "God, have mercy on me, a sinner." I tell you that this man, rather than the other, went home justified before God. For everyone who exalts himself will be humbled, and he who humbles himself will be exalted (Luke 18: 10-14).

The tax collector's prayer is the only kind the sinner can be sure that God will answer. One of the thieves being crucified at Calvary prayed with the same attitude and Jesus answered in the affirmative immediately.

> One of the criminals who hung there hurled insults at Him: "Aren't you the Christ? Save yourself and us!" But the other criminal rebuked him. "Don't you fear God," he said, "since you are under the same sentence? We are punished justly, for we are getting what our deeds deserve. But this man has done nothing wrong." Then he said, "Jesus, remember me when You come into Your kingdom." Jesus answered him, "I tell you the truth, today you will be with me in paradise" (Luke 23:39-43).

That is not to say that God will *not* answer any other kind of prayer for one who has not submitted humbly to Christ, but the unregenerate person has *no claim* upon Him to answer any other. God, in mercy, may *choose* to answer other prayers of one who does not know Him, but He has not obligated Himself to do so.

Three factors are pertinent to this first principle of effective prayer:

(1) God's *requirement* in order to hear and answer our prayers;
(2) Our *problem* which causes Him to hide His face from us and not to hear our prayers;
(3) Christ's *provision* to solve that problem.

GOD'S REQUIREMENT

> The eyes of the Lord are on the righteous and His
> ears are attentive to their cry; . . . The righteous
> cry out, and the Lord hears them (Ps. 34:15,17a).
> The prayer of a righteous man is powerful and
> effective (Jas. 5: 16b).

In any age, the requirement for an audience with the King of
kings is RIGHTEOUSNESS.

To get an appointment with the Prime Minister of Canada, the
President of the United States, or the Queen of England, one must
have impeccable credentials. To get an appointment with the Lord
God, Ruler of heaven and earth, also requires the proper credential—
just one: RIGHTEOUSNESS.

A young man in university was having financial difficulties.
The dean of the Faculty of Education referred him to a foundation
whose business it was to dispense grants to worthy students for
the largest chemical company in the world, the DuPont Company.
Glancing at the brief application form, and seeing no blanks for
the names of referrals, he asked the secretary of the foundation
whether some names should be given for character references.
She replied, "We have one referral for you already, that of your
dean. We don't need any others."

Likewise, only one credential is required for any who apply
for God's favour: RIGHTEOUSNESS.

OUR PROBLEM

But what encouragement is it that God makes only one
requirement if we lack it?

> When you spread out your hands in prayer, I will
> hide My eyes from you; even if you offer many
> prayers, I will not listen. Your hands are full of blood
> (Isa. 1:15). But your iniquities have separated you

from your God; your sins have hidden His face from you, so that He will not hear (Isa. 59:2). All of us have become like one who is unclean, and all our righteous acts are like filthy rags; . . . for You have hidden Your face from us and made us waste away because of our sins (Isa. 64:6, 7). Then they will cry out to the Lord, but He will not answer them. At that time He will hide His face from them because of the evil they have done (Micah 3:4).

Since all of us have sinned and made ourselves unrighteous (cf. Isa. 53:6; Rom. 3:23), we are unqualified to come into God's presence. Of what value to us, then, are all the promises regarding prayer? The sovereign God Himself has ruled us out.

F. J. Huegel summarizes the problem precisely:

No man can come into the presence of God and expect an audience standing on the ground of his own merits. His own righteousness will not avail.[1]

Queen Esther feared to go before the king, because Persian law forbade anyone to enter his august presence unless bidden. The penalty was death, but so great was Esther's anguish for her people that she took that risk and walked into the throne room. When Xerxes saw her, "he was pleased with her and held out to her the gold scepter" (Esther 5:2).

We, like Esther, are forbidden entrance. But will God be pleased to hear our request? Alas, He has already declared His displeasure and His refusal to grant us an audience.

But is there no mercy?

Mercy cannot defy justice. One attribute of God cannot fly in the face of another. Justice has declared us unrighteous; therefore, we are unfit for a hearing.

Can God declare the *unrighteous* to be *righteous*? Surely, He in His own *righteousness*, cannot disregard His *righteous* law and accept the

> *A sincere cry for mercy puts one on "praying ground."*

unrighteous – unless, of course, the demands of His law are fully met.

Obviously, we cannot meet those just demands, because even our "righteousness," our good works, our self-efforts, are like filthy rags to God. How inappropriate for an offering to Royalty. They are fit only to be thrown aside and burned.

Who then can pray? Who can be heard and answered? Whose request will God grant?

As it is written:

"There is no one righteous, not even one . . . " (Rom. 3:10). NO ONE RIGHTEOUS!

CHRIST'S PROVISION

Yet, the Scriptures abound with *invitations* to pray. Are they in the Bible to mock us? And what about all the *promises*?

The same verse which says that "the wages of sin is death" declares also that "the gift of God is eternal life in Christ Jesus our Lord" (Rom. 6:23). Hallelujah! All praise to the Lord Jesus! There is a light at the end of the tunnel. There *is* a way out.

> For He has rescued us from the dominion of darkness and brought us into the kingdom of the Son He loves, in whom we have redemption, the forgiveness of sins (Col. 1:13, 14). In Him we have redemption through His blood, the forgiveness of sins, in accordance with the riches of God's grace that He lavished on us with all wisdom and understanding (Eph. 1:7,8).

Only the wisdom of God could have devised such a plan. None of the philosophers of ancient or modern times ever conceived of such a plan for man.

How can justice and mercy be reconciled? *Through Christ and Him alone.*

How can God be just and the Justifier of the guilty? By providing the voluntary, sinless Substitute to bear our guilt and pay our penalty.

How can God extend to unrighteous persons the scepter and hear their requests without violating His own law? By providing the only acceptable Substitute to be punished in our place.

If RIGHTEOUSNESS alone qualifies a petitioner before the throne of Heaven, how can the UNRIGHTEOUS be heard?

> *"Prayer on any other basis than Calvary is a Satanic counterfeit."*
> —F.J. Huegel

But now a righteousness from God, apart from law, has been made known, to which the Law and the Prophets testify. This righteousness from God comes through faith in Jesus Christ to all who believe. There is no difference, for all have sinned and fall short of the glory of God, and are justified freely by His grace through the redemption that came by Christ Jesus. God presented Him as a sacrifice of atonement, through faith in His blood. He did this to demonstrate His justice, because in His forbearance He had left the sins committed beforehand unpunished — He did it to demonstrate His justice at the present time, so as to be just and the one who justifies the man who has faith in Jesus (Rom. 3:21-26).

All my sins have been charged to Christ's account and all His righteousness credited to mine.

FORGIVEN — CLEANSED — JUSTIFIED

Thank You, Lord Jesus.

"PRAYER on any other basis than CALVARY is a *Satanic counterfeit* for it is still a fact according to Christ's own avowed affirmation that *no man can come to the Father but by Him.*"[2]

S.D. Gordon said, "The blood of the cross is the basis of all prayer . . . . Only as I come to God through Jesus to get the sin score straightened, and only as I keep in sympathy with Jesus in the purpose of my life can I practice prayer."[3]

God's provision in Christ not only saves us from eternal punishment by the forgiveness of sins, but it also makes a way of access to God in prayer.

> But now in Christ Jesus you who once were far away have been brought near through the blood of Christ. He came and preached peace to you who were far away [Gentiles] and peace to those who were near [Jews]. For through Him we both have access to the Father by one Spirit (Eph. 2:13, 17, 18).

Jesus answered, "I am the way and the truth and the life. No one comes to the Father except through Me" (John 14:6).

In prayer we draw near to God (Heb. 10:22), we come before the throne of His grace (Heb. 4:16), and we address Him as "Our Father" (Matt. 6:9). But the Lord Jesus said, "No one comes to the Father except through Me" (John 14:6). These words introduce Jesus' teaching about praying to the Father in His (Jesus') name. To pray effectively, begin by receiving the Lord Jesus as your own Saviour and Lord of your life. "Yet to all who received Him, to those who believed in His name, He gave the right to become CHILDREN OF GOD" (John 1:12).

> Father, thank You for providing Christ's righteousness, taking away my guilt, and making me Your child. Now I can come to You in prayer because You are my Father, and I love You because You love me.

If you have already surrendered to God's love in Christ and yet you are not experiencing joy and fulfillment in prayer, remember that the Apostle John was writing to believers when he said, "If we confess our sins, He is faithful and just and will forgive us our sins and purify us from all unrighteousness" (1 John 1:9). Sin blocks prayer. God's requirement for our acceptance into His presence is righteousness. Positionally, we are made righteous and acceptable to God in Christ.

But practically, any known, unconfessed, unforsaken sin grieves the Holy Spirit, who has come to live in our bodies. Thus, fellowship is hindered, Satan is given a beachhead in the life, and prayer warfare is crippled.

> "But if we walk in the light, as He is in the light, we have fellowship with one another, and the blood of Jesus, His Son, purifies us from every sin" (1 John 1:7).

As a child of God, in fellowship with Him, you can claim the hundreds of promises, invitations, commands, and examples in Scripture concerning prayer.

I have read a wall motto which says, "Prayer is not a duty; it is a privilege." The second part of the saying is true, but the first part is a mistake. And the negative mistake is not necessary to stress the positive truth. Prayer is a duty. Prayer is also a privilege. The statements are complementary, not contradictory. The Prophet Samuel emphasized the duty of prayer in 1 Samuel 12:23. "As for me, far be it from me that I should sin against the Lord by failing to pray for you.

Dr. Ole Hallesby of Norway admitted: "The greatest sin that I have committed since my conversion, the way in which I have grieved my Lord the most, is in connection with prayer, my neglect of prayer. This neglect is the cause of my many other sins of omission as well as commission."[4]

It is God's
DESIRE, PURPOSE, DESIGN
that we use the
POWER OF PRAYER
to bring His
BLESSING and POWER
to our sin-cursed world . . . *to every part of it.*

PRINCIPLE:
We must be
RIGHTLY RELATED TO GOD
for our prayers to be effective.

"Let us then approach the throne of grace with confidence, so that we may receive mercy and find grace
to help us in our time of need" (Heb. 4:16).

Study and Discussion Questions

1. Since the requirement for effective prayer is righteousness, explain how God could answer the prayer of the publican (tax-collector) in Luke 18:10-14 and the prayer of the thief on the cross in Luke 23:39-43.

2. What hinders effective prayer in the life of a born-again Christian? Can you find verses of Scripture to support your answer?

3. When an unbeliever steadfastly refuses Christ, can that person have **assurance** that God will hear his or her prayer to spare a life in case of a tragic accident? Can we say for sure that God **will** hear that prayer or that He **will not** hear it (answer it)? Explain your answer.

4. If a Christian girl goes against the advice of her pastor and marries an unsaved man, why might that man remain unsaved even though his wife prays for his salvation?

5. Can you remember a situation in which your prayer was not answered for a long time because you had some unconfessed sin in your life? Perhaps you can share the experience with your discussion group and it will help someone else. However, if it is too private or too painful, just testify that you have found it to be true, but don't share the details.

3

ALONE WITH GOD

THE GREATEST THING
ANYONE CAN DO FOR GOD
AND FOR MAN
IS TO PRAY.
THE GREAT PEOPLE
OF THE EARTH TODAY
ARE THE PEOPLE WHO PRAY.

I do not mean those who talk about prayer; nor those who say they believe in prayer; nor yet those who can explain about prayer; BUT I MEAN THESE PEOPLE WHO TAKE TIME AND PRAY. . . IT IS WHOLLY A SECRET SERVICE.

—S.D. Gordon[1]

Oh, let the place of secret prayer become to me the most beloved spot on earth.

—Andrew Murray[2]

The first and the decisive battle in connection with prayer is the conflict which arises when we are to make arrangements to be alone with God every day. If the battle is lost for any length of time at this point, the enemy has already won the first skirmish.

—O. Hallesby[3]

> **PRINCIPLE:** Daily private prayer is spiritually productive.

It is vital to a Christian's walk with the Lord that there be some private time of intimate fellowship with Him every day. It is not a matter of law-keeping. The Lord will not love us less if we fail to meet with Him. But we might find, if we regularly neglect our quiet time, that we love Him less. In fact, lovelessness is both the cause and the result!

Dick Eastman of World Literature Crusade's *Change the World School of Prayer* reminds the thousands whom he has taught to pray more effectively that there are 96 fifteen-minute blocks of time in every day. How many of them can we afford to give to God in prayer? Can we afford not to give any?

Daniel faithfully knelt in prayer three times every day, and the threat of death could not deter him. It is unlikely that any of us face a more demanding daily schedule than this man who held the highest positions of trust and influence under a succession of world emperors. But no emperor or earthly responsibility was allowed to usurp God's time. It is all a matter of priorities!

There are two very simple, but very important, imperatives which will cause the principle stated above to function effectively.

I. HAVE A DEFINITE TIME

Satan will do everything he can to thwart your good intentions to keep your quiet time with God faithfully. He does not care how many classes you take on the subject of prayer, how many books you read on prayer, or how many assignments you complete on prayer so long as he can prevent you from actually engaging in effective prayer. He will, therefore, place many obstacles in the path of prayers. Some obstacles, of course, require no assistance from the adversary: our culture puts them there, or we do it ourselves.

A. Early Morning

There is no question among seasoned prayer warriors about

the best time for concentrated private prayer. One and all affirm that it is in the morning — especially early in the morning. Concerning our Lord, we read, "Very early in the morning, while it was still dark, Jesus got up, left the house and went off to a solitary place, where He prayed" (Mark 1:35). An unknown poet has expressed it well in the following lines:

The Morning Watch

The early morn with Jesus;
His happy, welcome guest!
The first glad thoughts for Jesus,
The brightest and the best!

Alone, alone with Jesus,
No other may intrude,
The secrets of Jehovah
Are told in solitude.

This is the time to worship,
This is the time for prayer;
The sweetest time for laying
The heart's petitions bare.

The time for holy wrestling.
The time to intercede;
The time to win from Jesus
The help and strength we need.

It doesn't take much effort for any of us to think of a number of good reasons for early-morning praying, but it takes a lot of effort and discipline to *do* it. Before the children are up, before the noises and busyness of the day, before the telephone's nerve-jangling insistence, while the mind is fresh and rested —this is prime time for quiet time.

...while the mind is fresh and rested— this is prime time for quiet time.

While the mind is fresh? Perhaps

not for all. Some awaken with vim, vigor, and vitality, but many find that just getting out of bed takes too much effort. (Yet, getting up is essential — as you so well know if you have ever tried having your quiet time while still in bed. It's *quiet* all right!) It takes a while to get moving, and the wheels of thought turn very slowly. To sit, meditate, and pray must be about the very quickest way to go to sleep again. And kneeling only facilitates the process — unless you kneel in the middle of the floor away from a bed, chair, or coffee table. So, while some folks may bounce out of bed and drop to their knees for a good alert prayer time, that is not for all of us.

How can sleepy heads have a meaningful early morning prayer time? Here are a few practical pointers. Try them, and use any which you find effective.

1. EXERCISE: a few deep-knee bends, running in place, toe-touching, etc.
2. SCALP RUB: vigorous rubbing with finger tips or knuckles, especially the back of the neck and temples.
3. BATH: not too warm!
4. COLD WATER: on the face and neck.
5. COFFEE.
6. A HARD CHAIR.
7. PRAYING OUT LOUD (to avoid day dreaming).

There is nothing particularly spiritual about having your time of devotions before you do anything else. It is a matter of practicality rather than spirituality which causes us to choose the early morning; so if your blood isn't oxygenating the brain when you first arise, do something to stimulate it before you pray. Weather permitting, Jesus' idea of going outdoors is ideal. If you are serious about prayer, you can find a way to meet God in the morning.

It is reported that J. Hudson Taylor, Founder of the China Inland Mission (now Overseas Missionary Fellowship) never let the sun rise while he was in China without finding him on his knees in prayer.

Of course, if there are circumstances which make early morning inconvenient or impossible for prayer time, one must choose a better time. Hudson Taylor's practice would pose some difficulties in the Arctic, where the sun does not set in mid-summer or rise in mid-winter! And many people working shifts must adjust their private time with God accordingly.

But for most, morning is a logical time to dedicate the day to God — to surrender all its activities, thoughts, and plans to Him — to ask for the re-filling of the Holy Spirit, for guidance, and for wisdom.

> Give ear to my words, O Lord, consider my sighing. Listen to my cry for help, my King and my God, for to You I pray.... Morning by morning I lay my requests before You and wait in expectation (Ps. 5:1-3). He wakens morning by morning, wakens my ear to listen like one being taught (Isa. 50:4b).

THE SECRET

I met God in the morning
When my day was at its best,
And His presence came like sunrise,
Like a glory in my breast.

All day long the Presence lingered,
All day long He stayed with me,
And we sailed in perfect calmness
O'er a very troubled sea.

Other ships were blown and battered,
Other ships were sore distressed,
But the winds that seemed to drive them
Brought to us a peace and rest.

Then I thought of other mornings
With a keen remorse of mind,
When I too had loosed the moorings,
With the Presence left behind.

So I think I know the secret,
Learned from many a troubled way:
You must seek Him in the morning
If you want Him through the day!
—Ralph Spaulding Cushman, 1879—[4]

A. Other Times

Psalm 55:17, "Evening, morning and noon I cry out in distress, and He hears my voice."

What a good time noon is to get one's spiritual second wind. It is an opportunity to fellowship with God and to renew alertness against temptation. When we have difficulty finding time to wait before God because of a busy schedule, it is well worth while to skip the noon meal and to take that hour for prayer. Most of us can get along quite well without lunch, at least some of the time. In addition to the daily morning quiet time, some Christians like to set aside at least one noon hour each week for prayer.

> *Jesus found that It was occasionally necessary to sacrifice sleep in order to have more time for prayer.*

Required in the priestly ministry of the Levitical system were both morning and evening sacrifices (2 Chron. 13:11). At the time of the evening sacrifice, Ezra fell on his knees, spread his hands out to the Lord, and prayed a prayer of bitter confession for his people who had married the idolatrous people of the land (Ezra 9).

Concerning Christ it is written, "Each day Jesus was teaching at the temple, and each evening He went out to spend the night on the hill called the Mount of Olives" (Luke 21:37). This was one of His favorite places of prayer, the one where He went in the hour of his betrayal. In the next chapter, Luke 22, it says, "Jesus went out as usual to the Mount of Olives . . ., knelt down and prayed . . ." It was obviously His regular practice to spend time in prayer in the evening as well as in the early morning.

What a blessed opportunity to talk over the events of the day with God, a time for confession and thanksgiving, a time for intercession.

> *If Jesus felt the need of special and regular prayer times, I certainly don't need them less.*

Jesus found that it was occasionally necessary to sacrifice sleep in order to have more time for prayer. "One of those days Jesus went out into the hills to pray, and spent the night praying to God" (Luke 6:12). The particular occasion mentioned was prior to the morning when He chose His twelve disciples. How much time and anguish we would save ourselves by following His example before making major decisions!

A sincere young lady said to me, "I just talk to the Lord any time; it's as natural for me to speak to the Lord throughout the day as it is to speak to anyone else. I don't see any need of having a special time for prayer."

Many of us, however, find that without the quiet time with God, our hearts do not turn to Him naturally all through the day. We are more liable to day-dream, talk to ourselves, or even "push the panic button" of worry than we are to pray. My experience has been that a good, unhurried time alone with God prepares me for a day of communion with Him.

Furthermore, if I did not have a definite time set aside for it, I doubt that I would have a very consistent and disciplined ministry of *intercession.* I would probably overlook many missionary needs, needs of the sick, and the problem of lost souls. Without disciplined times, I might just talk to the Lord about me and the things which concern me.

If Jesus felt the need of special and regular prayer times, I certainly don't need them less.

Of course, regulated times for prayer, although essential, are insufficient. God invites us to call upon Him especially in times of emergency. "And call upon Me in the day of trouble: I will deliver you, and you will honor Me" (Ps. 50:15). "May the Lord answer you when you are in distress . . ." (Ps. 20:1). Let us *not wait* until the time of trouble. If we dwell constantly in His presence, it is natural and easy to turn to Him instinctively in time of need.

Morning, noon, and night, special occasions, emergencies — all are great times for prayer. It all comes down to this: We need to *develop* the habit of continual prayer.

"Pray continually," urged the Apostle Paul in 1 Thessalonians 5:17.

He did *not* say, "Be in an attitude of prayer." An attitude is passive. Praying is active. The command is not to be in something, but to *do* something.

Luke says, "Jesus told His disciples a parable to show them that they should always pray and not give up" (18:1). All too often this matter of "being in an attitude of prayer" is a dodge, an evasion of the clear command to pray continually. Paul told the young pastor Timothy that he remembered him in prayer night and day (2 Tim. 1:3), and he told the Colossians that he had not stopped praying for them since the day he heard about them from Epaphras (Col. 1:9). He also asked the Colossian believers to *devote* themselves to prayer (4:2).

People object and say, "Well, you have some things to do other than to pray. You have to eat, sleep, work."

Of course — and Paul was as active as any of us — when he said that we are not to stop praying, he meant it in the normal sense of the language, like a doctor who tells his patient, "Don't stop eating." He does not mean that the patient is to eat constantly: nor does he mean to "be in an attitude" of eating! He means to *maintain the regular habit and don't give up.*

Develop the habit of praying about everything, of talking it over with God. And have regular prayer times. It need not be either/or. How much better to do both. Spontaneity in prayer grows out of discipline in prayer.

Dick Eastman reminds us, "God gives you 96 fifteen-minute periods every day. Will you give God at least one or two of these time periods in prayer for your loved ones, friends, and the world?"[5] (That would be a practical *beginning.*)

II. HAVE A DEFINITE PLACE

It is good to get alone to pray. Jesus did. "After He had dismissed them, He went up into the hills by Himself to pray. When evening came, He was there alone" (Matt. 14:23). In the Garden of Gethsemane, He separated Himself even from His disciples (Matt. 26:36-46). "One must get alone," said S.D. Gordon, "to find out that he never is alone. The more alone we are as far as men are concerned the least alone we are so far as God is concerned."[6]

Jesus teaches us to insure privacy for prayer: "When you pray, go into your room, close the door and pray to your Father, who is unseen" (Matt. 6:6). The context of this verse places the emphasis on privacy to avoid ostentatious praying. If our praying is for the glory of God and not self-glory, then secret prayer will take precedence over public praying. The strength of a mighty oak tree is not in its foliage but in its roots.

Praying in complete privacy also ensures freedom from distractions and enhances concentration. Jesus often departed from the crowds to a mountain top to pray. Or He went out alone early in the morning to some secluded spot.

Someone has pointed out that the One who told us to "go into your room, close the door" did not have a room to go into or a door to close. The birds and the foxes have their places of abode, but the Lord Jesus had none of His own. And a lot of Christians don't have a private room where they can go and close the door. They are in barracks, dormitories, bunk houses, and one-room mud-walled huts. There are all sorts of situations where a literal application of Jesus' admonition is impossible. But He found ways to be alone with His Father, and it is important that we should, too.

Some of my best times of communion with the Lord have been while hiking the trail on snowshoes. Is there a garden or park you can go to? If necessary, build a shed in your back yard. If you get up for prayer before anyone else in your family is up, perhaps the living room or the kitchen will be ideal for your rendezvous with God.

If you are in a situation where it is absolutely impossible to find privacy, ask the Lord to help you to erect four walls in your imagination and to shut out distractions. But determine in your heart that you are going to have that time alone with God at any cost.

In his *Quiet Talks*, S. D. Gordon observed, "A taught ear is as necessary to prayer as a taught tongue, and the daily morning appointment with God seems essential to both."[7]

Someone has said, "The secret of effective prayer is secret prayer."

And E.M. Bounds, who has done so much in his books on prayer to awaken preachers to the necessity of a powerful prayer life for a powerful pulpit ministry, shared this pointed observation from Carey's Brotherhood in Serampore, India: "Prayer — secret, fervent, believing prayer — lies at the root of all personal godliness."[8]

If you believe that God's promises are true, you will find a way to overcome every obstacle to prayer. You will get up earlier, stay up later, skip lunch, restrict your newspaper reading and television viewing, forego a social event, or even change occupations. Better to get rid of the TV or stop the daily paper than to miss the prayer time. Better to take a lower salary if it comes to that!

Once when Jesus was
PRAYING
IN PRIVATE... (Luke 9:18).
Jesus... withdrew again
into the hills
BY HIMSELF (John 6:15).

"Alone with God — that is the secret of true prayer; of true power in prayer: of real, living, face-to-face fellowship with God: and of power for service. There is no true, deep conversion, no true, deep holiness, no clothing with the Holy Spirit and with power, no abiding peace or joy, without being daily alone with God,"[9] said the saintly Andrew Murray.

However, the Bible nowhere says that we are to be bound by a law regarding the time or place to meet with God. There is freedom in Christ. The discussion questions at the end of this chapter will help you to think through common problems which illustrate the need for flexibility in *applying the principles* — not keeping them as law.

In conclusion to this chapter, let me share with you an incident that happened when I was visiting Sudan Interior Mission stations in West Africa. It points out the fact that as we intercede on a daily basis, God's Spirit works in accord with our prayers.

Rose Roth was exuberant when she rushed into Herb and Marcy Jones' dining room just as dessert was being served. No one had a chance to ask why she had not arrived for the beginning of the meal along with several other guests.

"Guess what! I've just led six of my boys to the Lord," she exploded without waiting for introductions.

So that was why she was late.

Rose teaches Religious Knowledge classes in Omu Aran, Nigeria. For three days the lessons in the prescribed curriculum for Form Three students (13 and 14 years old) had been from the third chapter of John's Gospel. Nigerians generally are very outspoken with questions and opinions, so Rose's boys' classes provided her with ample opportunity to explain the new birth. The discussions led to the need for personal acceptance of Jesus as Saviour.

That day, as Rose left her classroom at noon to go to Herb and Marcy's for dinner, two or three boys crowded around her with questions. As they stood on the schoolgrounds talking, the group increased to twelve or thirteen children.

"I want to have the new life," volunteered one.

Recognizing the possibility that he might want to curry her favour and enhance his grade for the course, Rose questioned him thoroughly. He assured her that he really meant it, and two or three others said that they wanted to be born again, too.

Although many Nigerian children call themselves Christian because they are born into Christian, not Moslem, families, few of Rose's students gave evidence of being new creatures in Christ Jesus. To have several ask to be led to Christ while other children on the playground were looking on was not an everyday occurrence.

"Right now?" asked Rose.

"Yes."

"Right here on the compound?" she persisted.

"Yes, I want the new birth now," they responded one by one.

So teacher and students bowed their heads. She prayed and had them repeat the prayer after her. Then, she instructed each boy to clinch the matter by talking to the Lord in his own words. When they had finished, six had prayed the penitent's prayer. Some others in the group, when asked whether they wished to pray, quite openly said, "No." Rose gave the new converts verses of assurance that Satan could not take away the salvation which Christ had given them, verses they would need when taunted by classmates.

As Rose related the incident to the friends gathered at the Jones' table, Marcy suddenly exclaimed, "Do you realize that today people around the world prayed for you?" Reaching for the S.I.M. Prayer Guide, she flipped the pages to "Day 17." One of the requests listed was: "Omu Aran: Teaching Bible in Government Schools."[9]

Study and Discussion Questions

1. List **several** reasons why morning would be a good time for **each** of the following people to pray:
    a. a mother
    b. a businessman
    c. a high school athlete
    d. a grade school child
    e. a honeymooning couple

2. If a mother has been kept awake most of the night by her sick baby and she has to get breakfast for her husband and school-age children, should she feel guilty about not getting up early to pray? Discuss a practical plan for her to have a meaningful quiet time with the Lord.

3. Discuss the difficulties a young married couple faces when trying to have prayer together if they must live in a small apartment with their unsaved relatives. This is often the case in Manila, Hong Kong, and many places. Furthermore, the relatives may be Muslims or Buddhists. They may forbid the Christian couple to read the Bible and pray.

4. Discuss other situations where it is apparently impossible to have a definite time and place to pray. In your group talk about ways of overcoming this difficulty.

4

PRAYING TOGETHER

They all joined together constantly
in prayer (Acts 1:14).
The Holy Spirit came..
the Church was born...
miraculous power was demonstrated...
three thousand souls were saved in a day...
the greatest force for good the world has ever
seen was unleashed...
the results are still multiplying 2,000 years later
and will endure throughout eternity...
BECAUSE A HANDFUL OF EARLY
BELIEVERS PRAYED TOGETHER!

Christians have many opportunities to pray together by two's and three's or larger groups in scheduled prayer meetings or in spontaneous prayer times. Praying-together occasions occur in churches, homes, schoolrooms, forest glades, *anywhere* at all. Yes, on board ships, in airplanes, and in prisons — *wherever* two or three believers are together is an ideal spot for a prayer meeting. Behind the Iron Curtain there were churches which met *daily* for prayer (in some places openly, in other areas secretly).

From the earliest days of the Church, believers have gathered together for prayer on regular occasions and in emergencies.

> **PRINCIPLE:**   United   prayer   brings   **SPECIAL SPIRITUAL POWER** into operation.

> *"No great spiritual awakening has begun anywhere in the world apart from united prayer. ..."*
> —J. Edwin Orr

They devoted themselves to the apostles' teaching and to the fellowship, to the breaking of bread and to prayer (Acts 2:42). So Peter was kept in prison, but the church was earnestly praying to God for him . . . many people had gathered and were praying (Acts 12:5,12b).

Prayer Meetings

"No great spiritual awakening has begun anywhere in the world apart from united prayer — Christians persistently praying for revival,"[1] insists J. Edwin Orr.

J.O. Sanders points us to a significant fact: "When a number of Christians unite in prayer for a given person or objective, it is the uniform teaching of Scripture that this brings special spiritual power into operation, for their gathering demonstrates that oneness that God delights to see and acknowledge."[2]

Watchman Nee focuses on *The Prayer Ministry of the Church* in his book by that title. He states, "Here lies a most important principle: God works through the Church today; He cannot do whatever He desires to do unless He does it through the Church . . .. God has put Himself in the Church . . .. What, then, is the prayer ministry of the Church? It is God telling the Church *what He wishes to do* so that the Church on earth can then pray it out . . .. The Church is to pronounce on earth that this will of God is what she wants . . .. The highest use of the Church to God is to allow His will to be done on earth"[3] (italics added).

And it is in his classic work, *The Ministry of Intercession*, that Andrew Murray insists, "We have far too little conception of the place that intercession, as distinguished from prayer for ourselves, ought to have in the Church and the Christian life.... The power of the Church truly to bless rests on intercession — asking and receiving heavenly gifts to carry to men."[4]

Again, I tell you that if two of you on earth agree
about anything you ask for, it will be done for you
by My Father in heaven. For where two or three
come together in My name, there am I with them
(Matt. 18:19,20).

S.D. Gordon comments: "Notice the place of prayer — 'on
earth'; and the sweep — 'anything'; and the positiveness — 'it
shall be done.' Then the reason why is given. 'For where two or
three are gathered together in My name, there am I in the midst of
them.' That is to say, if there are two persons praying, there are
three. If three meet to pray, there are four praying. There is always
one more than you can see.

When Peter and John were released from jail, they went back
to report to the believers the sufferings and threats they had
endured. Immediately, the whole assembly went to prayer. "After
they prayed, the place where they were meeting was shaken. And
they were all filled with the Holy Spirit and spoke the word of
God boldly" (Acts 4:31).

Should prayers in public be voiced in order to influence people?
Surprisingly enough, the scriptural answer is: Yes! Oh, not to make
an impression on people that we are very pious, to be sure. Jesus
warned against such hypocrisy in Matthew 6, but there is a clear
example in His own ministry of praying aloud in order to influence
people's faith. At the tomb of Lazarus, Jesus said, "Father, I thank
You that You have heard Me. I knew that You always hear Me,
but I said this for the benefit of the people standing here, that they
may believe that You sent Me" (John 11:41,42). God hears the
silent prayer of the heart just as well as the vocalized petition. But
"faith is infectious, and infection spreads where numbers
congregate. Unbelief, on the other hand, thrives more readily in
isolation."[6]

Evelyn Christenson suggests a helpful guideline for praying
in public. Her six S's should make any prayer meeting both
enjoyable and meaningful:

1. Subject by subject (one accord about one subject at a
   time)
2. Short

3. Simple

4. Specific

5. Silent periods (two-way conversation with God)

6. Small groups (best for shy and untrained newcomers).[7]

Conversational Prayer

"Prayer is the expression of the human heart in conversation with God."[8] states Rosalind Rinker. "Instead of each of us making a prayer-speech to Him," she advises, "let's talk things over with Him, including Him in it, as we do when we have a conversation."[9]

This method is especially helpful for any who may be unaccustomed to praying aloud in public. It guards against the traps of trying to impress people, assuming a false tone for prayer, daydreaming and praying long prayers that put people to sleep. Prayer as conversation is practical. It brings a new delight to praying in groups.

To get started, form a small group (two or three people, not more than seven or eight). Invite Jesus to join your group, and talk things over with Him. The smallness of the group provides an atmosphere of togetherness and encourages each member to participate freely.

Follow the rules of polite conversation. One person should not monopolize the conversation. Good conversation has a lot of give and take. It is lively, animated, spontaneous. Times of silence are good times to allow the Holy Spirit to speak to your own heart. Take turns, but stick to one subject until all who wish have had opportunity to pray about it. A person may pray as often as he is so inclined and without any particular order. There is no need to re-address God formally each time someone speaks. That is too stilted, and you would never do it in any other conversation.

Here is an example of conversational prayer from a Bible school class in Principles of Effective Prayer. Eunice was absent at the time and had been for several days because of her brother's accidental death. As the students prayed for her and her family, the conversation went something like this:

Karen: "Oh, Lord, I'm so concerned about Eunice. Please help her and comfort her."

Gordon: "And be especially near her this afternoon during the funeral."

Lorna: "Some members of her family aren't living for You. Help Eunice to know just how to help them spiritually."

Karen was Eunice's close friend and she knew the family, so she took up the conversation again: "In fact, Eunice is probably the only really strong Christian in the family. Her mom is really shaken by this. Eunice is going to be the one who will have to help the rest, so give her the strength, and don't let her go to pieces. Lord, she needs You now as never before."

Eunice was back in class in a day or two with a glowing testimony of the stability and guidance the Lord had given her.

If someone in your group prefers just to listen, that's fine. He or she will sense the reality of the presence of Christ and may soon begin praying spontaneously without any feeling of compulsion or embarrassment.

Conversation does not consist of a barrage of requests. When conversing with the Lord, you will often include praise, thanksgiving, confession, and expressions of love and commitment, as well as requests. Of course, requests for material needs are entirely appropriate. Jesus included "our daily bread" in the prayer guide He gave to the disciples.

As you open your mind and heart to the Holy Spirit, He will give many promptings which you may freely obey in conversational prayer.

"For where two or three come together in My name, there am I with them" (Matt. 18:20). The two-or-three-and-Jesus principle is a heart-warming experience. Look for many opportunities to put it into practice.

Prayer Partnership

My wife and I began praying together a year before we were married. Now, for fifty-two years of married life we have prayed together every night when we have been together unless some inconvenience, such as my late arrival home after a preaching engagement, made it impractical. This has always been our own time, after the children were in bed, for just the three of us — Jesus, Doloris, and me. We read God's Word, discuss it, talk over our problems, mention the needs of loved ones and friends, refresh our memories regarding missionaries' needs, and then bring all these matters to the Lord in prayer.

There are so many needs for prayer that we have some difficulty keeping up with them, so we use some reminders. For instance, we keep a list of some of my Bible school students who have requested prayer for various needs, and we have a looseleaf notebook with pictures of missionary families and their current prayer letters. This is as much a part of our daily life as eating and sleeping. I can't imagine a Christian couple going through life together without such a time. Yet it is not a ritual. We look forward to it eagerly.

Frequently, Doloris and I have had the joy of seeing some soul saved in direct answer to our prayers. Let me tell you about just one of them.

Faye asked us to pray for the salvation of her husband, Joe. One Sunday afternoon, a friend and I visited Joe and Faye and talked for a few minutes about the weather, sports, etc. Joe seemed friendly enough. Then, I asked Joe whether he had ever received the Lord Jesus as his Saviour. Immediately, he sat forward in his chair, clenched his fist, and said menacingly, "Don't you ever speak to me about Jesus again."

"Very well, Joe," I heard myself saying while hardly knowing what I would say next, "I won't speak to you about Jesus until you ask me to. Instead, I'll just talk to Him about you."

Without waiting for a reply, I dropped to my knees beside Joe's living room couch and prayed aloud for him. No preaching — just a short, sincere prayer for the work of the Holy Spirit in Joe's heart to draw him to Jesus.

When we were back in the car, I said, "What in the world have I done? I agreed not to speak to him about Jesus again!"

"Well, it shocked me, too," replied my friend, "but you didn't say that you would never speak to him about Jesus again, only that you wouldn't do so until he asks you to. Maybe that's just what he needed. I think the Lord is going to use it."

"I surely hope so, but I'm afraid I did the wrong thing. I should never have agreed to that. But I did say that I would talk to the Lord about him, and I'll surely have to do it every day until the Lord gets him."

Of course, as soon as I got home I told Doloris all about it and we began to pray.

Weeks turned into months and nothing happened, but we kept praying. Then, one day as I was mowing the lawn, a passing motorist honked his horn. Looking up, I was surprised to see that It was Joe and that he was waving to me in a friendly manner.

"Hey, Honey, guess what!" I exclaimed as I burst into the kitchen to share my excitement. "Joe's getting friendly. We've got to keep on praying. The Lord is working on him!"

Then Joe started occasionally attending the church I pastored. It was good to see him sitting with Faye and the children, but he did not come often. Then, one Sunday morning he showed up alone.

"Where are Faye and the children today, Joe? Hope they aren't sick," I volunteered.

"No, they're okay," he answered. "They've just gone down south to visit Faye's folks. I couldn't get away from my job right now to go with them."

As I went to the pulpit I was talking it all over with the Lord silently: "What does this mean, Lord? I can't imagine Joe coming to church when there is no one at home to persuade him to do it. Keep working on him. It's all up to You, Lord."

After church, Joe was standing to one side of the crowd in the church yard looking rather conspicuous with a cigarette between his fingers. When I spoke to him, he offered his car for Vacation Bible School that week if someone could take him to work and pick him up again. That was a bit strange, because my announcement had clearly asked for drivers for the cars I already had lined up for the week. Thanking him, I explained again that I already had plenty of driverless cars. He snuffed out his cigarette with his foot and shifted his weight from one side to the other. He wasn't really listening. It had been at least a year and a half, perhaps closer to two, since he had ordered me never to speak to him about

Jesus again.

"What's the trouble, Joe? Is there something else on your mind?"

"No, I don't guess so — well, not really. Oh, it doesn't matter." He was obviously very uncomfortable.

"Joe, do you remember the promise I made to you?"

"Yeah, I remember."

"Well, I've kept my agreement — both parts of it. Do you know what I mean?"

"Yeah, I understand."

There was a long pause. Then he said, "Okay, preacher, I've had it."

"Do you want me to come around to your house this afternoon, Joe?"

He nodded.

We sat in the same places we had sat that other Sunday afternoon, but this time there were just the two of

> *Having a prayer partner is an encouragement to pray.*

us. He talked for two hours. I asked an occasional question. There were sobs as Joe confessed the details of a sinful life. Then Joe knelt with me and received Jesus into his life.

When asked what brought him to Christ, Joe said that one Sunday his little boy had asked, "Daddy, aren't you ever going to take us to church again?" (Joe had been a churchgoer before he moved to our community.) That got to him, started him thinking, so he began going to church occasionally, and the preaching of the Word brought him under conviction.

Having a prayer partner is an encouragement to pray. The most obvious one is your spouse if you are both believers. If you are not married, ask the Lord to give you a friend who is likeminded with whom you can pray on a regular basis — if not daily, then at least weekly.

Family Devotions

The structure of family devotions should vary with the ages of the children and the parents' alertness to felt needs. As our family grew, we changed from the children's bedtime to the few minutes following the evening meal to avoid conflicting school activities. The content, too, had to be changed as the children grew.

Wide age differences made it difficult to keep the teenagers challenged without going over the heads of pre-schoolers. One help was to assign to *older* ones the responsibility of preparing and conducting family devotions for the *younger* ones. And in Bible memory work a little brother or sister can learn a meaningful clause or sentence from a longer portion which the rest of the family is studying.

When missionaries visit your church, invite them for a meal and include them in your family devotions. Ask that your name be added to their mailing lists for prayer letters. Then, share missionary prayer-requests and answers to prayer with the children regularly. A loose-leaf notebook for pictures and letters is an asset, or some families use a missionary bulletin board or a card file for names and needs.

Many families have found that daily devotional guides are helpful, such as *Our Daily Bread*, which is mailed free on a monthly basis from Radio Bible Class in Grand Rapids, Michigan.

Mission boards and other Christian organizations often provide monthly prayer bulletins with daily requests. *Operation World*, by Patrick Johnstone and Jason Mandryk, is a comprehensive guide to prayer for the nations of the world.*

Some activities which enhance family sharing are: Scripture memorization, Bible storytelling, role-play, singing. Role-play is especially good for very young children, who are thrilled to act out the parts of David and Goliath, Daniel and the Lions, and other Bible stories. It should be followed by a discussion of the qualities in the lives of the Bible characters which we should ask God to help us to develop in our own lives.

Gospel bookstores gladly provide guidance in purchasing various helps for family devotions: Bibles, Bible story books, devotional guides, books of Bible doctrine for children.

OPERATION WORLD and WINDOW ON THE WORLD (the family edition of Operation World) are available from Gabriel Resources, P.O. Box 1047, 129 Mobilization Drive, Waynesboro, Georgia 30830-2047, USA, email: gabriel@omlit.om.org, Tele: 1-8MORE-BOOKS (USA), 706-554-5907, Fax: 706-554-7444 (Int'l).

The basic ingredients are Bible reading (or Bible stories) and prayer. Wise parents will keep the time brief when children are small and increase it gradually as they grow older. Long, boring prayers can contribute to rebellious attitudes toward the things of God. But real, live missionaries, real-life answers to prayer, and enthusiasm on the part of parents can make this a highlight of the day and an important factor in shaping lives.

Study and Discussion Questions

1. Study Acts 3 and 4. With whole story in mind, consider 4:23-31.
   a. Why was it better for the believers to pray together instead of each one praying alone?
   b. How did the believers use their knowledge of what God is like to pray with confidence?
   c. How did they use the Scriptures to strengthen their faith?
   d. What was the main thing they wanted God to do for them in this threatening situation?
   e. How did God answer?
   f. What was the result?

2. Notice the Importance of the **united** prayers of early Christians in the following passages: Acts 2:42,46,47; 4:23-31;6:3,4: 12:5, 11-17; 13:1-4; 16:25; 20:17,36; 21:3-5. Use the following keyword questions to guide you in discussing the importance of united prayer in the early Church: "Who?" "What?" 'When?" "Where'?" "Why?" 'On what occasion?"

3. Why do you think it is easier for young people to try different ways of praying together (such as "conversational praying") than it is for older Christians? Does this mean that young, people are more spiritual? Does it mean that old people are more spiritual?

4. What do you think young people can learn about prayer from older, more mature Christians? Why does praying with young new believers sometimes spark new life into the prayers of older Christians?

5. Discuss ways to meet the needs of **all** members of the following family in family devotions:
   a. Father   c. John (12 years old)
   b. Mother   d. Sue (6 years old)
   Include such things as Scripture reading, who prays and for how long, memory work, praying for missions, and praying for each family member's needs.   **59**

5

SOME PRIMARY QUESTIONS ABOUT PRAYER

The High Priestly ministry of our Lord Jesus Christ, the priesthood of the believer, praying in the will of God, praying in Jesus' name, prayer warfare: such deep and thrilling Bible teachings form the contents of the great books on prayer. In teaching my first class in *Principles of Effective Prayer*, I started immediately lecturing on these and similar topics. Soon it was evident that we were in deeper water than some were ready for. The next semester, with a new group of students, I asked them to jot down questions and problems which they wanted answered. Not one asked about the things uppermost in my thoughts. Instead, they asked:

To whom should prayer be addressed?
Should we pray to Jesus and the Holy Spirit?
What position should we be in?
Are the words we use important?

Classic works on prayer take these matters for granted, as I did, so I had to search the Scriptures for answers. Early doubts about the practicality of these basic questions soon gave way to the realization that I, too, had some things to learn from them and that they should be discussed before going on to deeper things.

To Whom Should We Pray?

Mani and Raja, brothers raised in a Hindu family but won to Christ in their young manhood, have been students in my classes. So have many who grew up as Roman Catholics, nominal Protestants, unchurched pagans, and some who have been saved out of the cults. Almost any religious background imaginable is represented by the young born-again believers who comprise the student body of a Bible institute. Whereas the question, "To whom should we pray?" might seem unimportant to one who has attended an evangelical church all his life, it is more than academic to Mani and Raja and many others.

People pray to all sorts of things: the sun, the moon, a river, a spirit that is thought to live in a tree, an animal, idols, and fetishes.

> Elijah said to the prophets of Baal, "Choose one of the bulls and prepare it first.... Call on the name of your god...." Then they called on the name of Baal from morning till noon. "O Baal, answer us!" they shouted. But there was no response; no one answered.... "Shout louder!" he said. "Surely he is a god! Perhaps he is deep in thought, or busy, or traveling. Maybe he is sleeping and must be awakened." So they shouted louder and slashed themselves with swords and spears... until their blood flowed.... They continued their frantic prophesying until the time for the evening sacrifice. But there was no response, no one answered, no one paid attention (1 Kings 18:25-29).

God's Word is intolerant of prayer to any gods but the one true LORD God Jehovah, Creator of Heaven and earth. The prophets constantly reminded the nation of Israel that God forbad them to seek after other gods. The Israelites were commanded to drive out from the land the people who worshipped and served heathen gods. We should never pray to any "god," any person, or any thing other than the true and living God. "We know that an idol is nothing at all in the world and that there is no God but one" (1 Cor. 8:4b).

The Holy Spirit through the Apostle Paul declared the wrath of God against those who "exchanged the glory of the immortal God for images made to look like mortal man and birds and animals and reptiles," those who "exchanged the truth of God for a lie, and worshipped and served created things rather than the Creator —who is forever praised. Amen" (Rom. 1:23, 25).

We must also be careful not to participate in any dialogue or co-operative enterprise which might draw us into a public service in which we cannot freely pray to our heavenly Father in the name of the Lord Jesus Christ or in which prayer is offered to any other.

> Do not be yoked together with unbelievers. For what do righteousness and wickedness have in common? Or what fellowship can light have with darkness? What harmony is there between Christ and Belial? What does a believer have in common with an unbeliever? What agreement is there between the temple of God and idols? ...As God has said... "Therefore come out from them and be separate," says the LORD. "Touch no unclean thing. and I will receive you" (2 Cor. 6:14-17).

In early Church times some false teachers, who became known as Gnostics, professed great *knowledge* of spiritual things (Greek word *gnosis* = "knowledge"). In a great show of piety and humility they taught that we are never good enough to approach God directly, that we dare not come before the awesome, holy God, but that we must pray to the angels. However, the New Testament says. "Do not let anyone who delights in false humility and the worship of angels disqualify you for the prize" (Col. 2:18).

An angel was sent by God with an answer to Daniel's prayer (Dan. 10), but the prayer was addressed to God, not the angel. In the Bible, no angel ever accepts worship or prayer unless it be a Theophany, an appearance of God in human or angelic form (the "angel of the LORD").

There is not a single instance in God's Word of an endorsement of prayer to the deceased, nor to living saints.

Three men visited Abraham, and he prayed to one of them (Gen. 18). However, this was no mere mortal, but a Theophany. The Bible clearly calls Him 'the LORD" (verses 1,17, 20, 26, 33), that is, "the Judge of all the earth" (verse 25). This was none other than Jehovah

God.

Some pray to saints. By "saints" they mean people who did good works during their lifetime on earth and since their death have been canonized by their church. The Bible never uses the word "saints" in this way: all those who have been born again by faith in the Lord Jesus Christ are saints, as the Scriptures use the term. Neither is there a single instance in God's Word of an endorsement of prayers to the deceased, nor to living saints, for that matter. Prayer is a form of worship and any time in Scripture when worship was accorded to men or angels, it was forbidden by God (cf. Acts 10:26; 14:14, 15; Rev.19:10; 22:8, 9).

Some may argue that they do not actually pray to the saints, but seek the prayers of the saints on their behalf. But the Bible teaches that "there is one God and one mediator between God and men, the man Christ Jesus" (1 Tim. 2:5). Jesus taught His disciples to pray to the Father in His (Jesus') name, never to or through Mary or any other created being.

Moses addressed his prayers to the LORD, that is, to Jehovah (cf. Exod. 32:30-32). The title "LORD" (notice the capital letters throughout) or "Jehovah" comes from the Hebrew term "Yahweh" but "the original Hebrew was not vocalized: in time the 'tetragrammaton' YHWH was considered too sacred to pronounce: so 'adonay' ('my Lord') was substituted in reading and the vowels of this word were combined with the consonants YHWH to give 'Jehovah,'"[1]

It was this majestic Person to whom Old Testament saints prayed. So imposing, indeed, is He that He gave instructions to Moses for Aaron, the high priest, as follows: "Tell your brother Aaron not to come whenever he chooses into the Most Holy Place behind the curtain in front of the atonement cover... He is to put the incense on the fire before the LORD, and the smoke of the incense will conceal the atonement cover above the Testimony, so that he will not die" (Lev. 16:2,13). How awesome is the One who is to be addressed in prayer! All prayer in the Old Testament is addressed to the LORD God Jehovah. For instance, notice the opening words of Psalms 3-9.

Jesus prayed to God. "One of those days Jesus went out into the hills to pray, and spent the night praying to God" (Luke 6:12). He addressed Him as "Father" (John 17:1, 5, 25). He also taught His disciles to address their prayers to God the Father. "When you pray... pray to your Father who is unseen" (Matt. 6:6). "This is how you should pray: 'Our

> *Now awesome is the One who is to be addressed in prayer!*

Father in Heaven, hallowed be your name'"(Matt. 6:9).

"Prayer has an objective Referrent; it is addressed to God," states Spear.[2] Again he rightly insists, "Prayer is to be made to God alone...the *Second Helvetic Confession* says, 'since we do believe in God alone, and we do so through Christ.... For this reason we do not adore, worship, or pray to the saints in heaven, or to other gods, and we do not acknowledge them as our intercessors or mediators before the Father in heaven.'"[3]

Should We Pray To Jesus and the Holy Spirit?

The question then arises, "Should prayer be addressed only to the Father, or is it permissible to approach the other members of the Trinity, the Lord Jesus Christ and the Holy Spirit?"

Doris Salter expressed a principle which is applicable to this question. She said, "Our prayer plan must be like a protecting fence to save us from praying at random, but it must not be like a great high wall that shuts out the Spirit of God."[4] Likewise, I feel that we should follow the guideline indicated by our Lord when He said to pray, "Our Father ...," but we should not be so bound that we cannot freely express our love and admiration for the other two Persons of the Trinity.

Spear makes the interesting observation that the deity of Christ was not always recognized by those who petitioned Him and furthermore the "New Testament word for prayer (*proseuchomai*) is never used of requests made to Jesus while on earth, while the common term for asking (*erotao*), which is almost never used of prayer to the Father, is consistently used of requests made to Jesus."[5]

Nevertheless, as Spear gladly acknowledges, Jesus encouraged people "to pray to *Him* for such help as could come only from God."[6]

When I was a teenager, a young family man in the church Iattended prayed aloud frequently and used the words "dear Jesus" often. In my youthful ignorance and irreverence I often counted the number of times Simon said these words in prayer. I felt, rather smugly, to pray to the Father, in the name of the Son, and by the Holy Spirit — or something like that. Somehow, I shrugged off any discomfort I may have felt over my own arrogance.

One Sunday morning there was a new family in church, a small enough church so that such a phenomenon was noticeable. During one of the songs before time for the sermon I heard a sob and, looking around, saw the man of the visiting family making his way to the aisle and then down to the front. He knelt at the altar and the congregation sat quietly as the pastor counselled him. No invitation had been extended. The man acted spontaneously.

In a few minutes the pastor asked the visitor for a testimony of what God had done for him. Here is what he related in words as near to his as I can remember:

"For ten years I have lived next door to Simon B___. Every week he invited me to go to church with him. But I have laughed at him and told him that I didn't need his church. Yesterday, as I was mowing my lawn, Simon and his wife came out to get into their car and go shopping. Simon stopped by my yard and asked me to go to church with him today. I laughed at him as usual and told him that maybe I would go to church when I got old and ready to die, but I didn't need it now.

"After he left, I got to thinking how bad I had treated my neighbor. And I thought, 'In all the ten years I have known that fellow I have not seen one thing in his life that I could point a finger at and say that he doesn't live like a Christian ought to.' The more I thought about it, the worse I felt, and the more I realized that I do need what Simon has. So I came here this morning to get it. I've asked Jesus to save me and He has!"

Well, I was glad the man got saved, but I felt like going through the floor. Here was Simon's next-door neighbor, who, although unsaved, in ten years had never found a flaw in his Christian character, and here was I, a Christian, who had mentally mocked my brother in Christ because of the number of times he said "Dear Jesus" in his prayers. I quietly, but definitely repented of my sin and promised the Lord I would not again be guilty of criticizing other people's prayers.

I knew some little formula I had heard somewhere about prayer, but Simon knew the Lord. His prayers were more effective than mine.

Jesus Himself said, "And *I* will do whatever you ask in My name, so that the Son may bring glory to the Father. You may ask *Me* for anything in My name, and I will do it" (John 14:13-14, italics added).

> *"...in each of the Persons [of the Trinity] the whole essence of God is to be found. Since prayer to God is always proper, any of the Persons may be addressed in prayer."*
>
> —Wayne R. Spear

Stephen, the Church's first martyr, did not have any hangups about addressing his prayer to Jesus. The nearer he got to Heaven, the clearer became his vision, and he cried out, "Lord Jesus, receive my spirit" (Acts 7:59b).

Saul, on the road to Damascus, conversed directly with the risen Christ and so did Ananias (Acts 9).

The closing prayer of the Bible (Rev. 22:20) is. "Amen. Come, Lord Jesus."

What about the Holy Spirit? There is no example in the Scriptures where He is addressed directly in prayer. Nor is there any commandment to do so or not to do so, although He does intercede for us (cf. Rom. 8:26, 27). However, there is perfect unity in the Trinity. He is one God. I believe that Spear has good theological ground for his assertion "that in each of the Persons the whole essence of God is to be found. Since prayer to God is always proper, any of the Persons may be addressed in prayer. On this basis, prayer addressed to the Holy Spirit is proper even though Scripture does not speak explicitly of such prayer."[7]

What Should Be Our Posture in Prayer?

BOWING. Three times in Genesis 24 (verses 26, 48, 52) Abraham's servant is depicted as "bowing down" before the LORD in worship, but these seem to have been primarily times of praise and thanksgiving for God's clear answer to prayer. When he presented his request (verse 12; cf. verse 42), we are not told of a specific bodily position for praying. The servant did comment in his prayer, "See, I am standing beside this spring... (verse 13; cf. verse 43). Bowing is generally an act of worship of the LORD. It indicates humility, reverence, and obeisance, and although not specifically associated with *petitions* in Scripture, it is appropriate for one desiring an audience with the King.

FACEDOWN. A still more drastic symbol of unworthiness and utter subjection is falling facedown before the LORD. Ezekiel declares, "I fell facedown, crying out, 'Ah, Sovereign LORD! Are You going to destroy the entire remnant of Israel in this outpouring of Your wrath on Jerusalem?'" (Ezek. 9:8b; cf. also, Num. 16:22,45; 20:6; Josh. 5:14; 7:6; 1 Chron. 21:16; 2 Chron. 20:18). Jesus Himself prayed thus in the Garden of Gethsemane (Matt. 26:39; Mark 14:35).

KNEELING. During Solomon's great prayer of dedication of the Temple, which, except Psalm 119, is the longest prayer and certainly one of the most beautiful recorded in Holy Writ, he knelt (1 Kings 8:54; 2 Chron. 6:13). Ezra and the Psalmist David knelt to pray. Of Daniel it is clearly stated, "Three times a day he got down on his knees and prayed" (Dan. 6:10b). Luke 22:41 describes Jesus in the garden as kneeling. In the Book of Acts we find Stephen, Peter, Paul, the elders of the church at Ephesus, and the believers at Tyre (including wives and children) all kneeling on occasion to pray.

LOOKING UP. The King James Version translates the last part of Psalm 5:3, "and will look up," whereas the New International Version renders it, "and wait in expectation." Both express the same sense. It adds the attitude of expectancy to the attitudes expressed by the other positions. Several passages in the Old Testament speak of looking unto the LORD, but they are probably speaking figuratively and not describing an attitude of the body necessarily.

STANDING. Solomon stood for parts of his prayer of dedication of the Temple (1 Kings 8:22,55). Jesus said, "And when you stand praying, if you hold anything against anyone, forgive him ..."(Mark 11:25a). This position is an evidence of respect. Being an American, I was surprised in Nigeria when I entered a theological classroom and all the young "theologs" immediately stood up. They had been trained in the British system of etiquette.

TOWARD THE TEMPLE. An Old Testament practice, this apparently had special significance to God's people who were in captivity in a foreign land (cf. 1 Kings 8:35, 48; 2 Chron. 6:38; Dan. 6:10; Jonah 2:4). It, no doubt, indicated one's faith in Jehovah, the God of Israel.

LIFTING UP ONE'S HANDS. This beautiful symbol suggests beseeching, confession, openness, receptivity, and evidence of cleansing ("holy hands," 1 Tim. 2:8; cf. Neh. 8:6; Ps. 28:2; 134:2; 141:2; Lam. 2:19; 3:41).

SPREADING OUT HANDS. Moses said, "I will spread out my hands in prayer to the LORD" (excerpt, Exod. 9:29). This act accompanied Solomon's standing and kneeling (1 Kings 8:22, 54). Several Old Testament passages suggest this attitude in prayer. Whether there is any particular distinction to be made between this act and that of lifting up one's hands is not clear, although Franz Delitzsch, commenting on Psalm 88:9, says, "He calls and calls upon Jahve, stretches out his hands...towards Him, in order to shield himself from His wrath and to lead him compassionately to give ear to him."[8]

> *The positions are meaningful, but let It not be forgotten that "man looks on the outward appearance, but the Lord looks on the heart."*

CONCLUSION REGARDING POSTURE. The positions are meaningful, but let it not be forgotten that "man looks at the outward appearance, but the LORD looks at the heart" (1 Sam. 16:7b). Like the sacrifices and offerings of the Old Testament, which were deeply significant, positions in prayer are acceptable to God only when they are supported by right attitudes of heart. Joel said, "Rend your heart and not your garments" (Joel 2:13), and the Lord Jesus warned against the hypocrisy of the Pharisees, who were much concerned about outward observances, but had little regard for their hearts' wickedness.

Maybe there is something worth considering in this humorous poem:

> "The proper way for a man to pray,
> Said Deacon Lemuel Keyes,
> "And the only proper attitude
> Is down upon his knees."
> "Nay, I should say the way to pray,
> Said the Reverend Doctor Wise,
> "Is standing straight with outstretched arms
> And rapt and upturned eyes."
> "Oh, no, no, no," said Elder Snow,

PRINCIPLES OF EFFECTIVE PRAYER

"Such posture is too proud,
A man should pray with eyes fast closed
and head contritely bowed."
"It seems to me his hands should be
Austerely clasped in front
With both thumbs pointing toward the ground,"
Said Reverend Doctor Blunt,
"Las' year I fell in Hodgkin's well
Head first," said Cyrus Brown,
"With both my heels a-stickin' up,
My head a-pointing down;
An' I made a prayer right then an' there —
Best prayer I ever said,
The prayingest prayer I ever prayed,
A-standing on my head!"[9]

Are the Words We Use Important?

Since words are the vehicles of expression for the attitudes of the heart, the obvious answer to this question is, "Yes."

Old Testament prayers often addressed God in words of beauty and deepest awe and reverence. Words were carefully chosen for their worshipful value. They acknowledged major attributes of God. They expressed love, devotion, and adoration. They formed the argument, the theological basis for the request to follow. That is, the petition grew out of the attestation of the character of God. This usually involved a reminder of some promise of God related specifically to the request to follow. Take note of this feature, for instance, in Solomon's temple-dedicatory prayer:

> O LORD, God of Israel, there is no God like You in Heaven or on earth — You who keep Your covenant of love with Your servants who continue wholeheartedly in Your way. You have kept Your promise to Your servant David my father; with Your mouth You have promised and with Your hand You have fulfilled it — as it is today. Now LORD, God of Israel, keep for Your servant David my father the promises You made to him when You said, "You

shall never fail to have a man to sit before Me on the
throne of Israel, if only your sons are careful in all
they do to walk before Me according to My law, as
you have done." And now, O LORD, God of Israel,
let Your word that You promised Your servant David
come true (2 Chron. 6:14-17).

Read through to the end of the chapter for the poetic beauty of
the entire prayer. Then, take Nehemiah's intercession for Jerusalem
for another example:

O LORD, God of Heaven, the great and awesome
God, who keeps His covenant of love with those
who love Him and obey His commands, let Your
ear be attentive and Your eyes open to hear the
prayer Your servant is praying before You day
and night for Your servants, the people of Israel
(Neh. 1:5,6a).

Again, the words of the entire prayer (vv. 5-1 1) are worthy of
consideration. Then, meditate on Daniel 2:20-23:

Praise be to the name of God for ever and ever;
wisdom and power are His. He changes times and
seasons; He sets up kings and deposes them. He
gives wisdom to the wise and knowledge to the
discerning. He reveals deep and hidden things; He
knows what lies in darkness, and light dwells with
Him. I thank and praise You, O God of my fathers:
You have given me wisdom and power, You have
made known to me what we asked of You, You have
made known to us the dream of the king.

If we limit ourselves to the definition which sees prayer *only* as
"asking and receiving," these words of Daniel would not qualify,
because they *followed* the asking and receiving.

Ralph A. Herring believes, "The cycle of prayer concludes fittingly

> *The cycle of prayer concludes fittingly in praise to God.*
> —Ralph A. Herring

in praise to God."[10] He calls praise the most neglected arc in the cycle of prayer, and adds, "As echoes of the opening strain and movements of a symphony may be heard in the grand finale, so the varied elements in prayer become full orbed in praise. Nothing else in all the cycle can substitute for it. Every sensitivity of the soul is shocked by its absence."[11] With this in mind, many of the Psalms could serve as examples of prayers comprised of majestic and poetic words.

Are such examples limited to the Old Testament? One immediately thinks of the diadem of all prayers, the opening phrases of which excel in the enunciation of lofty concepts: "Our Father in Heaven, hallowed be Your name (Matt. 6:9).

Words, pregnant words! Yes, they are important. If we would give more care to wording our prayers, how enriched would be our private and corporate Christian lives! Our flippancy with the Creator-Judge-Saviour is not commendable. Early Christians knew nothing of the audacious praying which treats God as an equal.

> "Sovereign LORD," they said, "You made the heaven
> and the earth and the sea, and everything in them.
> You spoke by the Holy Spirit through the mouth of
> your servant, our father David..." (Acts 4:24, 25).

Hundreds of years between the Testaments, a change of dispensations, and Hellenistic culture replacing the ancient Hebrew civilization made no change in the practice of addressing God with the words of deepest reverence.

Yet, our Lord Jesus added a new dimension to prayer when He taught His followers to address God as "Father."

"What an intimate, personal, familylike approach to God," comments Phil Keller. "What a reassuring, comfortable way in which to address the Almighty, Creator of heaven and earth. Can it be that He, who is from everlasting, the infinite One, really regards me as His child? Does He care enough to consider me His son?"[12]

INTIMACY? YES!
FLIPPANCY? NO!

How do we maintain the correct balance in this matter? By surrendering our hearts fully to God and maintaining a right heart attitude of love and reverence. "For out of the overflow of the heart the mouth speaks" (Matt. 12:34b).

Although the Bible is replete with carefully worded prayers, let us not for a moment hesitate to come to Him for fear of inadequate terminology.

The disciples did not spend any time formulating regal phrases during the tempest. They put the matter to Jesus poignantly: "Lord, save us! We're going to drown!" (Matt. 8:25). Nor did Peter ponder pensively over the selection of words before crying out as he sank into the waves on another occasion, "Lord, save me!" (Matt. 14:30).

Nehemiah was not less reverent when he lifted his heart in a brief, silent prayer as he began answering the king of Persia (Neh. 2:4) than he had been in his well-worded intercession of Chapter 1.

The purpose of wording prayers with care is not to impress either God or man with our piety, nor to flatter God and psychologically prepare Him for our petitions. It is not to twist God's arm, not a sales gimmick.

The Pharisee in Jesus' parable (Luke 18:9-14) knew all about putting the pressure on God, but it was the irreligious tax collector who "stood at a distance" and "would not even look up to heaven, but beat upon his breast and said, 'God, have mercy on me, a sinner,'" who was justified before God.

God desires spontaneity from the heart. Jesus warned against hypocrisy in prayer: "But when you pray, do not be like the hypocrites, for they love to pray standing in the synagogues and on the street corners to be seen by men. I tell you the truth, they have received their reward in full. When you pray, go into your room, close the door and pray to your Father, who is unseen. Then your Father, who sees what is done in secret, will reward you" (Matt. 6:5,6).

John Bunyan put it well: "When thou prayest, rather thy heart should be without words than thy words without heart."

PRINCIPLES OF EFFECTIVE PRAYER

Throughout both Testaments we find examples of persons on such intimate terms with God that they reasoned with Him, persisted, and prevailed — often with no recorded formalities at all. Such were Abraham (Gen. 18:22, 23), Jacob (Gen. 32:9-12, 24-29), Moses (Exod. 32:31, 32), the centurion (Matt. 8:5-9), and the Canaanite woman (Matt. 15:21-28).

Scripture describes prayer as a cry, unutterable groanings, thirst, a sigh, panting. Whereas words are not without importance, they might be totally inadequate at times. "Hannah was praying in her heart, and her lips were moving but her voice was not heard" (1 Sam. 1:13a).

Some find archaic King James English such as "Thee," and "Thou" to be a hindrance to them in prayer. Very well, God is not confined to it. But beware of a critical attitude toward those who do pray thus. It is the language with which their Bibles have made them familiar, especially for approaching Deity. If a believer's mind is saturated with God's Word in archaic English, then it will be most natural to use it in prayer. God understands it quite as well as He does today's vernacular. A critical attitude is far more offensive to people, as well as to God, than language which you don't comprehend.

PRINCIPLE: **Keep your heart right with God and your prayers will be acceptable to Him.**

Study   and   Discussion   Questions

1. List as many names and expressions (titles) as you can remember
    which are used to address God in Scripture. Which ones do you
    prefer to use? Why? Do you think you might begin to use anythe
    others either in public prayer or private prayer?

2. What postures do you prefer in prayer? Are your preferences
    based on tradition (what you are used to in your home and church)
    or on the significance of the posture? Would any to which you
    are not accustomed be meaningful for you to try?

3. 1 Samuel 16:7 says, "Man looks at the outward appearance, but
    the LORD looks at the heart." In the light of this, why should we
    give any attention to postures in prayer and the words we use to
    address God? Try to discuss both positive and negative aspects.
    Other significant passages which may be considered are: Matthew
    6:5-8; 12:34b-37.

4. Do you prefer to say "Thee" and "Thou" when speaking to
    God, or would you rather say "You"? What should be your
    attitude toward Christians who don't agree with you about
    this?

5. How far should we go in our familiarity with God? What should
    we stop short of?

THE CONTENT OF PRAYER

We Westerners have a penchant for categorizing and outlining everything. The Bible, being Eastern literature, is not arranged that way, so no matter how we try to pigeon-hole certain types of prayer, we shall still have both gaps and overlaps. If you have read a few books on prayer, you have probably noticed that one author says that prayer consists of four parts and another lists five. Let's recognize that some other topical outline might serve just as well for this chapter, but for convenience we'll borrow J. Oswald Sanders' categories: "worship, or adoration; thanksgiving; confession; petition; and intercession."[1]

WORSHIP

Ours is a profane age. Its hallmark is irreverence. Not only because so many people have no interest in church. Not merely because so many churches have a back row of teenagers who whisper, giggle, and pass notes during the services. But because mature, adult Christians know no awe in the presence of Sovereignty, no hush before Transcendency.

The ear attuned only to country-and-western is not comfortable with classical music. Nor does our age with its buddy-buddy notion about God move easily into the Presence of the Shekinah glory.

We pride ourselves in a straw-hat-and-jeans approach to God, which would make Esau blush. Creatures of hurry and haste, we

---

PRINCIPLE: "It is written: 'Worship the Lord your God...'"(Luke 4:8).

> *Our age with its buddy-buddy notion about God does not move easily into the Presence of the Shekinah glory.*

hush and pitifully little of power in petition because we profane prayer and prostitute praise. In our rebellion against cold formality and dead liturgy we have thrown away our throne rights, the crown jewels of worship.

If all we know of prayer is asking, then let us use that knowledge to pour out our hearts in petition that we might be taught in the holy art of worship. Scripture offers abundant examples of worship in prayer. Abraham fell facedown in the presence of God (Gen. 17:3). Moses bowed to the ground and worshipped (Ex. 34:8).

It is all right, I suppose, to stress that "Abba" (Mark 14:36; Rom. 8:15; Gal. 4:6) is equivalent to our word "Daddy," but in our attempts to portray God as knowable and approachable we are in danger of becoming crassly familiar.

Listen to David as he prays: "I will exalt You, my God the King; I will praise Your name for ever and ever. Every day I will praise You and extol Your name for ever and ever. Great is the LORD and most worthy of praise; His greatness no one can fathom. One generation will commend Your works to another; they will tell of Your mighty acts. They will speak of the glorious splendor of Your majesty, and I will meditate on Your wonderful works. They will tell of the power of Your awesome works, and I will proclaim Your great deeds. They will celebrate Your abundant goodness and joyfully sing of Your righteousness" (Ps. 145:1-7).

The Word of God is replete with such worshipful prayers. Keller comments concerning Jesus' words, "Hallowed be Your name," "there was inherent in this four-word phrase, a whole world of respect, reverence, awe, and appreciation for the person of God His Father."[2]

"If God is not given the chief place in our praying," observes Sanders, "our prayers will be anemic. When our thoughts begin with Him, love is kindled and faith stimulated."[3]

The Lord Jesus told the woman at the well, "God is spirit, and His worshippers must worship in spirit and in truth" (John 4:24). There are three key words here: worship, spirit, and truth.

Worship." The Old English word was *worthship*. It denoted the worthiness of the one who receives such honor. How pertinent this is to the worship of the Lamb of God in Revelation 5:11,12, "Then I looked and heard the voice of many angels, numbering thousands upon thousands, and ten thousand times ten thousand. They encircled the throne and the living creatures and the elders. In a loud voice they sang: 'Worthy is the Lamb, who was slain, to receive power and wealth and wisdom and strength and honour and glory and praise!'"

Sanders says, "Worship flows from love, and where there is little love there will be little worship. But there can be an element of selfishness even in love. We can and should worship God in gratitude for what He has done for us, but it reaches a higher level when we worship Him simply for what He is, for the perfections and excellencies of His own being.

"'I have known men,' said Thomas Goodwin, 'who came to God for nothing else but just to come to Him, they so loved Him. They scorned to soil Him and themselves with any other errand than just purely to be alone with Him in His presence.'

"Worship, then, is the loving ascription of praise to God for what He is, both in Himself and in His ways. It is the bowing of the innermost spirit in deep humility and reverence before Him."[4]

Spirit. To pray in spirit or worship in spirit is more than to do so sincerely and earnestly.

"In spirit" shows clearly that outward posture is merely the expression, not the reality.

The woman at the well raised a question about the place to worship, but "true worship is not a question of place," says Charles R. Erdman, "but of faith and love, not a matter of form and ceremony, but of spiritual reality: its essence is found in a true knowledge of God and in fellowship with Him as a loving Father."[5] Not the Temple, not Mount Gerizim, but the heart, the innermost being.

Yet, "in spirit" includes more. Surely it means "by the Spirit" or "in the Holy Spirit." This is consistent with other passages of Scripture. Ephesians 6:18a, "And pray in the Spirit on all occasions with all kinds of prayers and requests." Jude 20, "But you, dear friends, build yourselves up in your most holy faith and pray in the Holy Spirit." And, of course, we must include Romans 8:26,27, which gives us so much insight into this ministry of the Holy

Spirit, "In the same way,... the Spirit Himself intercedes for us with groans that words cannot express. And He who searches our hearts knows the mind of the Spirit, because the Spirit intercedes for the saints in accordance with God's will."

Those who are born again have the Holy Spirit (Rom. 8:9; 1 Cor. 3:16; 6:19) and can by Him truly pray "in spirit" as they yield themselves to His control. He will instruct and add His own intercession to the believers' prayers. And Spirit-controlled praying will bring glory to Christ. who said, "But when He, the Spirit of truth, comes, He will guide you into all truth. He will not speak

> *Whether one kneels on a velvet-covered stool or at a rough-hewn bench . . . the physical accouterments of the sanctuary do not make worship acceptable to God.*

of His own; He will speak only what He hears, and He will tell you what is yet to come. He will bring glory to Me by taking from what is Mine and making it known to you" (John 16:13,14).

Finally, "in spirit" suggests the contrast between doing something, not in letter only, but in spirit. Not merely according to form, but in reality. If outward forms of worship, whether liturgical or charismatic or anything in between, are not supported by purity in the life, they are worthless. Whether one kneels on a velvet-covered stool or at a rough-hewn bench at the end of a sawdust trail, the physical accouterments of the sanctuary do not make worship acceptable to God. If worship is to be acceptable, it must be in spirit.

"Truth." "In truth" is in honesty. No shame, no hypocrisy, no pretense. Such reality is not the result of emotion, although feelings of awe and deep humility may be present, but of discipline and obedience.

Jesus said, "I am the way and the truth and the life. No one comes to the Father except through Me" (John 14:6). The significance of this verse did not end once you were saved. That was the beginning, not the end. Any time you come to the Father it is through the Son, for He is truth, and anything apart from Him is false and therefore unacceptable at the throne of grace.

The phrase "in spirit and truth" has but one preposition in the original Greek, and this makes it one idea, not two. Christ speaks of the inner being where truth dwells. Such inner honesty alone corresponds to the nature of God, who is Spirit and who is Truth.

THANKSGIVING

Praise and thanksgiving may both be considered forms of worship. They are not always completely distinguishable, but generally praise is considered to be the act of admiration and homage performed strictly because of *who* and *what* God is, whereas thanksgiving is an expression of gratitude for what *He has done*. They are constantly intertwined, in the Psalms particularly.

The Apostle Paul faithfully emphasized thanksgiving. "We always thank God...when we pray for you," he said in Colossians 1:3. In verse 12 he encouraged his readers to give "thanks to the Father" and he enumerated reasons for doing so. In chapter 3 he stressed the attitude of gratitude as a way of life: "And be thankful. Let the word of Christ dwell in you richly as you teach and admonish one another with all wisdom, and as you sing psalms, hymns and spiritual songs with gratitude in your hearts to God. And whatever you do, whether in word or deed, do it all in the name of the Lord Jesus, giving thanks to God the Father through Him" (Col. 3:15b-17). When he urged the Colossians to devote themselves to prayer, he specified, "being watchful and thankful" (4:2).

Notice particularly the close relationship of prayer to thanksgiving in 1 Thessalonians 5:17,18: "Pray continually; give thanks in all circumstances, for this is God's will for you in Christ Jesus." That is a relationship similar, not to pie and ice cream, but to pie and pie crust. Prayer and thanksgiving do not merely go well together; they are part and parcel of each other.

Have you noticed how the apostles stressed suffering as a cause for a thankful attitude? That's right, suffering! Especially suffering for Christ's sake. If the Lord Jesus counts us worthy to be persecuted for His sake, we should be grateful. We need not have a martyr complex, nor seek for suffering, but if we encounter it in our service for Christ, we may "count it all joy."

Dear friends, do not be surprised at the painful trial you are suffering, as though something strange were happening to you. But rejoice that you participate in the sufferings of Christ, so that you may be overjoyed when His glory is revealed. If you are insulted because of the name of Christ, you are blessed, for the Spirit of glory and of God rests on you. If you suffer, it should not be as a murderer or thief or any other kind of criminal, or even as a meddler. However, if you suffer as a Christian, do not be ashamed, but praise God that you bear that name (1 Pet. 4:12-16).

Our attitude in prayer need never be one of fretful care or worry. Such self-centeredness is the opposite of faith. By contrast, the Apostle Paul says, "Rejoice in the Lord always. I will say it again: Rejoice!... Do not be anxious about anything, but in everything, by prayer and petition, with thanksgiving, present your requests to God" (Phil 4:4-6).

Happy the person who has discovered that such rejoicing and thanksgiving is a matter of obedience to God's Word rather than a whim of the emotions!

It is not merely a matter of being in an attitude of thankfulness that we are talking about, but of the act of thanksgiving. *The principle of effective prayer* is: "always giving thanks to God the Father for everything, in the name of our Lord Jesus Christ" (Eph. 5:20).

CONFESSION

The recognition of God's sovereignty, holiness, love, and all His attributes, compels us to confess our unworthiness. It humbles us to the dust. Therefore, confession is understandably predominant in prayer. Can anyone truly enter into the austere presence of the Holy One and not feel as Job did? He said, "I am unworthy — how can I reply to You? I put my hand over my mouth" (Job 40:4), and again, "My ears had heard of You but now my eyes have seen You. Therefore I despise myself and repent in dust and ashes" (Job 42:5, 6).

Isaiah had a vision of the Lord on His throne such as few have ever beheld. His response was, " 'Woe to me!' I cried. 'I am ruined! For I am a man of unclean lips, and I live among a people of unclean lips, and my eyes have seen the King, the Lord Almighty'" (Isa. 6:5).

> *Let us realize in whose presence we enter when we pray . . . and let us speak only in humble confession... as is befitting vile sinners.*

In Daniel's confession (9:3-19) he identified himself with his people in their guilt. Verses 4-16 recount Israel's shame and blame and testify to God's justice in judgment. Only verses 17 through 19 contain any request, a request for mercy because the people of Israel bore the name of the Lord. What a powerful prayer! Anyone who has never prayed such a prayer of utter contrition has yet to learn the first principles of effective prayer.

Following an introductory portion given to worship, Daniel declared, "we have sinned and done wrong. We have been wicked and have rebelled; we have turned away from Your commands and laws. We have not listened to Your servants the prophets, who spoke in Your name to our kings, our princes and our fathers, and to all the people of the land. Lord, You are righteous, but this day we are covered with shame..." (9:5-7a).

We would do well, also, to personalize David's confessions in Psalms 32 and 51.

Ezra's prayer of confession (Chapter 9) contains no petition at all.

If we have never felt like Peter when he said, "Go away from me, Lord; I am a sinful man!" (Luke 5:8), perhaps it is because we have not realized in whose Presence we stand.

When John, that beloved disciple who leaned so intimately upon the Saviour's breast, saw Him in His splendour, he "fell at his feet as though dead" (Rev. 1:17).

Let us realize in whose presence we enter when we pray, let us lay our hands upon our mouths in silent awe and deep contrition, and let us speak only in humble confession from broken hearts, as is befitting vile sinners.

In one week in East Germany, when the communists ruled, I heard a pastor pray a number of times in words like these: "Oh, my God, we have sinned. Now our land is divided and we are under the heel of the oppressor. We live in a prison with grass. We are in bondage to our enemies, the atheists. But, God, we confess that we sinned against You. We dared to lift our fists against Your people, the Jews. But, Lord, we are Your people, bought with the blood of Your Son, Jesus, and You said, 'If My people, who are called by My name, will humble themselves and pray and seek My face and turn from their wicked ways, then will I hear from heaven and will forgive their sin and will heal their land' (2 Chron. 7:14). Lord, our land is divided; heal our land, dear God."

What is it going to take to bring the United States, Canada, Britain — the West — to our knees in such specific confession of national sin? I shudder to think! Most of us have never even remotely considered such a possibility as confession of *national* sin. Daniel did. Read Chapter 9. And both Daniel and the pastor in communist East Germany were just boys when their lands came under the heel of godless oppressors. We in the West are not yet under such oppression. But we have sinned grievously against God. May the terrorism of our new millenium be a wake-up call!

The principle of effective prayer is stated by David, "I said. 'I will confess my transgressions to the LORD' — and You forgave the guilt of my sin" (Ps. 32:5).

PETITION

We should not hesitate to make known our needs and desires to God. As a loving heavenly Father, He wants to supply our needs and fulfill our desires that are consistent with His will. Because He loves us He delights to give to us and to cause our hearts to rejoice.

Some preachers and authors tend to go to one of two extremes at this point. Some suggest that God wants us all to be affluent, if not wealthy. The idea seems to be that we, being children of the King, should live like kings, not only spiritually, but materially. "Just ask God for anything you want and He will give it to you," is the thought. Yet, no sensible parent would take that attitude toward his own children. Unless one presupposes some type of sinless perfection prior to the expression of our wants, we would all become spiritual pygmies. We would develop into warped, self-centered souls if we lived through the experience at all. No one ever yet developed character without being denied some of his wants. No, God is not in the catering business to satisfy our selfishness.

Then, there is the opposite extreme which says that prayer is not getting things from God, but only finding out God's will and saying "Amen" to it. But endorsing God's will is not contrary to asking Him for things. Jesus taught that God does want to give us things in answer to prayer. Of course, our requests should always be willingly subjected to God's will, but prayer does include getting from God good things, God-glorifying things, needful things, things that bring joy to our hearts and God's, spiritual things, and material things.

Take the requests in the model prayer for a case in point. There are petitions for spiritual matters and one for material need: "Give us today our daily bread." Should not the ratio in the Lord's prayer, six to one in favour of spiritual matters, also teach us something about priorities in prayer? Many of our prayers indicate that we have our priorities reversed. "So do not worry, saying, 'What shall we eat?' or 'What shall we drink?' or 'What shall we wear?' For the pagans run after all these things, and your heavenly Father knows that you need them. But seek first His kingdom and His righteousness, and all these things will be given to you as well" (Matt. 6:31-33).

I have compiled a collection of scores of answers to prayer from around the world. Two of them are included here to illustrate God's desire to grant our petitions.

Pappy Reveal, what a man! Once you heard him speak, you never forgot him. An accident had crippled him, but with braces on his legs and canes in his hands nothing could stop him. The Evansville, Indiana, Rescue Mission's dynamic little white-haired director talked to God so intimately and frequently that one often failed to detect in his sermons just where the preaching stopped and the praying started. But it wasn't difficult to recognize the unique closing he always used for his prayer. "Amen, Lord, amen!" he piped in his cheerful, boyish tenor.

One day the rescue mission had a bill due for $100 and no money with which to pay it. Because of his crippled legs in braces, Pappy stood for prayer while the rest of the staff knelt. As he prayed, hands behind his back, he rocked to and fro.

A friend, passing the mission, looked in and noticed Pappy's fingers opening and closing as he rocked and prayed. Thinking he would have a little fun, he tiptoed in and slipped a ten-dollar bill between Pappy's grasping fingers. Without a break in the rhythm of rocking and praying, Pappy swept the bill around in front of his eyes and said, "Thank You, Lord, now, where's the other ninety?" and continued opening and closing his hands behind his back. The teasing friend felt a sudden compulsion to join the prayer meeting.

In a few minutes the postman arrived with a stack of mail, both first class and second class. In the whole pile there was only one letter with a gift — a check for $90.00!

The friend marvelled when he realized how his teasing was actually God's way of supplying the exact amount that He knew was lacking.[6]

The next story, as told by Norene Bond, originally appeared in the magazine, *Africa Now*:

It happened on the shore of the Red Sea. We had just pitched camp on the beautiful white sand, and Bruce and the three boys had gone off to spear some fish for supper.

Or so they thought.

This was a very special adventure for our family. We had traveled three days from our SIM station in Ethiopia to visit this exotic place. Fancy us being on the shore of the Red Sea!

It only took a few minutes to pile out of the car and put our camp in order. The tide was receding, leaving shallow pools and swirling eddies, and the prospect of spearing a nice big fish was good. So the hunters hurried off while Becky and I got out the frying pan.

"There's a big one!" someone shouted, and four figures raced toward a shallow place, where something huge was churning around in an attempt to find deeper water.

"Come on, boys!" shouted an excited Bruce. "Watch your father spear supper!" He hefted the beautifully-balanced shaft and let it fly with a mighty swing. There was a rewarding thud as the point hit home. "Got him!" Bruce exulted. But before it could be captured, the intended victim flapped furiously over a sand bar and began its escape.

"It's a stingray!" the boys shouted in dismay. "And he's taking the spear with him!"

A chagrined foursome watched helplessly as the great, flat body slowly headed out to sea, the spear submerging like the periscope of a submarine.

"Oh. well," one of the boys said, "we wanted a real fish, anyway, not a stingray."

"But the spear!" another voice groaned. "It's not ours, you know!"

Missionary friends had urged the spear on us, insisting that we borrow it for our expedition. It was a beautiful, handmade instrument, quite expensive, and almost impossible to replace. We had accepted the offer hesitantly. There wasn't room in the car for such a long item, and we didn't want it to get broken.

Now the worst had happened.

As we lay in our sleeping bags on the sand that night — after a supper of beans — we had our evening prayers together. Before we finished, Becky's little voice broke the stillness. "Daddy, can't we ask God to give us back our spear?"

We have always taught our children that God answers prayer. Now Becky was putting us to the test — over a spear and a stingray, of all things. Our faith was rather weak, but we agreed. We asked the Lord for the spear back, and soon dropped off to sleep.

Early next morning, Bruce crept out of his sleeping bag and prowled along the beach, half hoping the spear had washed ashore during the night. It hadn't.

Simple family prayers followed breakfast, during which Becky again reminded us to pray about our loss. A couple of hours later we all went swimming in the warm, tropical waters. All but Bruce, that is, who elected to keep an eye on the camp. Anyway, the loss of the spear had taken the edge off his enthusiasm for water sports.

Suddenly a cry went up. "Stingray! Dad! A stingray!"

Bruce wasn't impressed. He'd seen enough stingrays for one holiday.

The cry persisted. "Dad! It's the one with the spear!"

That was different. Bruce leaped into action. Quickly, he dug out a large fishhook and tied it to the end of a long pole. He waded into the water, hardly believing his eyes. It had been sixteen long hours since that thing had swum away, with the whole Red Sea to disappear into. But here it was, back again, within half a mile of where it had left.

Another reason to marvel was that it stayed close to shore, gliding gracefully within Bruce's reach, while he angled for it. After a few attempts, Bruce managed to slip the hook around the shaft, and felt the point dig into the wood. A firm tug released the spear, and the stingray sped out to sea.

All we could think of was how God had made the iron ax head swim in the Jordan River for Elisha. Now God had done practically the same thing for us, making iron swim right out of the Red Sea and into our hands.

Becky, of course, was delighted. "Daddy," she said triumphantly, "God does answer prayer, doesn't He?"[7]

Yes, Jesus did encourage us to ask with expectation, even assurance, of an answer. A farmer who plants seed every spring expects a harvest every summer or fall. If he plants year after year and receives little or no returns, he will soon quit farming. And so the Lord does not expect us to keep asking but never receiving.

INTERCESSION

Beseeching God on behalf of others is called intercession. It should comprise a major part of our prayer life. This is real ministry in prayer. The Bible affords numerous examples and teaches us that both the Holy Spirit and the Lord Jesus intercede for us now (Rom. 8:26, 27, 34).

The Apostle Paul assured the churches of his constant intercession for them and frankly sought their prayers for him and his ministry. In spite of his many sufferings as a leader of the Christians, Paul never requested prayer that he might escape such persecutions and hardships. His great concern was for an open door of opportunity to proclaim the good news of salvation in Christ and that he might proclaim it effectively (Col. 4:3, 4).

Jesus Himself issued but one *command* regarding the content of prayer — many promises and encouragements, but only one command. He said, "Ask the Lord of the harvest, therefore, to send out workers into His harvest field" (Matt. 9:38). Prayer for the sending forth of missionaries is a crying need. Mission boards working around the world are constantly pleading for personnel to fill urgent needs immediately. Teachers, translators, church-planters, secretaries, accountants, maintenance men, evangelists, printers, doctors, nurses, farmers, mechanics — you name it, skills of all kinds are needed in the great task of bringing in the sheaves. There is no excuse for Christians to sit around talking about "closed doors."

Mission leaders continually

> *Jesus commanded us to pray that God would send forth labourers into His harvest field.*

assure us that there are far more doors opening than there are closing, and in many places they are not merely open, but are "clear off the hinges." Why, then, are there not sufficient personnel to fill the ranks of the missionaries who retire because of age, sickness, and circumstances beyond their control? "You do not have, because you do not ask God." If God's people were to take seriously Jesus' command regarding intercession for missionary candidates, we would be praying ourselves and our children out into the harvest fields and the needs would be met. Our generation can be reached for Christ. How? By obeying Matthew 9:38.

The moderator of the ministerial meeting before which William Carey urged the brothers to undertake the conversion of the heathen replied: "Sit down, young man, sit down and be still! When God wants to convert the heathen, He will do it without consulting either you or me."[8]

But Carey and the modern missionary movement which has followed the trail he blazed have proven the moderator wrong. God does use human beings to proclaim the Gospel to the unreached, and He does use humans to pray the labourers into the harvest field.

If God is omnipotent, can't He send missionaries forth without our prayers? The question evades the issue. God, in His omniscience, has willed that men and women cooperate with Him in both proclaiming and praying. Jesus commanded us to pray that God would send forth labourers into His harvest, because such prayer is absolutely essential in the plan which God has ordained for the reaching of the unreached and the winning of the lost to Christ. God puts Himself at our disposal and does not do His work apart from our prayers. This statement of fact does not abrogate the power of God. It honors God by acceding to His declared will rather than arrogantly assuming that we know

---

PRINCIPLE: *ASK!*
"*Ask* and it will be given to you;
   Seek and you will find;
      Knock and the door will be opened to you"
         (Matt. 7:7).

better than He does. If our prayers were not needed in order for God to send forth labourers, then He would not have ordered us thus to pray.

A.B. Simpson declared a wonder-inspiring truth: "Thou might'st have sent from Heav'n above angelic hosts to tell the story, but in Thy condescending love, on men Thou hast conferred the glory."[9]

And that glory which He has bestowed on us applies to intercession for missions, missionaries, and missionary candidates as much as to the telling of the story.

Of course, missions is not the only subject for intercession — merely the main one. The Apostle Paul prayed for the salvation of lost souls. He had a special burden for his fellow-Israelites: "Brothers, my heart's desire and prayer to God for the Israelites is that they may be saved" (Rom. 10:1). Prayer for God's ancient people is as timely today as it was in the first century of the Church. Prayer for unsaved souls is always timely.

Worldwide Journeys in Prayer includes several accounts of the salvation of souls in answer to prayer. Milton and Leora Eder had witnessed to her unsaved brother constantly, but with no results. So they prayed. They determined to pray for him daily — in family devotions, in private devotions, sometime each day — until he accepted the Lord Jesus as his own Saviour. For twenty-five years they prayed, and then he did come to the Lord for salvation. That was many years ago, and he is still living for the Lord today, a fine Christian man. Milton and Leora wonder what the end of the story would have been had they given up after twenty-four years.[10]

Fellow-Christians need our prayers. Read Romans 1:8-10; 15:30-33; 1 Corinthians 1:4; 2 Corinthians 1:11; 13:7, 9; Ephesians 1:15-19; 3:14-19; 6:18-20; Philippians 1:3-6, 19; Colossians 1:3, 9-12; 4:2-4, 12, 13; 1 Thessalonians 1:2, 3; 5:17, 25; 2 Thessalonians 1:3, 11, 12; 3:1, 2; 1 Timothy 2:1, 2, 8; Philemon 4-6, 22. See how constantly Paul prayed for the churches and asked for their prayers. If God has chosen this method to bring blessing into the lives of His saints and of furthering the ministry of the Gospel, let us heed His admonitions to pray for each other.

CONCLUSION

Worship is essential to a fully-effective prayer ministry.

Thanksgiving should occupy at least as much time in prayer as requests.

Confession establishes the right relationship with God necessary for effective prayer.

Petition is a God-glorifying form of prayer.

Intercession is the priestly ministry of every New Testament believer in Christ.

PRINCIPLE: "I urge, then,...that,...intercession...be made for everyone" (1 Tim. 2:1).

Study and Discussion Questions

1. Read some of the following prayers of worship: Psalm 145:1-
    7; Matthew 6:9-13; Revelation 4:11; Revelation 5:12. Do you
    pray worshipfully? It may help to write out your prayer of
    praise and adoration sometimes. It does not need to be long.

2. Read some of the following prayers and list features we should
    include in our prayers. Show the exact verse reference of each
    feature so you can share it and discuss it in your group. Exodus
    32:31, 32; Psalm 32:3-5, Psalm 51:1-19 (or any part of it): Daniel
    9, Ephesians 1:3-10: Ephesians 3:16-21: Colossians 1:9-14;
    Philippians 1:9-11. (Perhaps your leader can assign certain
    passages to certain individuals to prepare and discuss.)

3. In the 1980's Christians could not have realized that the Soviet
    Communist Bloc nations would be open to the gospel before the
    century was over. Yet, in 1989 the atheistic Soviet Empire
    disintegrated. The "Jesus" film has been shown in every school
    in Russia! What "closed" doors do we need to be praying open
    today?

4. Discuss ways to get the gospel to people who are in so called
    "closed" countries.

7

THE THEOLOGICAL FOUNDATION OF PRAYER — THE NATURE OF GOD

Effective prayer is addressed to God; all true prayer has as its goal the glory of God. Who is God? How do His attributes affect the nature and practice of prayer?

> How dread are Thine eternal years.
> O everlasting Lord!
> By prostrate spirits day and night
> Incessantly adored!
>
> How beautiful, how beautiful
> The sight of Thee must be,
> Thine endless wisdom, boundless power,
> And awful purity!
>
> O how I fear Thee, living God!
> With deepest, tenderest fears,
> And worship Thee with trembling hope.
> And penitential tears.
> —Frederick W. Faber, 1814-1863

Thee while the first archangel sings,
He hides his face behind his wings:
And ranks of shining thrones around
Fall worshipping, and spread the ground.

Lord, what shall earth and ashes do?
We would adore our Maker too,

From sin and dust to Thee we cry,
The Great, the Holy, and the High.

—Isaac Watts, 1674-1748

Man is finite and, realizing his limitations, recognizes his innate need to reach out to God in prayer. So all men pray — sometime — to someone — or something.

> *The ultimate basis of effective prayer is God Himself.*

God is infinite and has need of nothing. Man, by prayer, can add nothing to God — no power to His omnipotence, no knowledge to His omniscience. God has no need to be informed by our prayers. As for praise, if we fail, the very stones will cry out!

What right does the finite creature have to approach the august presence of the infinite Creator? By what authority can the sinner approach the awful, holy God, whom he has offended?

Does man have a claim on God?

On what ground can he expect an answer to his prayer?

In other words, what is the ultimate basis of effective prayer?

Faith? But faith requires an object.

The promises of God? But promises are only as good as the one who makes them.

The name of Jesus? But a name is worth only as much as the value of the character of its bearer.

The shed blood of the Saviour? But the shedding of blood works atonement only because of the absolute holiness of the sacrifice.

The ultimate basis of effective prayer, therefore, is *God Himself.* He is the bedrock foundation on which all else rests. In *Him* prayer finds its Source and its Fulfillment. God is the object of faith. The promises are valid because they are made by God. The name of Jesus is the authority by which we come to *God* in prayer, and His shed blood has made a way of access to the throne and assures the effectiveness of our supplication.

To pray intelligently, it helps to know the Person we are confronting, and to know Him requires some knowledge about Him. That does not mean that knowing theological terminology will necessarily enhance our prayers. Most of us have known some little old ladies who have never seen the inside of a seminary classroom or read a book of systematic theology who could pray circles around the professors. But those little old ladies had some good, sound, biblical theology down in their hearts — even if they couldn't sort it out systematically in their heads. What I do mean by knowing God and knowing about Him in order to pray well is that *the way we approach God in worship, thanksgiving, confession, petition, and intercession will largely depend upon what we know Him to be like.* Whether we come to Him in confidence rather than doubting, in reverential awe but not craven fear, in honesty and not hypocrisy will hinge upon what we are convinced He is like. The same is true of anyone who prays to any god!

When my students Raja and Mani were Hindus, they did not attempt to have communion with God. Such a thought never occurred to them, because they did not know a personal God. They might, on occasion, have requested that a priest ask a god for some favour for them, and they, themselves, might even have gone to a temple to prostrate themselves in worship, because, to them, "god" meant Siva ("god of destruction and reproduction"), Vishnu ("the preserver" who "is popularly believed to have had several human incarnations, most important of which is Krishna"), or Brahma ("the supreme and eternal essence or spirit of the universe")[1] but to commune personally with the Creator of Heaven and earth never occurred to them, nor would they have known how if it had. They might have even attempted to add some persuasion by bargaining with their god. If he would grant them favor, they would give a cow to the priest. You see, their concepts of prayer, meager as they were, totally depended upon their notions of "god" and what he is like. So do yours! *Do you pray to the capital-G God or to a small-g god?*

Now, let's look at two prayers to God. Although quite different, they are both to God, not to a god.

Dr. Tozer, whose books and whose editorials in the *Alliance Witness* (later *Alliance Life*) have blessed multitudes, prayed like this:

"O Lord God Almighty, not the God of the philosophers and

the wise but the God of the prophets and apostles; and better than all, the God and Father of our Lord Jesus Christ, may I express Thee unblamed?

"They that know Thee not may call upon Thee as other than Thou art, and so worship not Thee but a creature of their own fancy; therefore, enlighten our minds that we may know Thee as Thou art, so that we may perfectly love Thee and worthily praise Thee.

"In the name of Jesus Christ our Lord. Amen."[2]

"Pappy" Reveal prayed to the same God.

When Pappy prayed, he was on such familiar terms with God that others were sometimes embarrassed. Often, while preaching, he seemed to forget that he was talking to a congregation and carried on a running conversation with God. The Lord's presence was as real as that of any visible person, and Pappy talked to Him as casually and enthusiastically as he did to his congregation. Not infrequently, it was difficult to know when he was preaching and when praying. I have no doubt that he talked to God in his sleep. The two of them were constant companions and tremendous conversationalists!

Strangely enough, both Tozer and Reveal were intimate with the same Deity. They prayed to Him in a manner befitting God as they knew Him. To tell the truth, Dr. Tozer probably talked to His Heavenly Friend as enthusiastically at times as Pappy Reveal did. Not flippantly, but personally and lovingly. Both of these illustrations are entirely in keeping with the character of the Lord God Jehovah, our Father.

What is this God like to whom we pray? The Bible tells us many things about Him. As we meditate upon these truths and pray in accordance with them we shall find our prayer lives taking on new dimensions. Of course, we can never fully comprehend God, for He is infinite and our minds are

> **GOD IS.**
> *What implications does this greatest fact of the universe have for prayer?*

finite, but We can continually stretch our minds with the facts His Word reveals about Him. Let's consider, then, a few of the attributes of God and their implications for our prayers.

GOD IS

The person who prays must believe that God is. When Moses required God's identification (Exod. 3), the Lord answered, "I am." If you would enrich your prayer life, meditate on the fact that God is. You must start here, else all prayer is futile, all talk about principles of effective prayer foolish. Meditate on the name "God;" bring to mind all that you know about Him. Ask Him to reveal Himself to you, who He is, what He is, what He is like.

God is. What implications does this greatest fact of the universe have for prayer? Publishers do not print books large enough to contain the answer, but let's think about the question together to get the mental wheels turning. Then, you can carry on the exercise as often as you find time and strengthen your prayer ministry accordingly.

God Is Spirit

"GOD IS SPIRIT" (John 4:24). Therefore, we know that He is incorporeal (not limited to bodily existence), invisible, and unlimited by any physical barriers.

If we make a request of any human being, no matter how powerful or influential that person may be, there are physical limitations on his ability to provide what we ask. God has no such limitations. He can answer any request. Not limited by a body, He can answer prayer at any *place*. Space and distance offer no barriers. Not limited to physical strength, He has the *power* to answer any prayer. As a spirit, He can permeate the mind, affections, and attitudes of another person in answer to my prayer — not defying the will He gave that person, because that is in His own image, but influencing, convicting, appealing to that person's heart in answer to my prayers. He can go behind walls that shut me out, through locked doors, into the palaces of kings, into conference rooms where world issues are decided, behind enemy lines, into sick rooms. The possibilities are endless. It makes sense to pray to God, because He is Spirit and nothing can stop Him.

God Is Transcendent

God is transcendent — other than and far above all creation (Isa. 55:8, 9; Ps. 24:10; 1 Tim. 1:17; Isa. 6:1-5; 57:15). He is far above and other than the natural laws which He Himself has established. He does not have to "break" natural laws in order to perform the miraculous, because He transcends His own laws. Thank God for the laws. They are for our protection and convenience. But they do not limit Him in answering our prayers.

His power transcends our abilities. In answer to prayer He can do for us what we cannot do for ourselves.

He transcends our very thoughts. His ways are not our ways, nor His thoughts our thoughts. Therefore, when we do not know what is best to ask, but we desire His will, He can teach us His will or even answer in the way that is best, "far above all we ask or think." Meditate again on Romans 8:26, 27, "In the same way, the Spirit helps us in our weakness. We do not know how we ought to pray, but the Spirit Himself intercedes for us with groans that words cannot express. And He who searches our hearts knows the mind of the Spirit, because the Spirit intercedes for the saints in accordance with God's will."

It is logical to pray to such a transcendent God who is apart from, other than, and far above all human or natural causes and effects. It is reasonable that we should approach Him in holy awe. Dr. Tozer prayed to the God who is transcendent. Pappy Reveal did, too, but in a different style, and he knew that nothing in this world could meet his need, so he constantly turned to One who is above and beyond the world.

God Is Sovereign

God is sovereign — absolute Ruler over His creation (2 Chron. 20:6; Rev. 19:6; Ps. 59:13; Ps. 72:11; 103:19). Therefore, prayer is never a matter of persuading God to conform to our wills, but of total submission to His will. Anything else is absurd in the light of sovereignty. Surrender to His will is the starting point of prayer.

Do you think Nehemiah had sometimes meditated on the transcendency and sovereignty of God before he prayed, "O Lord, God of heaven, the great and awesome God, who keeps His covenant of love with those who love Him and obey His commands" (Neh. 1:5)? Did Jesus acknowledge God's sovereignty in the Garden of Gethsemane? And did Paul, when he accepted "the grace to bear it" instead of the healing he requested?

As we meditate on God's attributes, we may at times be confronted with some philosophical problem. If God is sovereign, can He not enact His will without my prayers? If He is truly sovereign, then He does not "need" anything in the ultimate sense of the word. He does not need my prayers.

But do not stop studying when you hit a problem. Go on until you see the answer in His Word. There, we find that God, in His sovereignty, has *willed* and *decreed* that we should pray. Commands, promises, and examples abound from Genesis to Revelation to support this fact. Now, if He is sovereign, does He have to give us, His creatures, a reason why He has thus willed and decreed? In His sovereignty He has made a way of access to His throne, into His august Presence. I cannot explain why the Sovereign of the universe has condescended to command our cooperation and has chosen to allow His finite creatures to move the arm of the infinite Creator. It is not my business to explain, but to obey.

God is Self-existent and Self-sufficient (Exod. 3:14; John 5:26; Acts 17:24-28). Not so man! Man is totally dependent for every breath, every heartbeat.

Consider the sunbeam coming through my window and warming my back as I write. When a cloud passes across the face of the sun, the sunbeam no longer warms me. It ceases to exist when it is cut off from its source. So we cannot exist apart from God, the Source of our life. We need Him, whether we acknowledge the need or not. However, He is complete without us. This is basic to a right concept of prayer. It is not a fellowship of equals, but of the utterly dependent upon the entirely independent. Any dependency He has upon our prayers is a depending which He sovereignly wills, not one that is essential to His Being.

Prayer is the reasonable activity of the dependent creature.

God Is Infinite

God is infinite — limitless, boundless, measureless, endless (Job 42:2; Ps. 115:3; 147:5). This fact applies to every attribute, to every truth about God. Contrariwise, man is finite in every realm. The logic of prayer is rooted in these two facts. God's infinity and man's finiteness.

God Is Eternal

God is eternal — infinite in relation to time (Ps. 90:2; Heb. 1:12; Rev. 1:8). He has no beginning, no progression, no ending, no past, no future. The "I AM" exists in the eternal now. Therefore, "my tomorrows are all known to Thee." He knows the end from the beginning. What inference does this have for prayer for guidance? For decisions? For plans?

God Is Omnipresent

God is omnipresent — infinite in relation to space (Jer. 23:23, 24; Ps. 139:7-10; Acts 17:24-28; Matt. 28:19, 20). "God is everywhere here, close to everything, next to everyone. The implications for prayer are staggering. Meditate on God's accessibility. Think of the significance for missions and for so-called "closed doors." Pray for absent loved ones and friends with new assurance.

Helen E. Martin, a high school teacher at Unionville, PA, in the Journal of American Scientific Affiliation, "Meditation: A Requirement," investigated reported physiological and psychological benefits of four types of secular meditation: Zen, Yoga, TM, and the Relaxation Response. Then she contrasted them to biblical principles of meditation. Her conclusions were as follows: "Encouraging the mind to be open, passive and boundless in an altered state of consciousness...is a disobedience to the Word of God." She also stated: "The purpose of Christian meditation must always be that of love of God. If it becomes a desire to reduce blood pressure or to achieve a mystical experience, it is not Christian meditation but humanism."

Meditate on the following seed-thoughts:

God is *omniscient* — infinite in relation to knowledge (Acts 15:18; Isa. 40:28; 1 John 3:20; Rom. 11:33; Ps. 147:5).

God is *all-wise* (Prov. 2:6; 3:19; 9:10; Ps. 33:10; 1 Cor. 2:7; Eph. 3:10; Jas. 1:5).

God is *omnipotent* — infinite in relation to power, strength, might (Job 42:2; Gen. 18:14; Matt. 19:26; Jer. 32:17).

God is *immutable* — unchangeable, without possibility of change in His character or attributes, apart from and above all change (Mal. 3:6; Jas. 1:17; 1 Sam. 15:29).

God is *love* (1 John 3:16; 4:8,16; Rom. 5:8).

God is *holy* — infinite in relation to purity, absence of all that defiles (Ps. 99:5, 9; Isa. 6:3; Josh. 24:19; John 17:11; 1 Pet. 1:15, 16).

God is *righteous* — or just... fair in all His dealings with His creatures (Ps. 11:4-7; 145:17; Ezra 9:15; Jer. 12:1; John 17:25; Zeph. 3:5).

God is *merciful* (Deut. 4:31; Ps. 62:12; 86:15; 103:8;145:8).

God is *gracious* (Exod. 34:6; John 1:14; Rom. 3:24; 2 Cor. 8:9; 9:8; Heb. 4:16).

God is *good* — kind, cordial, benevolent, full of good will toward men (Mark 10:18; Ps. 145:9, 15, 16; Matt. 5:45).

God is *faithful* — an essential presupposition when His immutability is considered (1 John 1:9; Deut. 7:9; 1 Cor. 1:9; 10:13; 1 Thess. 5:24).

God is *tri-une* — Trinity in unity; one God In three Persons (John 1:1; 17:22, 23; Matt. 3:16, 17; 28:19; 2 Cor. 13:14).

God is our *Father* (Matt. 6:6-18; Luke 22:42; 23:34; John 8:41; 12:28).

I highly recommend the reading of *The Knowledge of the Holy*, by A. W. Tozer. It is a small book of meditational and devotional studies of the attributes of God and their meaning in the Christian life. It will form a good foundation for your further meditations on the applications to prayer.

Remember, as the poet has written:

> Thou art coming to a King;
> Large petitions with thee bring.

Study and Discussion Questions

1. Discuss how the ideas people have about God determine the way they pray. The following list of types of people may help you. If you recognize some which you are familiar with, discuss those:

   a. children   b. Roman Catholics
   c. Hindus   d. Muslims
   e. Mormons   f. Jehovah's Witnesses
   g. Pagans   h. Satan worshipers
   i. Bible-believing Christians   j. parents
   k. teenagers   l. deep-sea fishermen
   m. astronauts   n. others you and your
                                         group think of.

2. Describe God as Dr. Tozer thought of Him. Describe God as Dr. Earnest ("Pappy") Reveal thought of him. Discuss the author's claim that **both** these illustrations are in keeping with the character of the true God.

3. Beginning with "God is omniscient" on page 100, discuss five of the attributes of God which are listed. How does knowledge of **each** one affect how we pray?

8

THE PRIESTLY MINISTRY OF BELIEVERS

New Testament believers are called a holy priesthood, a royal priesthood: "You also, like living stones, are being built into a spiritual house to be a holy priesthood, offering spiritual sacrifices acceptable to God through Jesus Christ.... But you are a chosen people, a royal priesthood..." (1 Pet. 2:5.9a). The Lord Jesus, "who loves us and has freed us from our sins by His blood... has made us to be kings and priests to serve His God and Father" (Rev. 1:5b,6a).

The Book of Hebrews makes it clear that the priesthood, the sacrifices, and all that pertained to the tabernacle ministry under the Law, served as an "illustration" (9:9), a "copy" (9:24), or a "shadow" (10:1) of that which was real. It speaks of "the sanctuary, the true tabernacle set up by the Lord, not by man" (8:2). This tabernacle in Heaven (8:1) is the real place of priestly ministry. All the Old Testament Levitical system of sacrificial and priestly ministry was but a "shadow" of this reality.

Even the articles of furniture associated with the Old Testament priestly ministry were highly significant as types of the substantive ministry of the New Testament priesthood. One of these, the golden altar of incense, placed before the curtain which led into the Holy of Holies, was the place where Aaron, the high priest, burned incense every morning and evening. It typified our High Priest's intercession. Revelation 5:8 identifies incense as a type of prayer when it speaks of "bowls of incense, which are the prayers of the saints." That it was the intercessory ministry of Jesus Himself, our High Priest, which was portrayed is clear from the fact that "none but the high priest was qualified to offer incense at that altar."[1] Furthermore, the Bible tells us that Jesus "always lives to intercede" for us (Heb. 7:25) and this is in the context of a discussion of His High Priestly ministry: "Such a high priest meets our need..." (verse 26) and, "The point of what we are saying is this: We do have such a high priest, who sat down at the right hand of the throne of the Majesty in Heaven" (8:1). Romans 8:34 declares, "Christ Jesus, who died — more than that, who was raised to life — is at the right hand of God and is also interceding for us.

Notice again the position of the altar: "in front of the curtain that is before the ark of the Testimony — before the atonement cover that is over the Testimony — where I will meet with you" (Exod. 30:6). Only one person went beyond that curtain, the high priest, and that only on one day of the year, the Day of Atonement.

The entrance of the high priest into the Most Holy Place is described in God's instructions: "He is to take a censer full of burning coals from the altar before the Lord and two handfuls of finely ground fragrant incense and take them behind the curtain. He is to put the incense on the fire before the Lord, and the smoke of the incense will conceal the atonement cover above the Testimony, so that he will not die" (Lev. 16:12.13). Keil and Delitzsch suggest that "as burning incense was a symbol of prayer, this covering of the *capporeth* with the cloud of incense was a symbolical covering of the glory of the Most Holy One with prayer to God, in order that He might not see the sin, nor suffer His holy wrath to break forth upon the sinner, but might graciously accept, in the blood of the sin-offering, the souls for which it was presented."[2]

What a sense of awe and wonder this brings upon us as we contemplate the ministry of intercession which our High Priest, the Lord Jesus, performs perpetually for us. For, although atonement has been completed once and for all in the shedding of the blood of our Sin-Offering, both types (sacrifice and high priest) being fulfilled in Christ, yet "He always lives to intercede" for us (Heb. 7:25).

Let us look more closely at the entrance of our Lord into the Holy of Holies to present His own blood as an expiation for our sins and become our ever-living Intercessor. The scene is Calvary,

"And when Jesus had cried out again in a loud voice, He gave up His spirit. At that moment the curtain of the temple was

We are invited to come confidently to God to perform our priestly ministry.

torn in two from top to bottom" (Matt. 27:50, 51a). The rending of the curtain represents the "new and living way opened for us through the curtain, that is, His body" (Heb.10:20).

Every board, every covering, every article of furniture in the Tent of Meeting and its Court is typical of some facet of the Person and Work of Christ. He is the antitype, the fulfillment of the pattern. The curtain was the type of His body. His body was the veil covering His glory. On the Mount of Transfiguration, Peter, James, and John were granted the unique privilege of catching a glimpse of His glory. When the physical body of Jesus was broken in death, the blood of the Sin-Offering was shed, atonement was made, there was no further need of a yearly Day of Atonement, nor of a high priest of the Aaronic order to represent us before God, so the veil was torn in two from top to bottom by the unseen hands of God. From that moment on, there has been no unapproachable sanctuary. It is open to all who will come by the blood of the Sin-Offering.

As we have seen, we New Testament believers are priests. Now in this age, there is no curtain barring entrance to the Most Holy Place. Nor do we need any temporal, human priests to mediate for us. "Let us then approach the throne of grace with confidence, so that we may receive mercy and find grace to help us in our time of need" (Heb. 4:16). "Therefore, brothers, since we have confidence to enter the Most Holy Place by the blood of Jesus, by a new and living way opened for us through the curtain, that is, His body, and since we have a great priest over the house of God, let us draw near to God with a sincere heart in full assurance of faith, having our hearts sprinkled to cleanse us from a guilty conscience and having our bodies washed with pure water" (Heb. 10:19-22).

We are invited to come confidently to God to perform our priestly ministry. Aaronic priests approached the sanctuary by way of the brazen altar and the laver, or basin of washing. The brazen altar, where sacrificial animals were slain, represents the cross. The basin speaks to us of the need for continual cleansing through the sanctifying, purifying work of the Holy Spirit by the Word of God.

Each time, before entering their place of ministry, priests washed their hands and their feet in the laver (Exod. 30:17-2 1). There had been a previous over-all washing (Exod. 29:4), so only the hands and feet needed it prior to each time of ministering. Their hands were soiled by handling the bloody sacrifices at the brazen altar. Their feet were dirtied by the dust in which they walked with sandaled feet.

> *We stand in need of cleansing before entering into the holy ministry of intercession.*

In the New Testament, when Jesus washed the feet of His disciples, He told Peter. "A person who has had a bath needs only to wash his feet" (John 13:10a). In our priestly ministry today we do not come with hands bloodied from repeated sacrifices, for Christ "has appeared once for all at the end of the ages to do away with sin by the sacrifice of Himself" (Heb. 9:26). Yet, our feet have trod in the dust of this world. Without any intention of sinning, without any willful sin, we have worked among people whose speech has been defiling. Our ears and eyes have taken in contaminating influences.

Although made positionally holy before God by the once-for-all sacrifice at Calvary, we stand in need of cleansing before entering into the holy ministry of priestly intercession. "But if we walk in the light, as He is in the light, we have fellowship with one another, and the blood of Jesus, His Son, purifies us from every sin. If we claim to be without sin, we deceive ourselves and the truth is not in us. If we confess our sins, He is faithful and just and will forgive us our sins and purify us from all unrighteousness" (1 John 1:7-9). The Apostle Paul speaks of Jesus' "cleansing" of the Church "by the washing with water through the word" (Eph. 5:26), and David, in Psalm 119:9 informs young men that the means of cleansing one's way is by heeding the Word of God.

Intercessory prayer is "heavenly" — not in the insipid use of the word which means "very nice" or "pleasant," but in the sense that it actually *takes place at the throne of God in Heaven.* It is the Holy Spirit's business, Christ's business, and our business as priests. It is not some trivial pastime of earth, but the serious business of Heaven. As we intercede, Christ adds the incense of

His own prayers to ours. Saved by His blood, clothed in His righteousness, washed by the continual cleansing of His blood and His Word, let us come with confidence and without ceasing beyond the rent veil into the presence of God.

Mrs. Matthews knew this kind of "heavenly" prayer ministry. It was no surprise to her when Ron Jordahl received the Lord Jesus Christ as his personal Saviour in 1959, because she had been praying that he would. She was getting along in years and her memory was poor, but she wasn't worried about it.

"Years ago, I asked the Lord to preserve my mind so I could pray," she remarked, "so I don't have to worry about that. I am very forgetful, but I remember the things I pray about."

> *"It is only when the Church gives herself up to this holy work of intercession that we can expect the power of Christ to manifest itself in her behalf."*
> —Andrew Murray

Ron shared with her the burden on his heart for the salvation of his father, Harry Jordahl.

When Ron and his wife Faye saw Mrs. Matthews in 1970, it had been several years between visits. They were able to visit her in the State of Washington, where she was living with her son. Her first words were, "Why, Faye! And Ron, is your dad saved yet?" By this time she was in her eighties, and Ron and Faye did not expect her to recognize them at all. In fact, they wondered whether she might be confused, because she asked that question in greeting as though she had seen them only the day before. Seeing Ron's hesitation, she added, "Your dad's name is Harry, isn't it?" When they told her that he had not yet come to the Lord, she assured them that he would.

Mrs. Matthews died in 1973. Her faith that God would answer her prayers for Ron's dad meant much to the Jordahls. It was obvious that God had kept her mind for prayer and would not let those years of faithful intercession be in vain.

During Christmas holidays in 1976. Ron Jordahl, Librarian and Faculty member at Prairie Bible Institute, received word that his father was dying of cancer. The family left hurriedly for Iowa as friends at Prairie prayed for Harry Jordahl's salvation before it was too late. He was 81 years old.

When Ron and Faye saw Harry, the transformation was evident. Yes, his roommate in the hospital had led him to the Lord.

When Ron's dad went to be with the Lord a day later, Faye's first thought was of the meeting between the faithful prayer warrior and the man she had never met on earth, but for whom she had prayed for so many years.

Such is the blessed priestly ministry of intercession which is committed as a sacred trust to every child of God in this Church Age. If you have trusted Christ Jesus as your Saviour, realize that He saved you for a purpose, that you might serve as a priest. It is a lifetime calling, and it is yours. Grasp it, cherish it, employ it faithfully.

Andrew Murray said, "It is only when the Church gives herself up to this holy work of intercession that we can expect the power of Christ to manifest itself in her behalf."[3]

E.M. Bounds adds this essential emphasis: "The praying which gives colour and bent to character is no pleasant, hurried pastime. It must enter as strongly into the heart and life as Christ's 'strong crying and tears' did; must draw out the soul into an agony of desire as Paul's did; must be an inwrought fire and force like the 'effectual, fervent prayer' of James; must be of that quality which, when put into the golden censer and incensed before God, works mighty spiritual throes and revolutions."[4]

The concept of priestly service is broadened still further by S.D. Gordon, who says. "It helps greatly to remember that intercession is service: the chief service of a life on God's plan. It is unlike all other forms of service, and superior to them in this: that it has fewer limitations. In all other service we are constantly limited by space, bodily strength, equipment, material obstacles, difficulties involved in the peculiar differences of personality. Prayer knows no such limitations."[5]

It soon becomes obvious in reading E.M. Bounds' books that his great burden was for *preachers* to get hold of the truth that secret, priestly intercession is essential to their public ministry, but his counsel holds good for all Christian workers and witnesses. He says. "Talking to men for God is a great thing, but talking to God for men is greater still. He will never talk well and with real success to men for God who has not learned well how to talk to God for men."[6]

Study and Discussion Questions

1. Read Matthew 27:45-54; Hebrews 10:19-22. Discuss what the torn curtain (rent veil) in the temple means to your prayer ministry. These verses are also significant: 1 Peter 2:5, 9 (about our priestly ministry).

2. Hebrews 4-10 describes Jesus' High Priestly ministry. Study the following verses especially: 7:23-8:5a; 9:11-14, 23-28. Tell how Jesus' high priestly ministry was much greater than that of earthly priests in the Old Testament.

3. Discuss Hebrews 10:19-22 thought-by-thought. Discuss what each phrase says, what it refers to in both the Old Testament and the New Testament, and why it is important for the priestly ministry of New Testament believers (that is why it is important for our prayer ministry).

4. What significance (meaning) does **each** of the following have for our prayer ministry?
    a. The gate to the Tabernacle's Outer Court
    b. The altar of burnt offerings (bronze altar)
    c. The laver placed before the door of the Tabernacle (Holy Place)
    d. The altar of incense
    e. The torn veil (curtain)
    f. The high priest
    g. The priests
    h. The ark with its mercy seat
    Feel free to discuss other parts of the Tabernacle in the Wilderness and later the Temple as they are helpful in understanding our priestly ministry in Christ our High Priest.

9

ASKING IN JESUS' NAME

I will do
WHATEVER
You ask in My name.

You may ask Me for
ANYTHING
in My name,
and I will do it.

A check with the signature of the world's richest man and the amount left blank for you to fill in as you wished would be as nothing compared with these astounding promises given by the King of Glory.

The doctrine of prayer would lack vital elements both in precept and example without Jesus' Upper Room Discourse in John 13-16. Here, in chapters 14-16, we are encouraged six times by the Lord Himself to *ask in His name*, and the assurance is given repeatedly that both He and the Father will stand behind the promise to honour anything thus requested. It is climaxed in chapter 17 with the tenderest prayer of intercession in all Scripture, Jesus' own High Priestly Prayer.

Let's look at the verses which advocate making request in Jesus' name. Some significant phrases and clauses are emphasized by using upper case letters.

> "I tell you the truth, anyone who has faith in Me will
> do what I have been doing. He will do even greater

things than these, because I am going to the Father. And I WILL DO WHATEVER

> *Jesus' name represents His Person.*

YOU ASK IN MY NAME, so that the Son may bring glory to the Father. You may ASK ME FOR ANYTHING IN MY NAME. AND I WILL DO IT. If you love Me, you will obey what I command... If you remain in Me and My words remain in you, ASK WHATEVER YOU WISH, AND IT WILL BE GIVEN YOU. ...You did not choose Me, but I chose you to go and bear fruit — fruit that will last. Then THE FATHER WILL GIVE YOU WHATEVER YOU ASK IN MY NAME. This is My command: Love each other... I tell you the truth, MY FATHER WILL GIVE YOU WHATEVER YOU ASK IN MY NAME. Until now you have not asked for anything IN MY NAME. Ask and you will receive, and your joy will be complete. Though I have been speaking figuratively, a time is coming when I will no longer use this kind of language but will tell you plainly about My Father. In that day you will ASK IN MY NAME" (John 14:12-15; 15:7, 16, 17; 16:23b-26a).

What Does It Mean to Ask in Jesus' Name?

1. *Jesus' name represents His Person.*

   "The name stands for the person," says J. Oswald Sanders. "To believe 'in the name of the only begotten Son of God' (John 3:18) means to believe in the person of Christ, in all that He is and has done.

2. *Praying in Jesus' name is praying in faith and in accordance with the will of God.*

   Charles R. Erdman agrees that it is "in virtue of, and in acceptance of, all that He has been revealed to be, as the divine Son of God, one with the Father." To this fact he adds, "The promises to answer prayer are unlimited, except by the clear statements made on other occasions that prayer must be, in faith, which includes submission, and in accordance with the will of God, both of which conditions are implied by the phrase. 'In My name.'"[2] Notice that Jesus spoke of "anyone who has faith in Me" (John 14:12) in the immediate context of His first utterance of the promise to do whatever we ask in His name. Moreover, the whole section on the true vine and the branches in chapter 15 implies, not only asking in His will, but abiding (remaining, living, continually acting) in His will.

3. "This is equivalent to saying *on My account, or for My sake*,"[3] says Albert Barnes.

4. *Christ's authority and union with Him are involved.*
    I believe that Everett Harrison stresses an important point when he says, "This involves at least two things: praying in the authority Christ gives (cf. Matt. 28:19; Acts 3:6) and praying in union with Him, so that one does not pray outside His will."[4]
    The matter of union with Christ was also uppermost in Samuel Chadwick's mind: "Prayer reaches its highest level when offered in the Name which is above every name, for it lifts the petitioner into unity and identity with Himself."[5]

5. *Jesus' name is the basis of our plea.*
    "We have been authorized," says Mr. Sanders, "to make Christ's name the basis of our plea. Our prayers are answered and we experience God's favour on the grounds of His merit, not our own."'

6. *When we pray in Jesus' name, we represent Him.*
    The saintly Andrew Murray agreed that "the name of Christ is the expression of all He has done and all He is and lives to do as our Mediator," and he saw clearly that "to do a thing in the power of another... is to come with the power and authority of that other, as His

> *To pray In Jesus' name is to claim the covenant blessings that are ours as heirs of God and joint-heirs with Christ.*

representative and substitute."[7]

Since we represent Him, we have His interest, His desire, His motive, and His purpose in each request. Otherwise, we are not praying in His name — no matter what cliche we tack onto the end of our prayer. It is because we come in Christ's stead, authorized by Him to use His name to accomplish His purposes that God can put Himself on the line to grant us anything we request.

7. *To pray in Jesus' name is to claim the covenant blessings that are ours as heirs of God and joint-heirs with Christ.*

This is the great truth highlighted by James William Thirtle. The Great Commission Prayer League has performed a real service in reprinting a condensation of Thirtle's classic work under the title, *In Jesus' Name, Amen!* in the foreword, Dr. Philip R. Newell summarizes the theme succinctly: "Far from being a mere matter of semantics, or just a ritualistic formula for concluding prayer, Dr. Thirtle insists that to pray in the Son's name is to invoke the issues of that covenant between the Father and the Son (Heb. 13:20) whereby our Lord Jesus in His triumph over Satan has been made 'Heir of all things,' and enables His redeemed ones to participate through prayer in that purpose for which the Son of God was manifested — 'that He might destroy the works of the devil' (1 John 3:8b)."[8]

It was Dr. Thirtle's conviction that no explanation of Jesus' commands to pray in His name was given because both He and His disciples would have clearly in mind the Jewish practice of presenting their petitions to God in the names of the patriarchs, with whom God had made covenants. For example, he declares, "In Psalm 132 there is a clear petition 'in the name': 'For Thy servant David's sake, turn not away the face of Thine anointed.' The name of David is pleaded. The Psalmist proceeds to plead the covenant made with the same king: 'The Lord hath sworn in truth unto David; He will not turn from it: of the fruit of thy body will I set upon thy throne.'"[9]

Of the nation which rejects Christ, we are told that to this day "they recite the covenants with their ancestors, in the hope that, on account of those who were more worthy than themselves, answer will be made to their prayers."[10]

"Now we see why there is power in the Name. At back of the Name there is a covenant, a divine undertaking which can never be set aside"[11] the New Covenant established in Christ by His shed blood, by which we have eternal salvation and "every spiritual blessing in Christ" (Eph. 1:3).

Who Can Ask?

Not everyone can ask in Jesus' name. Only the person who believes in Jesus can pray in His name. This is true even of the sinner praying the publican's prayer. The prayer is his expression of faith in the Saviour. But the person who asks for healing, guidance, money, or any other benefit who has not trusted and does not trust Jesus as his very own personal Saviour is not on praying ground. The name of Jesus is not his to use. Jesus has not granted the authority of His name to any except those who have accepted the revelation God has given of His Son. It was not to the Twelve that this privilege was extended, but to the Eleven; Judas had left the group. There is no way that a rebel against God and His Christ can pray in Jesus' name, so these promises are not for such. It is to "anyone who has faith in Me" (John 14:12) that the limitless promises are given, to those who "have loved Me and have believed that I came from God" (John 16:27).

R.A. Torrey says, "What does it mean to believe on Jesus Christ? To believe on Jesus Christ means to put our personal confidence in Jesus Christ as what He claims to be, and to accept Him to be to ourselves what He offers Himself to be to us. It means to accept Him as our Saviour, as the One who bore our sins in His own body upon the cross, and to trust God to forgive us because Jesus Christ died in our place, and also to accept Him as our Lord and Master to whom we surrender the absolute control of our lives."[12] John 1:12 clarifies it, "Yet to all who received Him, to those who believed In His name, He gave the right to become children of God." Believing in His name is essential to praying in His name.

Are All Christians Qualified?

Are all prayers offered by those who have been born again by faith in Christ necessarily offered in Jesus' name? Over and over in His last discourse the Lord qualified His

> *To pray In the name is to pray in full accord with the nature of the Person.*

promise regarding prayer in His name as applying to those who obey His commands and He summarized His commands in one, to love each other. Notice: "You may ask Me for anything in My name, and I will do it. If you love Me, *you will obey what I command....* If you remain in Me and *My words remain in you,* ask whatever you wish, and it will be given you.... If you *obey My commands*, you will remain in My love.... *My command is this: Love each other as I have loved you....* Then the Father will give you whatever you ask in My name. *This is My command: Love each other"* (John 14:14, 15; 15:7, 10, 12, 16, 17; italics added). Taking His words at face value, one quickly notices that loving Christ is evidenced by obedience to His commands, which are summarized in the command to love each other as He has loved us, and this is what He meant by remaining in Him. If this quality is not characteristic of our lives, we are not qualified to pray in His name.

If we hold smouldering resentments in our hearts or show our antipathy toward others, we are not living in accord with the revelation of Jesus Christ and therefore cannot pray within the sphere of that revelation. The name reveals the Person; to pray in the name is to pray in full accord with the nature of the Person; if we are not in harmony with Him, having a oneness of attitude with Him toward others, then our use of His name becomes a forgery.

Let us obey all His words. They include not only quotations from Him in the Gospels, but all His Holy Word from Genesis through Revelation. To do so will require the saturation of our minds with it. There are no promises of answered prayer for a disobedient child, only for an abiding child. Torrey summarizes it succinctly: "The promise of God to give to a certain class of people whatever they ask in a certain way, is made to those who are united to Him by a living faith, and an obedient love, to them and to them alone."[13]

On What Grounds Can We Use Jesus' Name?

As we have already observed throughout this chapter, the basis of our requests which God promises to grant unconditionally is the name of the Lord Jesus. All my life I've been praying "in Jesus' name," but God hasn't given me all my requests. (Thank the Lord!) Why? What did I do wrong? If praying in Jesus' name means merely to tack "in Jesus' name, amen" to the end of our prayers, why aren't all such requests granted? Interestingly enough, not one prayer recorded in the Bible ends with "in Jesus' name" or "for Jesus' sake." Don't get me wrong. I'll probably go right on saying it. I'm fascinated, though, with the praying of a friend who often *begins* with, "In Jesus' name, we come to Thee, our Father," or words to that effect. What I'm endeavouring to emphasize is that the phrase does not constitute a formula which makes prayers work. "In Jesus' name" is not a Christian incantation, not an abracadabra to insure success. Yet, how often we as Christians subconsciously assign it such superstitious mumbo-jumbo powers. Or else we use it thoughtlessly.

However, the name of Jesus does carry with it all the authority of Heaven and earth. By way of illustration, imagine yourself going into a strange bank, filling in a savings account withdrawal slip in the amount of ten dollars and presenting it to the teller. She asks for your account number.

"I don't have one," is your reply.

"Well, I'm sorry, sir," she says, "but I cannot give you ten dollars if you have no account here!"

"But there is my name on the withdrawal slip. The signature is genuine; here, I have identification."

There is no need to take that illustration further. Its ridiculous nature is obvious.

Let's try another imaginary scene: same bank, same person (you), same teller. This time you present a check made out to you in the amount of $10,000 and certified by the president of the bank. Your identification is verified and the money paid to you. No argument.

What made the difference? There were no funds behind your

name. Your name in a bank where you had no account was worthless. But when you presented a check properly certified by the president of the bank, the teller knew that the money was there to back it up. It was the president's name that carried authority, not yours. When you need to draw on Heaven's bank, there is only one name which carries authority: Jesus Christ.

Let's try one more example. Prairie Bible Institute has accounts with the major gasoline companies. When I am sent out as a speaker by the Extension Department of the school, an automobile and credit cards are supplied. Any time I need gasoline, an oil change, or a lubrication job, I merely present a card with the name of Prairie Bible Institute on it. My name does not appear on it, but it is always honoured. The school authorities have entrusted me with the use of the school name. They trust me not to abuse the privilege by running up a bill for my personal expenses. I use the school credit card for school business.

So our wonderful Lord Jesus has entrusted us with His name. His character stands behind it. He trusts us to use it for His purposes. What a glorious principle of effective prayer!

An ambassador goes to a foreign country to represent his government. He goes in the name of his president or prime minister. It is not his business to make a profit for himself, to pursue his own interests. And so, we witness and pray "in the name of" our Lord, that is, we represent His interests, not our own. We will, therefore, pray only for those things which He approves. We will seek only those things which will further His kingdom and bring glory to His name.

It was in the context of service for Christ that He gave the promises regarding answers to prayers offered in His name: "I tell you the truth, anyone who has faith in *Me will do what I have been doing. He will do even greater things* than these, because I am going to the Father. And I will do whatever you ask in My name, so that the Son may bring glory to the Father" (John 14:12, 13). And again, "You did not choose Me, but *I chose you to go and bear fruit — fruit that will last.* Then the Father will give you whatever you ask in My name" (John 15:16; italics added). We dare not lift the promises out of context to apply them to selfish interests. We only pray in Jesus name when we go forth for Him, bearing His name unashamedly before His enemies, witnessing in His name to those who know Him not, bearing lasting fruit, and glorifying the Father through our loyal service to His Son. That is a far cry from the habit of hanging His name like a magic amulet to the end of our prayers with the notion that it will make any request work. When truly asked in Jesus' name, every request is granted.

To What Extent Are We to Use His Name?

Not only is prayer "In Jesus' name." Jesus said, "...repentance and forgiveness of sins will be preached in His name to all nations, beginning at Jerusalem" (Luke 24:47). Miracles were wrought in Jesus' name; Peter said to the crippled beggar, "Silver or gold I do not have, but what I have I give you. In the name of Jesus Christ of Nazareth, walk" (Acts 3:6). In explaining the miracle to the Sanhedrin he re-emphasized the point, "It is by the name of Jesus Christ of Nazareth, whom you crucified but whom God raised from the dead, that this man stands before you completely healed" (Acts 4:10). The name represents the Person, all He is and does. That which is done in His name is done with reliance upon His power. Paul adds that we should be "always giving thanks to God the Father for everything, in the name of our Lord Jesus Christ" (Eph. 5:20). And in Colossians 3:17 he gets it all together, "And whatever you do, whether in word or deed, do it all in the name of the Lord Jesus, giving thanks to God the Father through Him." Pray, witness, wash dishes, preach, saw a board, supervise a construction gang, serve a meal, entertain guests, sing a song, go on a date, get married — do *all* in Jesus' name, in His stead, as His representative, in the light of the revelation we have of Him, for His glory. It's a way of life, not an incantation.

A young woman who is not enamored with the Bible-contradicting features of Women's Lib is delighted to take her husband's name. She is in love with him and wants to be fully identified with him, to merge her identity into his. When she is so completely his and so obviously has his interests at heart, he gladly establishes a joint checking account, gives her copies of his credit cards, and stands good for her bills. Jesus does the same with His bride and for the same reasons.

PRINCIPLES OF EFFECTIVE PRAYER

Samuel Chadwick sums it all up: "To pray in Christ's name means something more than adding 'for Jesus' sake' to our petitions. The name expresses personality, character, and being. The Person is in the name. Prayer in Christ's name is prayer according to the quality of His Person, according to the character of His mind, and according to the character of His will. To pray in the name of Christ is to pray as one who is at one with Christ, whose mind is the mind of Christ, and whose purpose is one with that of Christ."[14]

> *"To pray in the name of Christ is to pray as one who is at one with Christ, whose mind is the mind of Christ, whose desires are the desires of Christ, and whose purpose is one with that of Christ."*
> —Samuel Chadwick

To discover what Christ wants and how He prays so that we might follow suit, we would do well to begin with His High Priestly Prayer in John 17 and His Gethsemane Prayer in Matthew 26:36-46. Notice that the glory of God and the will of God are foremost in His requests.

In the following two songs I have tried to capture the truths of this lesson:

IN JESUS' NAME
(To the tune of "Under His Wings")

In Jesus' name we can come to the Father,
'Though in ourselves we have nothing to bring,
Nought to redeem us and nought to commend us,
Yet in His name we can come to the King.

Chorus:
In Jesus' name, in Jesus' name,
We are as one with the Saviour,
In Jesus' name, the Father approves.
Bestows on us all His favour.

In Jesus' name there's a clear way of access

Unto the throne of our heavenly King;
Into the presence of God in His glory,
For to our Saviour in faith we will cling.

In Jesus' name we can pray with assurance,
And know God hears us in Heaven above,
Know He receives us, and know He will answer.
In our dear Saviour, the Son of His love.

In Jesus' name, representing His Person,
All of His nature, authority, too,
All of His holiness, and all His power.
All of His glory, our prayers to endue.

JESUS, WHAT A NAME!
(Matt. 1:21; John 14–16)
(To the tune of Austrian Hymn:
"Glorious Things of Thee Are Spoken."
or Hyfrydol: "Our Great Saviour")

Jesus! What a name of power!
Jesus! What a name of love!
For the sinner full salvation
In that name from God above.

Chorus:
Jesus! Jesus! Name of glory!
Jesus, Jesus, pleads my case,
For "Jehovah is salvation,"
And His name is full of grace.

Unto Him is all authority;
Unto us He gives His name,
That we might in faith have access
Just as though 'twere He who came.

Anything we ask in Jesus' name,

Anything, the promise is true,
Unto us that we might bear fruit,
And our joy may be full, too.

(Words of both songs © Wentworth Pike)

Study and Discussion Questions

1. Discuss what praying In Jesus' name means to you. Make it personal by using "I." "me," "my," "mine."

2. Why is praying in Jesus' name so effective?

3. **Each** person in your group may discuss one of the 7 items under "What Does It Mean...?". Tell how your item is meaningful and helpful for your own prayer life. If some are more difficult than others, discuss them more. See whether you can find helps, Scripture, and greater development of the ideas than the author of this book gives.

4. Discuss some hindrances born-again believers might have to claiming the wonderful promises of Jesus in John 14-16 about praying in His name.

5. Discuss ways in which we might use Jesus' name **illegally** in prayer. What would be the **result**?

10

THE BELIEVER'S POSITION OF AUTHORITY

(ATTENTION! Study this chapter with an OPEN BIBLE! Turn to Ephesians. You will need to refer to it often.)

Our prayer in Jesus' name is effective because God accepts us in union with His Son. He accepts us as He does His own beloved Son and grants our petition as readily as He does a plea from the One at His right hand. He sees us as being *in Christ.*

This "in Christ" position of the believer is mentioned frequently in the Scriptures. Paul uses it much, especially in the Epistle to the Ephesians. The knowledge that we are in Christ and that the Father accepts us in Him is a sure foundation for effective prayer.

Now, stop and read Ephesians 1:1-14 and notice the many blessings which are ours "in Christ," in Him," in the One He loves."

1 Corinthians 1:30 declares, "It is because of Him that you are IN CHRIST JESUS, who has become for us wisdom from God — that is, our righteousness, holiness and redemption."

When one places his faith in the Lord Jesus as personal Saviour, he is baptized into Christ's Body (the Church comprised of all true believers) by the Holy Spirit (1 Cor. 12:13). Christ Himself is the Head of the Body and the believers are parts of the Body which all function in harmony under the direction of the Head. As an arm, a hand, a leg, or a foot is in the body, so Christians are in Christ's Body, one with Him and with one another. We are "in Christ," not in the sense that we might be in Toronto or Chicago, nor in the sense that the water is in the glass. We are in Christ in that we are in union with Him, united with Him, under His guidance and control, sharing His life. As a human body is served by the same vascular system, nervous system, respiratory system, etc., so there is a living unity in the Body of Christ. We are not merely on His team or in His club, we share His life. His life is our life, we receive it from Him. If there is a lack of unity, a lack of harmony, it is because some members of the body refuse to take direction from the Head.

The Bible follows through on this analogy by teaching us that what happens to the Head happens to the Body. We are united with Christ. His crucifixion is our crucifixion: "I have been crucified with

> *The knowledge that we are in Christ and that the Father accepts us in Him is a sure foundation for effective prayer.*

Christ..."(Gal. 2:20a). His resurrection is ours: "and I no longer live, but Christ lives in me..." (Gal. 2:20b). This crucified, resurrected life has been called "the deeper life," "life on a higher plane," "the crucified life," and "the exchanged life." Actually, it is the normal Christian life. It is not something mysterious or some super-spiritual life for which Christians are to strive. It is a fact that is true by virtue of our placement into Christ when we were born again. Not all believers live in the light of this truth. Some are not even aware of it. But it was accomplished by Christ in the crucifixion–resurrection event, and it was appropriated by faith in Him when we were born again.

This identification of believers with the Lord in His death and resurrection is traced to its logical and practical conclusion in Ephesians 1 and 2. Here the Apostle Paul, by the Holy Spirit, shows us that we are not only raised, but also ascended with Christ so that our rightful position is in Christ in the seat of authority and intercession at the right hand of the Father. Ephesians 2:6, "And God raised us up with Christ and seated us with Him in the heavenly realms in Christ Jesus."

In Ephesians 1 we have Paul's prayer for believers that we might know "His [God's] incomparably great power for us who believe" (v. 19). In the following verses we have that power illustrated in the resurrection-ascension-exaltation of Christ. When we understand that we are in Christ, seated with Him in heavenly places at the right hand of the Father, we are ready to understand a new aspect of prayer.

The right hand of the Father is the place of intercession (cf. Rom. 8:34). We have not merely the glorious truth that our Lord is there interceding for us, but also the fact that we are united with Him in the ministry of intercession. Jesus prayed "that all of them may be one, Father, just as You are in Me and I am in You, May they also be in Us so that the world may believe that You have sent Me. I have given them the glory that you gave Me, that they may be one as We are one: I in them and You in Me" (John 17:21-23a). God is in Christ: Christ is in us: we are in Him — and at no time does this mystical truth take on such practical application as when we are united with the Saviour in intercession.

The right hand is also the place of authority — "far above all rule and authority, power and dominion, and every title that can be given, not only in the present age but also in the one to come" (Eph. 1:21). Now, since we are seated with Christ, we, too, are in this position of authority above Satan and all his hosts. We are united to Him, as the head and the body are united, and it is for the benefit of the Body that the Head, Christ, is placed above all things, as the next two verses in Ephesians tell us: "And God placed all things under His feet and appointed Him to be head over everything for the Church, which is His Body, the fullness of Him who fills everything in every way (Eph. 1:22,23). Where the Head is the Body is. The Church, then, is in the position of authority and intercession.

Theodore H. Epp has dealt with this truth well in the small book, *Praying with Authority*. He declares, "Our identification with Christ was not confined to His death but includes His resurrection (Eph. 2:5) and ascension also... (v. 6). He sits in the place of authority at the right hand of the Father (Rom. 8:34), and we with Him. From this stem our present throne-rights. These carry with them potential powers and privileges altogether too few of us have entered into."[1]

It is this union which puts us, with Christ, at the right hand of the Father in the position of authority over the powers of Hell.

For the sake of Jesus and the salvation of the souls for whom He died, Dr. Epp insists: "We have been raised together with Jesus Christ and made to sit together in heavenly places (Eph. 2:5,6).

This is why we have throne-rights. To fully enter into them the self-life must be completely dispossessed, and we must share the mind of Christ and join with Him in suffering. All that is Christ's is ours now, if all that we possess and are, is His now."[2] My friend, will you please stop and re-read the last two sentences of that quotation. They are so important. They point out the path of effective intercession with the true authority of Christ.

The truth of this Ephesians' portion was clarified and stressed for me by a former Bible school teacher now with the Lord, Rev. J.A. MacMillan. Mr. MacMillan had been on the mission field only a short time when the doctor ordered him home because of a "nervous breakdown." In those days it was not so easy to get transportation halfway around the world, so he had to wait for quite a while. One day, while in deep depression, MacMillan was reading Ephesians and the truth became clear to him. Although he felt he must be the lowest member of Christ's body, the sole of His feet so to speak, yet he saw himself in Christ at the right hand of the Father, above — yea, "far above" — "all rule and authority, power and dominion," far above anything with which Satan could attack him. On his knees, therefore, he accepted his position in Christ and claimed victory. He did not go home, but spent a lifetime serving the Lord in great power.

Mr. MacMillan shared what he learned about our authority from our "in-Christ" position in a booklet entitled *The Authority of the Believer*, published by Christian Publications. In it, he says, concerning Ephesians 1:19ff. "behind the fact of the resurrection of the Lord Jesus there lay the mightiest working recorded in the Word of God."

"Having been thus raised from among the dead, Christ Jesus was exalted by God to His own right hand in the heavenlies. Then was seen the reason for such mighty working. The resurrection had been opposed by the tremendous 'powers of the air': — 'all principality, and power, and might, and dominion, and every name that is named, not only in this world (*aioni*, age) but also in that which is to come.' The evil forces of the 'age to come' had been arrayed against the purpose of God. They

> *"All that is Christ's is ours now, if all that we possess and are is His now."*
> —Theodore Epp

had, however, been baffled and overthrown, and the risen Lord had been enthroned 'far above' them, ruling with the authority of the Most High.

"In calling attention to the 'exceeding greatness of His [God's] power,' we passed over without comment four words. These are: 'to usward who believe.' All the demonstration of the glory of God, shown in the manifestation of His omnipotence, pointed manward. The cross of Christ, with what it revealed of obedience to God, of atonement for sin, of crushing defeat of the foes of divine authority, shows us a representative Man overcoming for mankind and preparing, through His own incumbency, a throne and a heavenly ministry for those who should overcome through Him.

"Observe in this connection the identification of Christ's people with Himself, in this crisis of the resurrection. In the first verse of chapter 2, the words read literally: 'And you, *being dead* in trespasses and sins,' or, perhaps, to bring out better the thought: 'And you, *when ye were dead in trespasses* and sins.' It will be noticed that we have left out the verb 'hath He quickened' which appears in our Bibles. This verb is not in the original; the sentence is incomplete, 'being left unfinished,' says one expositor, 'in the rapidity of dictation.' We do not accept this as the explanation of the omission, for we believe that the Holy Spirit so arranged the structure of the whole passage, that the fact might be emphasized that *Christ and His people were raised together* [italics mine].

"Where, then, do we find the verb that controls this passage? It will be seen in verse 20 of chapter 1: 'According to that working of the strength of His might *when He raised Him from the dead...* (then, putting a parenthesis around the words to the end of the chapter)... *and YOU when ye were dead.*' The same verb which expresses the reviving of Christ expresses also the reviving of His people. That is to say *the very act of God which raised the Lord from among the dead, also raised His body* [italics mine]. Head and body are naturally raised together: Christ, the Head: His Body, the Church (*ho ekklesia*, the assembly of believers in Him). This is a most important statement, and one of which the definite significance cannot be overestimated."[3]

It is one thing to be in Christ positionally, but it is another matter to abide in Him. In the first, authority is potentially ours; in the second it is worked out in practical application. In John 15 Jesus talks about our "in-Christ" position, comparing it to the branch in the vine, but He admonishes us to maintain it actively and in this context promises to give whatever (cf. John 15:5-7) we ask.

What is the way to abide in Him? Be sure that His Word abides in us, that we abide in His love through obedience to His commands, which are condensed into one: to love as He has loved us.

The purpose of this union is the production of fruit, much fruit (cf. John 15:4,5,8), Lenski comments, "The vine orders the branches to ask of it all that it is able to give. And there is no question about the receiving: 'it shall be done for you.' No limits exist for the vine: the only limit is in our faith, which may not ask though it has the right to ask."[4] As we maintain our relationship with Christ by holding His words obediently, we may ask for whatever is necessary to produce fruit, the fruit of the Spirit, in our lives and God will give it. This is the principle of effective prayer taught in Jesus' allegory of the vine and the branches. There is no other way, for we draw sap to produce fruit from the true vine and from Him alone.

Too often we look upon salvation merely as something which took place instantaneously at some point in our past and fail to consider its continuing, sanctifying aspect. Jesus' saying, "Whoever eats My flesh and drinks My blood remains in Me, and I in Him" (John 6:56), expresses this continuing relationship. "If we walk in the light, as He is in the light, we have fellowship with one another, and the blood of Jesus, His Son, purifies us from every sin" (1 John 1:7). Every verb in these verses stresses *continuous action*: eats, drinks, remains, walk, is, have, purifies.

This then is the principle: Our new-birth experience placed us on praying ground with authority over all powers which oppose Christ, and our continual adherence to His words qualifies us to ask for anything we need to produce fruit for His glory.

Therefore, let us ASK LARGELY!

Study and Discussion Questions

1. In the light of the believer's **position** in Christ and His **authority**, discuss the following idea: The intercessor/prayer-warrior does not send his prayers **up to Heaven** but **down from Heaven**.

2. Discuss how our position in Christ (Ephesians 1:18-2:7) will help us pray victoriously in the following situations:
    a. Times of temptation
    b. Times of discouragement and depression emotionally and spiritually,
    c. Times of satanic/demonic attack against our bodies and minds, our families, our ministry.

3. Study John 15:1-7. Discuss how **asking in Jesus' name** is related to the idea of **the-Vine-and-the-branches**. Show the relationship between verses 7 and 16.

---------------- **11** ----------------

THE WARFARE OF THE BELIEVER

Two and a half million Israelites, by conservative estimate, followed the pillar of cloud by day and fire by night, crossed the Red Sea on dry land, drank of the water miraculously made palatable, gathered manna sent down from Heaven, and quenched their thirst at a stream which flowed from a rock when their leader struck it. The staff which Moses raised above the sea to divide the waters, and with which he struck the rock to provide drinking water, was the symbol of God's authority.

At Rephidim, the Amalekites attacked the Israelites, Joshua hastily drafted an army of sorts from the undisciplined masses. As they fought in the valley, Moses took Aaron and Hur to the top of a nearby hill. He raised the staff of God toward Heaven in a gesture of dependence upon God and of authority over the enemy. In the valley, swords clashed and blood flowed. The battle progressed favourably for Joshua and the Israelites.

Moses, the acknowledged commander-in-chief of Israel, and his two priestly helpers, did not issue military directives from the hill. Yet, it soon became obvious that there was a definite connection between the outcome of the battle in the valley and the activities atop the hill. Moses' arms grew weary as the day wore on. When he lowered the staff of God, the battle turned against Joshua's army. So the help of Aaron and Hur was enlisted to hold Moses' hands aloft. With Moses sitting on a stone, Aaron on one side and Hur on the other held his hands steady until sunset, and Joshua completely routed the enemy.

This true incident from Exodus 17 is more than a mere historical novelty. It has stood through the ages as a clear illustration of the reality of spirit warfare behind the visible strife on this earth and of the powerful influence exerted through the identification of the intercessor with those for whom he makes supplication. While Joshua's involvement in the thick of the fray was essential and very real, the deciding factor in the victory was obviously Moses' definite and persistent use of spiritual authority.

T.S. Rendall observes, 'The uplifted hand represents Moses interceding on behalf of his people. We reject completely the theory that the uplifted hand was some kind of superstitious gesture or magical action on the part of Moses. It was, rather, an act of faith in exercising his authority as a prince with God. He was identifying himself with the purpose of God for Israel, and was interceding for the power of God to be manifested in total triumph for Joshua and his soldiers."[1]

Further insight is gained into this strange incident and its spiritual significance through Dr. Rendall's questions and incisive comments: "What, then, incited the Amalekites to attack Israel? Can we doubt that it was evil angels, princes of Satan, who moved Amalek and his soldiers to pounce upon the people of Israel? This vitriolic anti-Semitism had no basis other than hatred for God's people and opposition to His redemptive plan for Israel. Thus God declared perpetual enmity against Amalek and his descendants because he became the instrument of these wicked angel princes in their attempt to wipe out the chosen people."[2]

Let's look at another example of prayer warfare in Scripture. Read 2 Kings 18 & 19 for the full dramatic story.

> In 18:19-22, Sennacherib's army field commander taunted Hezekiah's officials for depending on their own strategy and military strength, on Egypt, or on the LORD (Jehovah). In 18:23-25, he belittled them, saying that he would give them 2000 horses - if they could even put riders on them! And the final insult was to claim, "The LORD himself told me to march against this country and destroy it" (18-25b).
>
> Chapter 19, verses 14-17, we find Hezekiah receiving

an insulting message from the Assyrian king in the form of a letter. Hezekiah spread the letter out before the LORD in the temple, appealed to Him with lofty recognition as the only "God over all the kingdoms of the earth," and called attention to the fact that Sennacherib's words were sent to him to "insult the living God."

That night the angel of the LORD put to death 185,000 men in the Assyrian camp. When those who still lived awoke in the morning they were surrounded with dead bodies! Sennacherib broke camp and returned to Nineveh. He had never stepped foot in Jerusalem - just as God had promised through His prophet Isaiah (see 2 Kings 19:20-34).

Lord Byron's poem, "The Destruction of Sennacherib" retells the story dramatically:

THE DESTRUCTION OF SENNACHERIB

The Assyrian came down like the wolf on the fold.
And his cohorts were gleaming in purple and gold;
And the sheen of their spears was like stars on the sea
When the blue wave rolls nightly on deep Galilee.

Like the leaves of the forest when summer is green.
That host with their banners at sunset were seen;
Like the leaves of the forest when autumn hath blown,
That host on the morrow lay wither'd and strown.

For the Angel of Death spread his wings on the blast.
And breathed in the face of the foe as he pass'd;
And the eyes of the sleepers wax'd deadly and chill,
And their hearts but once heaved, and forever grew still!

And there lay the steed with his nostrils all wide,

But through it there roll'd not the breath of his pride.
And the foam of his gasping lay white on the turf,
And cold as the spray of the rock-beating surf.

And there lay the rider distorted and pale,
With the dew on his brow and the rust on his mail;
And the tents were all silent, the banners alone,
The lances unlifted, the trumpet unblown.

And widows of Ashur are loud in their wail,
And idols are broken in the temple of Baal;
And the might of the Gentile, unsmote by the sword,
Hath melted like snow in the glance of the Lord!

—Lord Byron

Here are two outstanding examples of prayer warfare directed against flesh-and-blood armies. Then consider the unusual story in 2 Chronicles 20.

A vast army was marching against Judah. The secret of the outcome is recorded in verses 3 and 4: "Alarmed, Jehoshaphat resolved to inquire of the Lord, and he proclaimed a fast for all Judah. The people of Judah came together to seek help from the Lord; indeed, they came from every town in Judah to seek Him." Jehoshaphat put singers at the head of his army "to sing to the Lord and to praise Him for the splendour of His holiness" (excerpt from 2 Chron. 20:21). The Lord, then, set ambushes against the enemies and they began to destroy each other. When the men of Judah arrived on the scene all they found was a battlefield of dead bodies. It took them three days just to haul away the plunder!

And on we could go with examples of battles on earth which were won by God in Heaven in response to prayer warfare waged on earth. But these still would not illustrate the whole story of prayer warfare.

Perhaps the biblical account which best indicates something of the nature of the unseen warfare in the heavenlies is Daniel 10. Daniel prayed for three weeks, a full twenty-one days. He gave himself so entirely to prayer that he forfeited choice foods and bodily comforts, depriving himself of the satisfaction of all fleshly appetites that he might devote himself solely to the task at hand.

Then a vision came to Daniel, a vision of a man who is not named, but who in appearance was very much like the revelation which John had of Christ on the Isle of Patmos hundreds of years later (cf. Dan. 10:5,6: Rev.

> *"...angels contend for the rule over nations and kingdoms, either to guide them in the way of God or to lead them astray from God..."*
> — F. Delitzsch

1:13-16). The heavenly visitor strengthened Daniel, who had passed out at the overwhelming sight, and informed him that he had come from God in response to Daniel's words. Furthermore, his message included the fact that Daniel's prayer had been heard from the very first day that he had set his mind to gain understanding and to humble himself before God.

There had been no delay whatsoever in Daniel's prayer reaching God, but delivery of the answer had entailed a twenty-one day delay. It is the explanation of this aspect of prayer that startles us. It is given in one simple sentence, but this sentence is a door set ajar through which we glimpse the true battlefield of prayer: "But the prince of the Persian kingdom resisted me twenty-one days" (Dan. 10:13a). The answer was sent by personal messenger from God immediately when Daniel began to pray, but the messenger was intercepted and the message delayed.

Now, what is meant by "the prince of the Persian kingdom"? The rest of verse 13 gives a clue: "Then Michael, one of the chief princes, came to help me, because I was detained there with the king of Persia." Here, Michael, the archangel, is referred to as a "prince." In fact, he is called "one of the chief princes." An *archangel* is a *chief* prince. The prefix "arch" and the word "chief" mean the same thing. And in verse 21, the heavenly visitor designated Michael to Daniel as "*your prince.*" In Daniel 12:1 he is referred to as "Michael, the great prince who protects your people." So Michael, the archangel, is apparently the chief prince assigned especially to the Jewish people. He was therefore Daniel's prince and perhaps had a special appointment to Daniel personally because of his influence in regard to the Jewish people.

The antagonist in 10:13 is also called a prince. Daniel 10:20 mentions still another antagonist, the prince of Greece, who would join the prince of Persia in the battle against the heavenly messenger and Michael. Obviously, each personage designated as a "prince" is an angelic being. Since some princes fight against the angels of God and do their utmost to hinder answers to prayer, they must be evil angels.

Isaiah referred to two distinct realms of power: "In that day the Lord will punish the powers in the heavens above and the kings on the earth below" (Isa. 24:2 1). Ironside refers to the Authorized Version of this verse when he comments, "The 'host of the high ones that are on high' evidently refers to those wicked spirits in the heavenlies who attempt to control the minds of men in such a way as to set them in opposition to God and in the vain endeavour to thwart His unchanging plans. They and their dupes, who have given them such willing service, will be shut up together in prison, awaiting the time when the Lord will deal with them in the final judgment."[3]

Delitzsch agrees: "... 'the host on high' refers to personal powers... the angelic army... the reference must be to a penal visitation in the spiritual world, which stands in the closest connection with the history of man, and in fact with the history of the nations. Consequently the host on high will refer to the angels of the nations and kingdoms.... Just as, according to the scriptural view, both good and evil angels attach themselves to particular men, and an elevated state of mind may sometimes afford a glimpse of this encircling company and this conflict of spirits: so do angels contend for the rule over nations and kingdoms, either to guide them in the way of God or to lead them astray from God....

This is what the Apostle Paul directs our attention to in Ephesians when he says. "For our struggle is not against flesh and blood, but against the rulers, against the authorities, against the powers of this dark world and against the spiritual forces of evil in the heavenly realms" (Eph. 6:12). The unseen enemy in prayer is real. Satan himself is the prince over a host of spirit-princes. In John 12:31; 14:30; and 16:11 he is called "the prince of this world," and in Ephesians 2:2, "the ruler of the kingdom of the air." They are his hosts, and they do their utmost to conquer prayer and the pray-er.

But, praise God, that is only one side of the coin. "Those who are with us are more than those who are with them" (2 Kings 6: 16b). When Elisha's servant was severely frightened by the sight of an army with horses and chariots surrounding the city, Elisha prayed and the Lord opened the servant's eyes to see "the hills full of horses and chariots of fire all around Elisha" (2 Kings 6: 17b). Have you caught sight of them?

When Joshua was preparing to do battle against Jericho, he looked up and saw before him a man with drawn sword. When he questioned this stranger, Joshua learned that he was none other than "the commander of the army of the Lord" (Josh. 5:14). Wasn't the army of Israel the army of the Lord, and was not Joshua its commander? Yet, Joshua fell facedown to the ground in reverence to this Self-revealed Commander, who then demanded that he take off his sandals as a sign of further reverence. This was the same procedure demanded of Moses by the I AM of the burning bush episode. Who is this Commander? In the following verses (Josh. 6:2ff) He is identified as the Lord Himself. In Isaiah 9:6, He is the *Prince* of Peace.

> *We must recognize prayer as more than conversation, more than petition, but as God's means of victory over Satan and his evil hosts.*

The New Testament word *archon* and its derivatives are applied not only to Satan, as in the passages studied earlier, but also to the Lord Jesus Christ. They are variously translated "author," "Prince," and "ruler" in Acts 3:15; 5:31; Hebrews 2:10; and Revelation 1:5.

What is the believer's part in all this? To pray unceasingly. Paul referred to it as fighting, wrestling, agonizing, struggling. Jesus told the parable of the persistent widow in order to show the need of always praying and not giving up (cf. Luke 18:1). What if Daniel had given up before the end of the twenty-one days? We can only conjecture.

The putting on of the warrior's armor in Ephesians 6 is in order that we might stand our ground, but standing, we are to engage in battle. The action is designated in verse 18; "And pray in the Spirit on all occasions with all kinds of prayers and requests. With this in mind, be alert and always keep on praying for all the saints." Then Paul gives instruction regarding prayer for himself as God's servant.

Heaven is on our side, but are we engaging in the battle? There is a mystery here. We do not fully understand why or how our participation turns the tide of battle, but Moses with his uplifted rod on the hillside proves that it does.

> *"Prayer concerns three, not two but three: God to whom we pray, the man on the contested earth who prays, and the Evil One against whom we pray."*
> —S.D. Gordon

The principle of effective prayer here is: We must recognize prayer as more than conversation, more than petition, but as God's means of victory over Satan and his evil hosts.

Scholars who accept the plenary, verbal inspiration and authority of the Bible are unanimous in their acceptance of this literal spirit warfare. Here is what some of them say:

S.D. Gordon: "...to define prayer adequately one must use the language of war."[5]

"Prayer from God's side is communication between Himself and His allies in the enemy's country."[6]

"Prayer concerns three, not two but three: God to whom we pray, the man on the contested earth who prays, and the Evil One against whom we pray. And the purpose of the prayer is not to persuade or influence God, but to join forces with Him against the enemy."[7]

"In its simplest meaning prayer has to do with a conflict. Rightly understood, it is the deciding factor in a spirit conflict in the earth. The purpose of the conflict is to decide the control of the earth, and its inhabitants."[8]

Theodore H. Epp: *(concerning principalities)* "princes in Satan's kingdom who have sections or provinces of this world under their control... special reference to political realms in which evil spirits work to influence earthly rulers, kings, presidents, parliaments, legislatures, judges, civil officers, voters, party politics, office holders, office seekers, and the entire range of men and things connected with the government.... No wonder we are instructed to pray for those in government. When we do, we resist and thwart the efforts of the Evil One in persuading men to follow the path he has mapped out for them."[9]

(Concerning powers) "... an exceeding large section of Satan's forces who are evil spirits of great energy and force. Their particular method of operation is to attack the personal feelings and thought-life of Christians. Unbelievers are also attacked in this way, and the terrible crimes we repeatedly read about...are...inspired by these evil powers.... They operate under disguises such as self-interest, self-revenge, and self-gratification."[10]

(Concerning the rulers of the darkness of this age) "The evil spirits spoken of are those who foster superstition, fortunetelling, and false teaching of various kinds. They delude people into watching for signs, seeking the interpretation of dreams or to follow mental suggestions or emotional impressions they receive, regardless of the source."[11]

> *"Briefly, prayer warfare simply means holding unceasingly the power of 'the finished work of Christ' over the hosts of evil... until the victory is won."*
> —Jessie Penn-Lewis

(Concerning wicked spirits in heavenly places) "... religious demons who intrude into the highest religious experiences. They come as angels of light, sometimes speaking through men behind pulpits.... The program of these evil spirits is to attack the most conscientious religious people and get them to accept heresy and follow impressions to where they become puffed up with self-conceit and self-righteousness, fancying themselves to be above others."[12]

F.J. Perryman: "There are some striking passages of Scripture which make it abundantly clear that in the unseen world there is daily in progress a tense battle for supremacy (Dan. 10:12-21). That is the foremost reason why prayer may be difficult. The Devil opposes it."[13]

Jessie Penn-Lewis: "Briefly, prayer warfare simply means holding unceasingly the power of the 'finished work of Christ' over the hosts of evil, in their attack upon some place or person, until the victory is won. Just as Moses lifted his hands steadfastly until the victory was won, so the prayer warrior holds up steadfastly the victory of the Cross — the finished victory of Christ over Satan — until the forces of evil retreat and are vanquished."[14]

"Prayer warfare against the powers of darkness can only be

understood and entered into by those who are 'spiritual,' i.e., who 'walk after the spirit,' and not 'after the soul'; for it is distinctly a spirit warfare against spirit foes."[15]

> *"In this conflict only spiritual weapons are effective."*
> —J.O. Sanders

A. Sims: "Real prayer is opposing a great spiritual force to the onslaught of evil, and asking God to put into operation the work done by His Son on the Cross, which was not only the redemption of man, but the defeat of the prince of this world."[16]

J. Oswald Sanders: "The Spirit-controlled Christian, Paul asserts, is involved in spiritual warfare with powerful but intangible forces. In this conflict only spiritual weapons are effective. But they are available and are 'divinely powerful for the destruction of fortresses' (2 Cor. 10:4). Of these weapons, the most potent is that recommended by Paul: 'pray[er] at all times in the Spirit' (Eph. 6:18)."[17]

F.J. Huegel: "Oh, for soldiers who will buckle on the armor of God and face the foe! Oh, for soldiers who will grasp the weapons which are not carnal but mighty through God to the pulling down of strongholds of Satan, the prince of darkness! Oh, for soldiers who will believe that Christ the Lord has spoiled principalities and powers and made a show of them openly, triumphing over them through the Cross; who will, in the name of Jesus, exercise authority, execute judgment that is written in Psalm 149, and so move mountains of oppression that are crushing peoples and nations today.

Study and Discussion Questions

1. From the following Scripture portions list all the names and titles under the three headings (A, B, & C):
   A. Our main enemy
   B. The beings under our main enemy who fight against God
   C. Our Captain

   Eph. 1:21; 2:1-6; 6:10-20; Dan, 9:25: 10:13-15; 1 Pet. 5:8; Exod, 3:13-15; Heb. 2:2,10; Josh. 5:13-15; Rev. 1:5-12; 5:5-8; 9:11; 11:15; 12:7-17; 19:9-16; Psalm 18:1-3; 24:7-10; Mark 1:23-27; Isa. 9:6,7; 31:1-5, John 1:29; 12:13-15; Acts 5:31; 1 Cor. 1:24

   Discuss your list with your group. Tell them what you learned about Christ, Satan, and spiritual warfare.

2. Discuss Colossians 2:15. Use helps if you can get some.

3. Tell what you learned about prayer warfare in each of the following passages:

   Exodus 17:8-15; 2 Kings 18:17-19; 36; Daniel 10; Ephesians 6:10-20.

12

WAGING THE WARFARE

The first time I visited Niagara Falls was a moving experience. I was informed that two of the world's mightiest hydroelectric plants received their power from water diverted from the river. Besides great nearby electrochemical industries, various cities within a radius of 350 miles receive energy from the plants. As I stood on the Canadian side enjoying the imposing scene and trying to contemplate the tremendous energy potential, I heard a policeman's whistle behind me. It was July 4th, a major American holiday, and throngs of tourists streamed across the bridge. Traffic was very heavy. When the policeman's whistle sounded and his hand was upraised, automobiles, buses, trucks, and motorcycles came to a halt. I thought, "My, what power!" Turning back to gaze at the falls, I repeated to myself, "My, what power!"

There was a difference, of course: one was inherent power, the other, delegated power.

Christ has power, all power, inherent omnipotence. His also is the authority to exercise the power. "With authority and power He gives orders to evil spirits and they come out!" (Luke 4:36b). "Then Jesus came to them and said, 'All authority in Heaven and on earth has been given to Me'" (Matt. 28:18).

We have no inherent power, but Christ has delegated to us His authority. It is not only our privilege but also our spiritual, and moral obligation to exercise the power of God on earth. As soon as Jesus declared His all-encompassing authority, He commanded His followers to go and make disciples of all nations and promised His personal accompaniment: "And surely I will be with you always, to the very end of the age". (Matt. 28:20b).

After the healing of the cripple at the gate Beautiful, Peter inquired of the gawking crowd, "Why do you stare at us as if by our own power or godliness we had made this man walk?... By faith in the name of Jesus, this man whom you see and know was made strong" (Acts 3:12b, 16a).

The policeman at Niagara had no power in his arm to stop the flow of traffic, but behind his upraised hand was the authority of government. This pictures our authority in Christ. Theodore Epp stresses this truth: "He has delegated us His authority in order that we might perform His work. God has vested this authority in us for a purpose. Having it is not something for us to be proud of, but it is something we must accept and that with all humility.... God has chosen to work through men and women yielded to His will. Unless He finds such, His work is hindered."[1]

The work is to wage war by prayer. Jessie Penn-Lewis explains it: "Briefly, prayer warfare simply means holding unceasingly the power of the 'finished work of Christ' over the hosts of evil, in their attack upon some place or person, until the victory is won. Just as Moses lifted his hands steadfastly until the victory was won, so the prayer warrior holds up steadfastly the victory of the Cross — the finished victory of Christ over Satan — until the forces of evil retreat and are vanquished."[2]

F.J. Huegel concurs: "It is that prayer must be aimed against God's great foe, the Adversary, who is forever on the march mobilizing his forces with keen strategy to thwart the Christian's cause and to turn souls against His Christ, the world's Saviour.

"The god of this world has blinded the minds of unbelievers, so that they cannot see the light of the Gospel of the glory of Christ, who is the image of God" (2 Cor. 4:4). It is against this foe that we must wage war in order that souls may be freed to see and accept the light.

This was well illustrated in the ministry of J.O. Fraser, pioneer missionary to the Lisu people along the China/Burma border. How he longed to see a great ingathering of souls and the Church of Jesus Christ established in that land of ignorance, fear, and demon-worship. At his request, his mother, back home in

> *We have no inherent power, but Christ has delegated to us His authority.*

England, got a small group of people together who made themselves Fraser's partners in the work, by means of regular prayer meetings on his behalf. However, he became depressed in spirit. At first, he sought the reason in his circumstances, but as the weeks passed and the depression did not lift, he realized he was under attack by other influences. His mind was filled with tormenting questions of doubt regarding prayer and God's care. The realities of Scripture truth began to seem unreal and his prayers were apparently of no avail. Lack of spiritual results forced him deeper into gloom.

In the words of Fraser's biographer, Mrs. Howard Taylor, "Deeply were the foundations shaken in those days and nights of conflict, until Fraser realized that behind it all were 'powers of darkness,' seeking to overwhelm him. He had dared to invade Satan's kingdom, undisputed for ages."[4]

While Fraser was in the depths of despondency, a messenger arrived with letters and papers. Among them was a copy of *The Overcomer*, a periodical with which he was unfamiliar, in which was an article emphasizing Christ's triumphant victory over Satan. Through this article Fraser recognized Satan's design upon him.

Later, he said, "The Lord Himself resisted the Devil vocally: 'Get thee behind Me, Satan!' I, in humble dependence on Him, did the same. I talked to Satan at that time, using the promises of Scripture as weapons. And they worked. Right then, the terrible oppression began to pass away."[5]

In later times of trial and temptation he continued to use Scripture aloud to resist Satan. He advocated shouting a determined note of defiance against the enemy and spoke much of "fighting prayer."

It was after Fraser learned to withstand Satan that many souls began to turn to Jesus in saving faith. Families by the scores and eventually by the hundreds came to the Saviour.

"Be self-controlled and alert. Your enemy the Devil prowls around like a roaring lion looking for someone to devour. Resist him, standing firm in the faith, because you know that your brothers throughout the world are undergoing the same kind of sufferings" (1 Pet. 5:8,9). It is against this Adversary that we must wage war that believers might be released from suffering or that, suffering in the will of God, Satan's purposes of doubt, discouragement, despair, and depression might be thwarted and God's purposes of patience, meekness, faith, and Christ likeness might be accomplished.

F.G. Perryman has a balanced perspective on sufferings instigated by our Arch-Foe. He says, "Admitting all that may be said as to the divine permission and purpose of suffering, and of mental affliction, I am obliged, by the bare facts of life, to say nothing of divine revelation in the Word itself, to see that much of it is caused by failure to obey the divine command: *Resist the Devil, and he will flee from you.*"[6]

How? How do we resist? Ephesians 6:10-20 answers our question.

1. (Verses 11,13) "Put on the full armor of God," without which we have no defence but are totally vulnerable to every attack.

2. (Verses 11,13, 14a) "...take your stand against the Devil's schemes...stand your ground and after you have done everything...stand. Stand firm then..." Plant your feet. Make no provision for retreat. Rigidly resist every subtle scheme, such as:

   —situations which make compromise look easy and faithfulness appear intolerant;

   — "innocent" pastimes: ouija boards, tea leaves, "harmless" drugs — which draw one into occultism and thence under demonic power;

   — the "everybody's-doing-it" syndrome;

   —the "be-A-good-sport" taunt;

   —plausible explanations of prophecy, of obscure verses, and of Bible history which gradually ensnare one in false teaching;

   —the "social" drink;

   —attractions to the opposite sex which are outside God's boundaries;

   —appeals to self-glory in Christian service. (The variations are numberless.)

3. (Verse 12) Recognize that the battle is not against flesh-and-blood opponents, but against Satan and his

ranks of spirit-being forces. Otherwise, we cannot understand his tactics nor thwart his advances.

4.   (Verse 14) Buckle up "the belt of truth." Jesus said to His Father, "Your Word is truth" (John 17:17). Reject any shade of dishonesty, untruth, deceit, guile, misrepresentation, distortion, exaggeration, pretence, half-truth, double meaning — whether by word, raised eyebrow, shrug of the shoulder, silence — or whatever.

5.   (Verse 14) Fix "the breastplate of righteousness in place." Having received Jesus' imputed righteousness in justification, accept also His imparted righteousness in sanctification for the daily walk.

6.   (Verse 15) Fit your feet with "the readiness that comes from the gospel of peace." "Feet," "readiness," and "gospel" all speak of carrying the good news to others. It is not the "gospel" for those who never hear it whether they are primitives in far away places or your next-door neighbors.

7.   (Verse 16) "Take up the shield of faith, with which you can extinguish all the flaming arrows of the evil one" — arrows such as:

—the temptation to ask "Why me?" In times of suffering and sorrow;

— ridicule;

— being ignored;

— misunderstandings;

— personality conflicts;

— lack of appreciation of one's services;

— discouragement and depression;

— irritations;

— a series of failures;

— bitterness;

— lust.

(Again, the possibilities are endless.)

8.   (Verse 17) "Take the helmet of salvation." As 2

PRINCIPLES OF EFFECTIVE PRAYER

Corinthians 10:5 declares, "we take captive every thought to make it obedient to Christ."

9. (Verse 17) "Take...the Sword of the Spirit, which is the Word of God." Take it. Positively lay hold of it in study, memorization, meditation, and obedience in order to wield it as a two-edged sword in effective warfare.

10. (Verses 18-20) "And pray in the Spirit on all occasions with all kinds of prayers and requests. With this in mind, be alert and always keep on praying for all the saints." Take the offensive. "Withstand'" and "stand" are defensive words, but now we are urged to go on the offensive, to take positive action against the enemy. Resist him and he will flee. Drive him back. Engage in massive frontal assault while remaining ever on the alert for flanking movements. Verses 19 and 20 continue to urge prayer, and Paul specifies his personal request that he might fearlessly declare the gospel. Both the prayer and the preaching are offensive action.

" F o r though we live in the world, we do not wage war as the world does. The weapons we fight with are not the weapons of the world. On the contrary, they have divine power to demolish strongholds" (2 Cor. 10:3,4).

> "God answers prayer on the ground of redemption and on no other ground."
> —Oswald Chambers

The armor, the weapons, and the action (prayer) are all essential for waging warfare and are therefore interwoven in such passages as Ephesian 6.

One more word must be added concerning the basis of our prayer warfare, which is the redemption Christ purchased on Calvary. Oswald Chambers Insisted, 'Immediately you try to explain why God answers prayer on the ground of reason, it is nonsense; God answers prayer on the ground of redemption and on no other ground. Let us never forget that our prayers are heard, not because we are in earnest, not because we suffer, but because

Jesus suffered."[8]

The Scriptures reveal clearly that it was at Calvary that Christ won a total victory over the hosts of Hell.

Approaching the time of His death, He said, "But this is your hour — when darkness reigns" (Luke 22:53b).

Earlier, in predicting His death, He stated, "Now is the time for judgment on this world: now the Prince of this world will be driven out" (John 12:3 1).

The Apostle John explained, "The reason the Son of God appeared was to destroy the Devil's work" (1 John 3:8).

It is the victory of Christ to which the Apostle Paul refers in Colossians, "And having disarmed the powers and authorities, He made a public spectacle of them, triumphing over them by the Cross" (Col. 2:15). This is one of the most important and picturesque verses on the subject. Paul drew much of his imagery from Rome's military might, especially in his prison epistles, written when he was a prisoner of Rome and under the guard of Roman soldiers. So it was that he vividly portrayed the Christian's battle garb in terms of the armor of a soldier in Ephesians 6. Here in Colossians, also, he depicts Christ's victory in terms of the Roman triumph.

The triumph in ancient Rome was the highest honor accorded a victorious general. (By the days of the empire it was reserved for the emperor.) It was a spectacular parade along the Via Sacra (Sacred Way) to the capitol. First, came the senators, followed by the trumpeters, carriages bearing spoils of war, oxen to be sacrificed, and captives in chains. The general, crowned with laurel, and accompanied by his children and friends, then came in a triumphal car drawn by four horses. Finally, the general's soldiers came, cheering and singing as they marched.[9]

In the light of this description we see easily the picture Paul is painting of Christ's victory. It is a triumph. Jesus triumphed over all the powers of Hell. He made a public spectacle of them. He did this by means of His crucifixion.

God, through Christ's crucifixion, also "has rescued us from the dominion of darkness and brought us into the kingdom of the Son He loves" (Col. 1:13).

The writer of Hebrews summarizes it for us: "Since the children

> *"God waits for us to put into force the victory of His Son at the cross against Satan..."*
> —A. Sims

have flesh and blood, He too shared in their humanity so that by His death He might destroy him who holds the power of death — that is, the Devil — and free those who all their lives were held in slavery by their fear of death" (Heb. 2:14,15). Through Christ's *death* the Devil's *destruction* is assured and we are *delivered*. Praise God!

A. Sims testifies: "God waits for us to put into force the victory of His Son at the Cross against Satan, and under the guidance of the Holy Spirit we should honestly seek to do so. The greatest thing I have ever learned about prayer is to use the *Scriptures in prayer*."[10]

In the next chapter we shall consider this wielding of the Sword of the Spirit.

Study and Discussion Questions

1. Discuss ways to claim victory when Satan tempts us to discouragement, depression, or even suicide. What practical steps can we take to restore the joy of the Lord?

2. What should spiritual insight reveal to us when bitter feelings threaten to split a church? What can we do about it in prayer?

3. If our faithful prayers have not brought revival, what should we suspect? What course of prayer-action should we take?

4. Why does Satan fight terribly against the following types of prayer?
   a. Prayer for specific lost individuals;
   b. Prayer for unity of the Body of Christ;
   c. Prayer for pioneer missions where paganism and false religious have held sway for centuries.

5. How should we wage warfare in each of the situations in Question 4?

13

USING THE SWORD OF THE SPIRIT
IN PRAYER WARFARE

The believer's weapon, the Sword of the Spirit, is the Word of God, and His method of warfare is prayer in the Spirit (cf. Eph. 6:17, 18). To neglect either the Word or prayer is to abandon the means of effective warfare and forsake the hope of victory. Stress upon the objective Word without the subjective element of prayer makes for dead orthodoxy. Prayer without the control of Scripture leads to fanaticism.

Both the weapon and the method are given by the Spirit. The Bible is the authoritative Word of God inspired by the Holy Spirit. Prayer is the Holy Spirit's intercession for us according to the will of God. Our participation in the Spirit's intercession requires our use of the Spirit's Sword. Prayer "in the Spirit" is based upon the Spirit-revealed principles of the Bible, saturated with the Spirit-inspired words of the Bible, and guided by the Spirit-illumined thoughts of the Bible.

J.O. Sanders quotes H.W. Frost on this aspect of prayer. "There is an inseparable union between the Spirit, the Word and prayer, which indicates that the Spirit will always lead the saint to make much of the Word, and especially God's promises in the Word... This explains the fact that the great pray-ers have always been great students of the Word."[1]

I see five basic ways of using the Scriptures in prayer:

Obeying

Remaining in Christ, His words remaining in us, and obeying His commands are concepts interwoven in Christ's upper-room discourse in such a mutually-interdependent way as to make them equivalent to each other. They are essential to the principle of praying in Jesus' name (cf. John 14-16) and together they form the condition of answered prayer (read especially John 15:1-10).

The song writer captured this important principle in "Trust and Obey." One missionary often had his congregations sing it as "obey and trust" in order to call attention to the aspect of obedience. Certainly, the two cannot be divorced. Obedience is basic to praying in faith.

If we allow God's Word to set our standards and shape the moral fiber of our lives, then we will see Him work on our behalf in response to our prayers.

> *First*, we must obey the commands and accept the invitations regarding prayer itself: "Pray continually "(1 Thess. 5:17). "Devote yourselves to prayer" (Col. 4:2). "Do not be anxious about anything, but in everything, by prayer and petition, with thanksgiving, present your requests to God" (Phil. 4:6). "And pray in the Spirit on all occasions with all kinds of prayers and requests. With this in mind, be alert and always keep on praying for all the saints" (Eph. 6:18).
>
> *Second*, we must obey, not only the commands *to pray*, but *all* of Christ's commands. (cf. John 15:9-17).

Someone will complain, "But that's law-keeping and we are under grace." True, on both counts. It is law-keeping. Is that bad? If someone objects to law-keeping, do you want him for your next-door neighbor? Jesus came, not to abolish the law, but to fulfill it (Matt. 5:17). Although we are saved by grace, not law, God's grace does not make us lawbreakers. Instead, He puts within us the desire and the power, the will and the enabling, to obey Christ's commands.

In response to the question of a teacher of the law, Jesus summed up God's law in two commandments of love: "Love the Lord your God with all your heart and with all your soul and with all your mind and with all your strength.... Love your neighbor as yourself" (Mark

12:30,31a).

In John's first epistle we have an explanation of the relationship of these two commands: "If anyone says, 'I love God,' yet hates his brother, he is a liar... And He has given us this command: Whoever loves God must also love his brother" (1 John 4:20a,21). The proof that one loves God is his love for his brother. Therefore, Jesus emphasized this aspect in His "Vine and Branches" discourse, "My command is this: Love each other as I have loved you.... This is My command: Love each other."

Not only the command, but the enablement to obey it is from the Lord. In His High Priestly prayer Jesus requested of His Father "that the love You have for Me may be in them and that I Myself may be in them" (John 17:26b).

To the extent that we allow God's love to be manifest in us we are obeying Christ's command. To that extent we are remaining In Him and His words are remaining in us. And to that extent we can expect to have our prayers answered. "If you remain in Me and My words remain in you, ask whatever you wish, and it will be given you" (John 15:7).

> *Faith is tremendously enhanced by claiming the promises, because we knew that we are thereby praying in God's will.*

Claiming

Taking the sword involves *claiming* the promises that the Lord will grant "whatever you wish," "whatever you ask in My name," "anything in My name." There are also scores of *specific* promises to be claimed in prayer, such as these:

> How much more will your Father in Heaven give the Holy Spirit to those who ask Him! (Luke 11: 13b). If any of you lacks wisdom, he should ask God, who gives generously to all without finding fault, and it will be given to him (James 1:5). If My people, who are called by My name, will humble themselves and pray and seek My face and turn from their wicked ways, then will I hear from Heaven and will forgive their sin and will heal their land (2 Chron.

7:14).

In all your Bible reading, watch for the promises, meet the conditions, and claim the promises in prayer. "For no matter how many promises God has made, they are 'Yes' in Christ. And so through Him, the 'Amen' is spoken by us to the glory of God" (2 Cor. 1:20). That is what prayer is — our "Amen" to God's promises, which are assured in Christ! Amen: so be it!

Faith is tremendously enhanced by claiming the promises, because we know that we are thereby praying in God's will. "This is the assurance we have in approaching God: that if we ask anything according to His will, He hears us. And if we know that He hears us — whatever we ask — we know that we have what we asked of Him" (1 John 5: 14,15). This truth is illustrated by the following account.

It was in Durban, South Africa. Missionary Will Dawn was spending the bright Friday afternoon in study and meditation when the telephone rang. "Hello, Brother Dawn. Will you be so kind as to go to the hospital and pray for my son, George? He has been in a terrible car accident."

The whole side of the young man's head had been smashed when his car overturned. He was picked up and rushed to the hospital, but no hope was given that he would live through the afternoon. His parents had been called to come to his "death bed."

Will's reaction was to think, "Who am I to be asked to pray for the sick?" and he voiced his fear by saying to the distraught mother, "I have no special gift from the Lord in praying for the sick."

Very firmly, yet graciously, she replied, "I didn't ask if you had a gift of praying for the sick. I only asked if you would please come and pray for my son."

With profuse apologies, he assured her that he would go immediately. He confesses that he went with fear and trembling and with not much faith. The family was standing around the bed. After hearing the details from the mother and brother, the missionary prayed a simple prayer that God's will be done and that this would be a means of speaking to each of the family about the brevity of life. He was able to speak to the relatives about

Christ before leaving and asked to be called should there be any change in the young man's, condition.

During his nearly five years of ministry with Worldwide Evangelization Crusade in the city of Durban, Will had become well-known in evangelical circles. The accident victim. George, and his brother were both members of an evangelical church. That evening when the Dawn family prayed for George, it was primarily that God would comfort the family in their sorrow.

Saturday, they prayed again. Sunday morning, they prayed with more faith that God would perform a miracle.

Will's usual procedure each Sunday afternoon was to go down to the main Durban beach with a group of Christian businessmen to hold an open-air meeting. But on this particular Sunday he said to his wife, "I feel strongly that God would have me go down to the hospital to anoint George and pray for his healing." Replying that she, too, had the same conviction, she encouraged him to go.

On arrival at the private ward where George lay in a coma, he saw that God had prepared the way by placing a Christian nurse on special duty with the injured lad. The boy's sister, also a believer and a registered nurse, was there, too. But when Will explained his errand, both exclaimed, "Mr. Dawn, we feel it would be better if you would pray that God would take him Home. He is a Christian. Three doctors have been on the case, one a Christian, and all three say it is absolutely impossible for him to live. It would be better for him to die than to be healed in body and be a cabbage mentally for the rest of his life."

The missionary, who at first had himself been reluctant to pray, asked, "Do you believe that God would heal only the body and not the mind? He made the whole man, and although the head is the part that is injured, if God heals, He will do a perfect job."

With their doubts somewhat assuaged, the little group anointed George and prayed. They simply reminded God that the prompting had come from Him and that they stood upon His promise, "If two of you shall agree on earth as touching anything that they shall ask, it shall be done for them of My Father which is in Heaven" (Matt. 18:19).

Exactly twenty-one days later, Will answered the phone to hear the Christian nurse on special duty exclaiming, "Mr. Dawn, please come down to the hospital. George is conscious and is trying to talk."

He rushed downtown and ran up the hospital steps to the ward. He could hear George slowly forming words as he went in and marvelled at the goodness of God.

Will could remember having met George on only one occasion when preaching at his church. He asked, "George, do you remember me?"

After several minutes, from behind a mass of bandages, a faltering voice said, "Yes, I remember you. You came first to our school and spoke to the Christian Association about a passage in Isaiah which talks about seeing the King in His beauty."

"Molly," Will said through tears of joy as he turned to the nurse, "do you remember what I said about God healing the whole body? Certainly, there is no question about a perfect healing."

George was completely restored. The firm for which he worked sent him to Britain to take a comprehensive course in their line of business. Today, he is well up in the business world, married with a family, and walking with the Lord. Praise His wonderful name![2]

In claiming God's promises it is necessary to meet His conditions. Matthew 28:20 records Christ's amazing promise, "And surely I will be with you always, to the very end of the age." But the only way to claim the promise is first to fulfill the conditions of the Great Commission set forth in verses 18-20.

A promise we all like to claim is: "And my God will meet all your needs according to His glorious riches in Christ Jesus" (Phil. 4:19). But God has not obligated Himself to meet everyone's needs. The promise was made to those who had faithfully and sacrificially met the needs of God's servant, Paul, as he took the Gospel to the unreached.

A box of Precious Promise cards, which itemizes promises without giving contexts, is of less value than an open Bible, because one needs to know the conditions as well as the promises.

> *Our spontaneity in prayer, while commendable, if relied upon entirely, often produces shallowness.*

Including

Praying saints in the Bible sometimes incorporated portions of Scripture in their prayers. Often they praised God for His attributes and quoted His promises. As a basis for his request, Moses reminded the Lord, "You have said, 'I know you by name and you have found favour with Me'"(Exod. 33: 12b).

Nehemiah quoted God in his prayer: "Remember the instruction You gave Your servant Moses, saying, 'If you are unfaithful, I will scatter you among the nations, but if you return to Me and obey My commands, then even if your exiled people are at the farthest horizon, I will gather them from there and bring them to the place I have chosen as a dwelling for My name'"(Neh. 1:8, 9).

Psalm 90 is a prayer of Moses to be quoted or sung by all the people. And, of course, many of the Psalms are David's prayers and are given that they might be repeated often.

Daniel (9:4) and Nehemiah (1:5) both quote Exodus 20:6 and Deuteronomy 7:9 in their adoration of God as "the great and awesome God, who keeps His covenant of love with all who love Him and obey His commands" (Dan. 9:4).

Jesus' cry on the cross, "My God, My God, why have You forsaken Me?" comes directly from Psalm 22:1. And the early believers in Acts 4:25, 26 quoted Psalm 2:1, 2.

Our spontaneity in prayer, while commendable, if relied upon entirely, often produces shallowness. Our prayers are lacking in inspired poetry and scriptural principles. Let us so saturate our minds with the Word of the living God that the spontaneous phrases which fly to our lips will frequently be the lofty phrases of Holy Writ. We will thus honor God and His Word and strengthen our faith and the faith of those who pray with us.

The secret of effective use of Scripture in prayer is hiding God's Word in our hearts. Jesus said, "For out of the overflow of his heart his mouth speaks" (Luke 6:45).

You can personalize a passage like Psalm 116 or Psalm 139 by merely reading it aloud to God from a sincere heart while on your knees. The personal pronouns throughout will make it applicable. Don't rush. Mix meditation with thanksgiving as you pray, "For You, O Lord, have delivered my soul from death, my eyes from tears, my feet from stumbling, that I may walk before the Lord in the land of the living" (Ps. 116:8, 9). Make every inspired word your own praise of God or your own plea to Him as you personalize Psalm 139, "O Lord, You have searched me and You know me. You know when I sit and when I rise: You perceive my thoughts from afar... Search me, O God, and know my heart; test me and know my anxious thoughts. See if there is any offensive way in me, and lead me in the way everlasting" (Ps. 139).

You can make Psalm 46 your own by deliberately personalizing the pronouns: "God, [You are my] refuge and strength, an ever present help in trouble. Therefore [I] will not fear, though the earth give way..." (Ps. 46:1, 2a).

Doctrinal truth becomes rich in meaning when it forms the structure of our prayers. We may apply it to ourselves, to unsaved loved ones, to the unreached millions, or to whoever weighs upon our hearts. My personal prayer based on Ephesians 2:1-7 follows:

> My Heavenly Father, I was once dead in my transgressions and sins, in which I used to live when I followed the ways of this world and of the ruler of the kingdom of the air, the spirit who is now at work in those who are disobedient. I lived according to the cravings of my sinful nature and followed its desires and thoughts. Like the rest, I was by nature an object of wrath. But because of Your great love for me, God, You who are rich in mercy, made me alive with Christ even when I was dead in transgressions — it is by grace I have been saved.
>
> And You raised me up with Christ and seated me with Him in the heavenly realms in Christ Jesus, in order that in the coming ages You might show the incomparable riches of Your grace, expressed in Your kindness to me in Christ Jesus.
>
> But, dear Lord, some of my friends and loved ones are still disobedient, still walking according to the course of this world, still dead in their

transgressions and sins. Because of Your great love, O God, convict George of sin so that he might be made alive with Christ and in the ages to come You might demonstrate the exceeding riches of Your grace through him.

And, Father, there are millions who have not heard this Good News. Your mercy in Christ Jesus has never been presented to them. Strengthen Your servant June Duguid in Niger Republic. Give her fluency in the French language and a good understanding of the culture so that she might lead people away from the ways of this world and of the Ruler of the kingdom of the air, so that those who are dead in transgressions might be made alive with Christ, saved by Your grace.

Especially bless the Bible clubs she teaches and the young people she trains as Bible-club teachers.

Accept my thanksgiving and my requests in Jesus' name. Amen.

Now, why don't you try turning some of these passages into personal prayer?

Ephesians 2:8-13
Colossians 1:9-14
1 Corinthians 13
Psalm 23
Matthew 5:13-16
Matthew 6:5-15
Romans 3:19-28
Romans 1:14-18

Instead of verse-by-verse application, some longer portions lend themselves more to meditation on the whole passage. Then one can

> *We like to think of prayer as conversation, but then we make it a lecture, a recital, or an appeal.*

PRINCIPLES OF EFFECTIVE PRAYER

incorporate the lessons of the story into purposeful prayer. In the account of Naaman (2 Kings 5) you can apply to yourself lessons from the servant girl's witness. Naaman's need of humility and obedience, and Gehazi's deceit and punishment. Other passages which provide rich prayer material with this approach are:

> Genesis 24
> Joshua 14:6-15
> Ruth 1
> Daniel 1
> Luke 4:1-13
> Acts 5:1-11

Practice turning Scripture into prayer for your own spiritual edification.

Listening

"The Sovereign Lord has given me an instructed tongue, to know the word that sustains the weary. He wakens me morning by morning, wakens my ear to listen like one being taught" (Isa. 50:4). To be an effective prayer warrior one must learn to listen with the inner ear of the spirit. We like to think of prayer as conversation, but then we make it a lecture, a recital, or an appeal. Appeals are all right but would be more in accord with God's will and more effective if we would be quiet and listen some of the time. "Lord, teach us to pray" (Luke 11:1). A person who is constantly talking is not learning very much! One reason we are not better taught in prayer is that we get up talking and go to bed talking in order not to feel guilty for having missed our morning and evening prayers.

Andrew Murray introduces his beautiful little treatise, *Waiting On God*, with this poem by Freda Hanbury:

> "Wait thou only upon God"; my soul, be still,
> And let thy God unfold His perfect will,
> Thou fain would'st follow Him throughout this year.
> Thou fain with listening heart His voice would'st hear,
> Thou fain would'st be a passive instrument
> Possessed by God, and ever Spirit-sent

Upon His service sweet — then, be thou still.
For only thus can He in thee fulfil
His heart's desire. Oh, hinder not His hand
From fashioning the vessel He hath planned.
"Be silent unto God," and thou shalt know
The quiet, holy calm He doth bestow
On those who wait on Him; so shalt thou bear
His presence, and His life and light e'en where
The night is darkest, and thine earthly days
Shall show His love, and sound His glorious praise.
And He will work with hand unfettered, free,
His high and holy purposes through thee.
First, on thee must that hand of power be turned,
Till in His love's strong fire thy dross is burned,
And thou come forth a vessel for thy Lord,
So frail and empty, yet since He hath poured
Into thine emptiness His life. His love.
Henceforth through thee the power of God shall move
And He will work *for* thee. Stand still and see
The victories thy God will gain for thee;
So silent, yet so irresistible,
Thy God shall do the thing impossible.
Oh, question not henceforth what thou canst do;
Thou canst do *nought*. But He will carry through
The work where human energy had failed,
Where all thy best endeavours had availed
Thee nothing. Then, my soul, wait and be still;
Thy God shall work for thee His perfect will.
If thou wilt take no less, *His best* shall be
Thy portion now and through eternity.[3]

God calls special attention to three Old Testament characters for their might in prayer: Moses and Samuel, mentioned in Jeremiah 15:1, and Elijah, mentioned in James 5:17,18. S.D. Gordon points out that all three were trained to *listen*. Moses spent forty years "wearing the noise of Egypt out of his ears so he could hear the quiet fine tones of God's voice."[4] Samuel learned early in childhood to say, "Speak, for Your servant is listening" (1 Sam.

3:l0b). Elijah first heard the word of the Lord, then undertook his Mount Carmel conflict with the priests of Baal.

Jerome Hines, world-renowned basso with the Metropolitan Opera Association, who has sung for presidents and kings and has toured the Soviet Union, unhesitatingly witnesses of his faith in Jesus Christ and relates accounts of God's guidance and protection in answer to prayer. He especially emphasizes the need for discerning God's voice. The following article from *Guideposts* contains two stories of answered prayer in regard to the Lord's guidance in Jerome's life.

The Voice Within — by Jerome Hines[5]

"How can you be certain that the guidance you receive from God is not just your own thoughts?" a friend asked me not long ago.

I told him that before I act there are three checks I run against my inner guidance.

First, does it run contrary to God's Word?

Second, are my own desires getting in the way?

Third, am I ready to act on any alternative if God so instructs me?

Actually I was totally unaware that a loving God would communicate with His children until that night back in 1952 when I committed my life to Jesus Christ. No sooner had I put myself under His sovereignty than His voice began to direct me in some remarkable ways.

Now, of course, I don't mean I hear an actual sound. His voice is simply a thought in my thoughts, but one that stands out from them with a conviction my own thoughts never have.

From the time I began to act on His guidance, it was like stepping out of the fog into warm sunlight. There was meaning and purpose and new joy in every area of my life. Most of my difficulties came on those occasions when I preferred to rely on my own reason or what I thought to be common sense.

[Then Hines tells of an occasion when his wife had a miscarriage and nearly died while waiting for an ambulance, whereas she would have had prompt medical care had he sent her home earlier in the afternoon as he felt the Lord prompting him to do.]

This experience and several others like it have taught me an important fact about guidance. *If I'm really to identify His voice in my heart, I have to shut out all the other ones that I might mistake for His.*

Then there was the occasion in Detroit early in my Christian life when God first spoke to me about working on skid row. I say first because it was the first of many such assignments He was to send me on.

After checking into my hotel room, I asked God just where He wanted me on skid row. The answer came back.

"Come with Me and I'll show you.

Soon I was wandering through an area of bedraggled flophouses and dingy bars. "God, what in the world am I doing here?" I asked, as I passed a drunk dressed in rags. I tugged self-consciously at my tie. Then I saw a familiar sign: SALVATION ARMY.

I decided to enter, but to my astonishment as I reached the building the voice said, "Not here. Keep walking."

I started to argue: I knew people in the Army, I could give names to introduce myself — but I caught myself in time and kept walking.

At last, many blocks later, I came to a building on which were the words: RESCUE MISSION. And now the voice inside me said unmistakably, "Here."

So this was my job for tonight! A little embarrassed I walked inside, introduced myself to the minister and asked if I could help out at the mission in any capacity. He looked at me oddly and the answer was a cold "No."

After an embarrassed silence I asked awkwardly if I could sing for their service that evening, adding hastily. "You see, I'm in town on a singing engagement.... I sing at the Metropolitan Opera House."

He was unimpressed. "No." he said again.

I started to leave when he called after me: "Do you think you can work your way into Heaven by doing good deeds?"

In answer, I simply said, "I came here because God sent me."

This statement aroused his interest and led me to tell him of the experiences which had brought me to know Jesus Christ.

His attitude was totally changed. He told me that an outside church was coming to hold the evening service and that he had not wished to interfere with their program. Now he felt God really had a place for me in that service. It was quickly arranged that I should sing.

That evening I was about to leave for the mission when my accompanist, Emil Danenberg, arrived at the hotel — four hours ahead of schedule.

"Where are you off to, Jerry?" he said.
"I've ... ah ... we've got a concert," I told him. "Come on.

Without a word he followed me through shabby streets to the mission. The man leading the program greeted us with great relief.

"Thank God!" he cried. "Thank God you came!"

He almost dragged us inside. "There's been a mix-up," he said. 'No one has showed up for our program tonight and the men are getting restless." Then his face fell.

"Oh, but my wife's sick! There's no one to play the piano!"

"The Lord has taken care of that," I said, pointing to Emil.

"Can he play hymns?"

"I'll try," answered Emil — a world-famous concert pianist.

So Emil played, and we had a meeting there none of us will ever forget. Not only were there a great many men, but they were ready, eager, waiting with expectancy that charged the air. Lives were changed that night and hearts opened — our own included — in a way that left no doubt whose meeting that was and who had called each of us to that place.

So I know with great certainty that I have and do hear His voice — and receive His help. It comes as long as I continue to turn to Jesus, as long as I continue to ask for His guidance, and as long as I am willing to obey His instructions when I receive them.

We are so accustomed to din and clatter that most of us find silence intolerable. We do anything to escape it. When we have it, we do not know how to use it constructively. Having not trained the ear of the spirit to listen to God, we daydream.

The secret of learning to listen to God is to read, study, and memorize His Word and then to discipline our minds to meditate upon it. S.D. Gordon recommends for this purpose not studying the Bible as a textbook (although that certainly has its place), but seeking to know God through His Book. In prayer, ask Him what He wants to say to you through the passage on which you are meditating.

Meditation is not a mind-emptying technique, but is a careful, devotional "chewing" of the Word of God to get the full benefit from it. The literal meaning of the word "meditate" pictures a cow chewing its cud. We can bring back to mind again and again the

> *"The enemy yields only what he must ... only what is taken."*
> —S.D. Gordon

Scripture we have hidden there and "chew" it for its rich flavor and nourishment.

Conquering

The sword is a weapon of conquest. Jesus used the Sword of the Spirit to overcome Satan's temptations. Every thrust was prefaced with, "It is written."

S.D. Gordon says, "Prayer is insisting upon Jesus' victory, and the retreat of the enemy on each particular spot, and heart and problem concerned. The enemy yields only what he must. He yields only what is taken. Therefore the ground must be taken step by step. Prayer must be definite. He yields only when he must. Therefore the prayer must be persistent. He continually renews his attacks, therefore the ground taken must be held against him in the Victor's name."

"Resist the Devil, and he will flee from you" (Jas. 4:7b). As well as claiming the promises before the throne, let us wage a counter-attack in the field of battle against the usurper, Satan. We must offset every flaming arrow with a mighty sword-thrust of God's own Word. Address the *claims* to God. Aim the *sword-thrusts* at *Satan* himself. Jesus did. He said, "Away from Me, Satan! For it is written: 'Worship the Lord your God, and serve Him only'" (Matt. 4:10). And the Devil left. On another occasion Jesus, recognizing the real source of Peter's suggestion that He avoid the cross, again said. "Out of my sight, Satan!" (Matt. 16:23).

Although prayer is *addressed* to God, it is also scriptural to address Satan, to resist him, to withstand him with Scripture. Prayer to God and Scripture used directly against Satan are two vital aspects of spiritual warfare.

To use God's Word effectively in prayer, let us obey it, claim its promises, include it in our prayers, listen to God's voice, and conquer Satan with it.

Study and Discussion Questions

1. Choose one of the passages of Scripture suggested and personalize it in a written prayer.

2. Collect 10 or more promises from God's Word which you would like to memorize for use in prayer. Type them or print them individually on cards of a size that will be convenient for you to carry around with you. Include references.

3. (Group work to be done in class) For each of the following topics, share Scripture portions (verses or longer portions) and then use some of them in a season of prayer before going on to another topic. *Use portions that come to your own minds,* but if you need help, some references are listed. You'll find it best to group yourselves in groups of only three or four members for this exercise.

    a. PROMISES: (*Claim* them in prayer.) Jas. 1:5; 2 Chron. 7:14; 1 John 5:14,15; Phil. 4:19 (From the context, consider who qualifies for this.); Matt. 7:7-11; John 14:27; Jer. 29:12,13.

    b. PERSONAL NEEDS: Matt. 6:11; John 15:11,16; Gal. 5:22,23; 1 John 1:9; Jas. 1:5 (again).

    c. PRAISE, ADORATION: (Select some Psalms to personalize in prayer.)

    d. THANKSGIVING: Ps. 105:1; 1 Cor. 1:4; Phil. 1:3; 1 Cor. 15:57; 1 Thess. 5:18; Col. 1:12; Phil. 4:6.

    e. CHRISTIAN CONDUCT: (Promise the Lord you will obey specific matters and ask God for inner strengthening to keep your promises.) Phil. 4:4-6; 2 Tim. 3:12-15; Tit. 3:9; 2 Tim. 2:24; Phil. 4:8; 1 Thess. 5:11-22 (verse-by-verse); James 1:21; 1 John 2:15-17; 2 Cor. 5:20; Mark 16:15; Col. 3:17-24.

    f. INTERCESSION: (Apply the principles to requests shared by your group or to persons for whom you feel a sense of responsibility in prayer.) Col. 1:9-12; Eph. 1:16-20; 3:14-21; Dan. 9:3-19; Gen. 18:23-33; 1 Thess. 3:1,2; Rom. 10:1.

    g. SELECTED PASSAGES TO PERSONALIZE IN PRAYER: Ps. 23; 1 Cor. 13; Matt. 6:5-15: Rom. 1:14-18.

14

CONDITIONS OF EFFECTIVE PRAYER

If we are to wage effective warfare, we must follow proven procedures. God will bless only the means which He has ordained. Let's take a closer look at the kind of praying which claims Christ's victory over Satan and receives God's answers. Some of these aspects have been suggested in earlier chapters, but they should be emphasized. As a student of prayer, you would do well to review the chapter, "Asking in Jesus' Name," before studying this chapter.

Praying in faith

> FAITH HONORS GOD.
> GOD HONORS FAITH.

Faith is implicit trust in the immutable God, who is unchangeable in righteousness and whose promises are "Yes" in Christ (cf. 2 Cor. 1:20), who is faithful and true, who can do all things, and who never fails.

Praying in faith is not a groping and grasping, after some floating plank when we feel we are sinking. Although the Lord in mercy responds to such cries of desperation ("Lord, save us! We're going to drown!" Matt. 8:25), He wants us to progress rapidly beyond this grabbing-at-a-plank stage. Jesus rebuked the winds and the waves in response to the disciples' cry of terror, but He first reprimanded them: "You of little faith, why are you so afraid?" (Matt. 8:26).

Consider another illustration. When an infant is learning to walk, the elbows are bent and the hands held instinctively at

> *Faith is a disciplined act of obedience based on the fact of God's Word, not on the fickleness of feeling.*

shoulder level to provide balance and to grab for the nearest support when the toddler topples. Too many believers toddle along in their Christian walk as babes in Christ, never acquiring any skill in trusting prayer, never knowing the security of the walk of faith.

James cautions regarding the petitioner: "But when he asks, he must believe and not doubt, because he who doubts is like a wave of the sea, blown and tossed by the wind. That man should not think he will receive anything from the Lord; he is a double-minded man, unstable in all he does" (Jas. 1:6-8).

Jesus frequently scolded His disciples for littleness of faith and promised, "If you believe, you will receive whatever you ask for in prayer" (Matt. 21:22).

We have already noted that Jesus has provided a way of access to the throne of God by shedding His own blood. Our means of appropriating this surpassing privilege is faith. "In Him and through *faith* in Him we may approach God with freedom and *confidence*" (Eph. 3:12). "Let us then approach the throne of grace with *confidence*..." (Heb. 4:16). "Therefore, brothers, since we have confidence to enter the Most Holy Place by the blood of Jesus, by a new and living way opened for us through the curtain, that is, His body, and since we have a great Priest over the house of God, let us draw near to God with a sincere heart in *full assurance of faith*... So do not throw away your confidence; it will be richly rewarded" (Heb. 10:19-22a,35). (Italics added in preceding Scripture portions.)

Faith is instilled in the heart by the message of the Lord through His Holy Word. "Consequently, faith comes from hearing the message, and the message is heard through the word of Christ" (Rom. 10:17). Whether we *feel* we have faith or not is irrelevant. Faith is a disciplined act of obedience based on the fact of God's Word, not on the fickleness of feeling. As we saturate our minds with Scripture, memorize it, and meditate upon it, we shall be enabled to pray in faith.

In that great hall of faith, Hebrews 11, we are told in verse 6, "And without faith it is impossible to please God, because anyone who comes to Him must believe that He exists and that He rewards those who earnestly seek Him."

So, go to the fountainhead of faith, the Word of God, imbibe its principles, and faith will be born in your heart. Only thus can our prayers as well as our behavior please Him.

Sanders stresses the fact that there are two kinds of faith, natural and spiritual, and only born-again Christians possess spiritual faith, which is a gift of God's grace (cf. Eph. 2:8). By natural faith he refers to such matters as believing that the postal authorities will deliver one's letter and believing in the moral integrity of a businessman. By spiritual faith he is speaking of viewing things through spiritual eyes and perceiving things invisible to the natural eye.[1] Let us accept the gift of spiritual faith, appropriate it for God's glory, develop it by claiming the promises, and strengthen it by constant use in prayer.

Praying in the Will of God

Faith is not drummed up by a stirring of the emotions or even by a mere act of the will. But it thrives when one knows that his prayer is in the will of God and can be substantiated by the Word of God. It could hardly be put more succinctly or clearly than 1 John 5:14, "This is the *assurance* we have in approaching God: that if we ask anything *according to His will*, He hears us. And if we know that He hears us — whatever we ask — we *know* that *we have* what we asked of Him" (italics added).

Praying according to God's will is coming to Him in faith without any unconfessed sin and in purity of motive and attitude. "I will therefore that men pray everywhere, lifting up holy hands, without wrath and doubting" (1 Tim. 2:8).

The very first step in praying in the will of God is to surrender to His will. One might think that the first step is to discover the will of God, but that is not so. Discovery follows surrender. Without surrender to God's will, one will probably never know what it is. I repeat: the way to pray in the will of God is not to seek to know what His will is and then decide whether to follow it. That is not faith; it is audacity.

> *The very first step in praying in the will of God is to surrender to His will.*

We must keep in mind that God is GOD. You and I are His creatures. God is *good*; His will is good. We accept God's will — not on the basis of our enjoyment, understanding, or judgment — not because we have found out what it is and have decided in favor of it — but because it is *God's* will. Furthermore, it is good, whether we think we like it or not. By faith we say with Jesus in Gethsemane, "Yet not as I will, but as You will" (Matt. 26:39). Faith accepts the ultimate outcome as good because it is God's will regardless of immediate consequences, as Jesus added, "My Father, if it is not possible for this cup to be taken away unless I drink it, may Your will be done" (Matt. 26:42).

THERE IS NO SUCCESSFUL PRAYER ASIDE FROM SURRENDER TO THE WILL OF GOD.

And yet, I am not satisfied with that word "surrender." I have used it, because it is essential to convey the concept of the conquest of self-will and of the idea of total submission. Yet, it is not entirely satisfactory, because its implications are negative. The will of God is positive and for it we need the word "embrace." Embrace the will of God, for it will only do you good. "Therefore, I urge you, brothers, in view of God's mercy, to offer your bodies as living sacrifices, holy and pleasing to God — which is your spiritual worship. Do not conform any longer to the pattern of this world, but be transformed by the renewing of your mind. Then you will be able to test and approve what God's will is — His good, pleasing and perfect will" (Rom. 12:1,2).

Jesus taught His disciples to pray. "Your will be done on earth as it is in Heaven" (Matt. 6:10). This is not a gimmick to use to evade the responsibility of praying specifically, definitely, and in faith. "If it be Thy will" may too often be a mere escape hatch used to avoid praying positively with firm assurance for that which God has clearly shown to be His will. Not so in scriptural references to the will of God in prayer. Many thousands who have sat under L. E. Maxwell's ministry have thrilled to hear him pray: "Thy will BE done" with the clear implication, "We *desire* Your will and we *will* it to be done." That is consistent with the Bible's teaching.

Having surrendered unequivocally to God's will, and having embraced it gladly, one then sets about determining what it involves. This is spelled out for us in so much detail in such passages as the Ten Commandments, the Sermon on the Mount, the Great Commission, and the exhortations to godly and prayerful living in the epistles that there can be no doubt remaining as to the kind of holy living which constitutes its content and its course. We have no excuse for a prayerless life because of a lack of knowledge of God's will. If we pray faithfully about the application of all the *revealed* will of God, we shall have more to pray about than we'll have time for.

We know we are praying in God's will when we pray for the salvation of a lost person, because 2 Peter 3:9 tells us clearly that He is "not wanting anyone to perish, but everyone to come to repentance." Likewise, we are sure of God's will in praying for the sending forth of missionaries, because Jesus said, "Ask the Lord of the harvest, therefore, to send out workers into His harvest field" (Matt. 9:38). We know, too, that confession, repentance for sin, thanksgiving and praise are always in accordance with His will. Intercession for fellow-believers is, too. And so is prayer for those in governmental authority over us. And on we could go selecting examples of those matters which are revealed as God's will and for which we should pray.

Daniel prayed concerning the restoration of the Jews to Jerusalem because he knew it was God's will and God's time. Jeremiah's writings told him so. Nehemiah prayed concerning the rebuilding of the city walls for the same reason.

All too often Christian young people are very concerned about finding God's will when they have not entered a life of prayer about the revealed will of God. A simple principle of effective prayer here is: Get your priorities straight.

Yet, of course, the Bible does not tell us what school to go to, what specific profession or trade to train for, or whom to marry. It does not even tell one in which part of the world to serve or under which mission board to enlist. These are important matters for prayer. We need to know God's will before making such choices. Before Jesus chose His twelve disciples, He capped His daily devotions with a whole night in prayer (cf. Luke 6:12,13). We would make far fewer blunders if we would follow His example when faced with decisions.

God's will in specifics is learned from the guidance of the Holy Spirit. It will always be consistent with His inspired Word, so the all-important activity, as has been repeatedly emphasized, is to soak up Scripture like a sponge. To direct our thoughts, the Spirit may use such things as prayer requests, circumstances, a sermon, the daily newspaper, or a handbook for world intercession entitled *Operation World*.[2] He may give an inner prompting with no evident outward cause. But the Holy Spirit's guidance will always be consistent with His Word. It could not be otherwise. The Bible is His message without error; therefore, He will not (yea, *cannot*) prompt any prayer contrary to it.

A few years ago I came upon the scene of a one-car accident. Witnesses said the automobile had been traveling at an excessively high speed when a front tire blew out. Hitting the concrete curb of the centre median, the vehicle catapulted through the air and hurtled end over end as it spewed bodies along the way.

When I crested the slight hill only moments later, I saw the body of a man lying flat on his back in the median. Quickly pulling off the road and stopping my car, I ran to the man. There was blood oozing from all the orifices of his head, but there were no visible wounds. He was breathing spasmodically.

Suddenly, I was aware of an officer of the U.S. Air Force kneeling beside me. Silently, we loosed the unconscious man's collar, belt, and cuffs. We did not dare move him. Within moments a large crowd had gathered. Someone assured us that an ambulance was on the way from a nearby Air Force base. A woman began to scream, "Pray for him, oh, pray for him, somebody pray for him!" The Air Force officer, straightening, quieted the hysterical woman and said loudly enough for all to hear, "All right, lady, I'll pray for him, but I'm afraid it's too late. I know this man. Just this afternoon before he left the base I asked him to receive Jesus Christ as his personal Savior, but he laughed and said he had plenty of time." He prayed and I prayed. All we could do was ask that God's will be done.

> *Let's not suppose that we have glib answers to every problem...*

The accident victim was dead on arrival at the hospital. God did not give the officer or me faith to pray that the man might live and be healed. It is perfectly all right to pray for God's will to be done even when we do not know what it is, but there is no need to pray contrary to His will. All our wishful thinking about another chance, all our natural inclinations to wish life into a dying man, would not constitute a prayer of faith which God could honor.

Sanders says that the prayer of faith, which finds its warrant in the promises of the Word of God, "is a divinely given intuition and assurance that God has answered our prayer and granted our request. It is not the outcome of trying to believe, but is effortless confidence in God.... For it is impossible for a believer to exercise faith for something that is beyond the scope of the will of God. If faith is the gift of God, and it is, He will not give it to someone in order to encourage him to do something contrary to His will."[3]

Let's not suppose that we have glib answers to every problem that arises in regard to praying in God's will. The fact remains that God's thoughts are not man's thoughts; His ways are not ours. He alone sees the end from the beginning. Some things He allows are too mysterious for our understanding, and the only proper posture of faith is the humble acknowledgment that God knows what He is doing. If we truly desire God's will, we will pray for it even if we cannot understand it. Else, what is faith for? If we insist on understanding everything, we are walking, not by faith, but by sight.

Sometimes, after a period of months or even years, we are permitted to catch a glimpse of what God is accomplishing. His will is that we should "be conformed to the likeness of his Son" (Rom. 8:29), and that is the "good" toward which He is working all things (verse 28).

At other times, we are not shown what God is doing. Apparently, it is part of His process of molding us in Christ's likeness to allow us to trust Him without seeing His purposes. But, oh, how many precious prayer-warrior-saints have testified to the fact that it was in the valleys that He made His presence felt and drew His child close to His breast, that it was at such times of testing that new insights were given into His Word, new lessons taught, new character traits developed.

But one may ask, "Can I pray specifically when I do not know

> *"Prayer is difficult, I object to facile solutions."*
> —Donald Cole

God's will?" The answer is, *"Yes."* We can pray specifically and submissively *for His will* — whatever it is. Remember, the order is not first to find out God's will, and then to surrender to it. It's exactly the other way around. In fact, it is to embrace His will whether I ever understand it or not.

Donald Cole, radio pastor of Moody Bible Institute, said to Don Bjork of Worldteam, "Prayer is difficult; I object to facile solutions."[4]

Bjork goes on to suggest as explanations for unanswered prayers: human selfishness, human sinfulness, and divine sovereignty. Then, he suggests the kinds of prayer God does want to answer: contrite prayers, character-of-Christ prayers ("in My name"), confessional prayers, and conditional prayers ("if it be possible... nevertheless, not as I will, but as Thou wilt").

Paul frankly acknowledges that we are dependent entirely upon the Holy Spirit, not only to teach us to pray as we ought, but to take over for us because of our ignorance. "In the same way, the Spirit helps us in our weakness. We do not know what we ought to pray, but the Spirit Himself intercedes for us with groans that words cannot express. And He who searches our hearts knows the mind of the Spirit, because the Spirit intercedes for the saints in accordance with God's will" (Rom. 8:26,27). What a blessed truth. This is the last word on praying in God's will: the Holy Spirit intercedes for us according to God's will. Praise the Lord! When my finite mind cannot comprehend the infinite plan and purpose of God, I can rest in this fact. I can commit even my limitations to Him and let Him re-word my prayer according to God's will.

God's Word teaches us His will on many subjects. Commands, promises, and principles abound to assure us of His will for our own lives and the lives of those for whom we intercede. So, to pray in God's will, it is necessary that we saturate our minds with Scripture. As we read, memorize, meditate, and study, the Holy Spirit will have material from which to draw when we pray — material to use in teaching us God's will. He will bring Scripture quotations and principles to bear on our requests. Then, when we are unsure of His will, it is a comfort to know that the Holy Spirit takes over.

Praying Definitely

When one knows God's will in a matter, one can pray specifically and positively. This is a point emphasized by Mrs. Mary Moynan, daughter of the famous pioneer missionaries to China, Jonathan and Rosalind Goforth.

In regard to prayer, Mrs. Moynan told me, "Looking back over my seventy-five

> "He [husband Bob] believed, and I do, too, in very specific requests to God."
> —Mrs. Mary Goforth Moynan

years, I feel that this is the most rewarding type of ministry that I had a part in. I maintained liaison between the women's prayer groups in our various churches and the minister, my husband. Bob would give me a list of specific requests for prayer. He believed, and I do, too, in very specific requests to God. There are so many problems that come up in the ministry of the church. Bob would share a problem with me without mentioning the name and I would take it to the women's prayer group and we would pray."

On one occasion Pastor Bob Moynan went personally to the ladies' group at Collingwood Presbyterian Church in Toledo, Ohio, because he was very agitated in his spirit about a certain case. He told them, "This is the hardest nut I've ever had to crack." A doctor in the congregation had called him with a request that he visit Mr. Leslie Middleton, who was in the hospital with terminal cancer. Middleton was an atheist.

Bob had made the visit, but could get nowhere with the man. He had been an atheist all his life. He said, "I've been planning all my life for my retirement, and now that I know I have cancer, I haven't any retirement. I haven't got a thing to look forward to."

As Bob tried to persuade him to put his trust in Christ, he said, "How do I *begin* to believe in God when I haven't believed all my life?"

So Pastor Moynan visited the ladies' prayer group and asked them to pray specifically: "Please pray that I will be given the passage of Scripture that will reach that man's heart."

On the way to the hospital it was as though a light from Heaven came to him. The passage from Mark 9 concerning the boy

PRINCIPLES OF EFFECTIVE PRAYER

possessed with an evil spirit flashed into his mind. The father of the boy had cried to Jesus, "Lord, I believe; help Thou mine unbelief."

Pastor Moynan told the Bible story to Leslie Middleton. When he got to the verse, "Lord, I believe; help Thou mine unbelief," the atheist's face lit up, and he said, "Bob," for by then they were on a first-name basis, "you've gone 'round and 'round with me, but this time you've hit the bull's-eye; I can pray that prayer." From that moment he was a saved man. He asked Pastor Moynan to preach at his funeral and to tell everyone of his salvation. He gave instructions to put on his tombstone the words, "Lord, I believe."

Leslie Middleton was known throughout Toledo as a businessman, an atheist, and a man with a mean disposition. His funeral was well-attended, and the story of his salvation made a profound impact.[5]

Read Psalm 51 again and see how specific David's request was for forgiveness and cleansing. Notice how direct and definite are the requests of the Lord's Prayer. "Give us today our daily bread:" today — the time is indicated precisely; our daily bread — the object desired is specified. Check Jesus' parabolic teaching on prayer: "Friend, lend me three loaves of bread..." (Luke 11:5b). Review Paul's explicit intercession such as. "I pray that out of His glorious riches He may strengthen you with power through His Spirit in your inner being" (Eph. 3:16).

How ineffective it is to pray: "Dear Lord, bless the missionaries and the pastor and the Sunday school teachers, and bless Aunt Sue and Uncle Bill and Mother and Father and all our loved ones. Be with us through the day in all we do. In Jesus' name, Amen." What an uncertain sound!

John R. Rice masterfully illustrated the point: "In the matter of daily living, we make our requests definite. We never go into a restaurant and say. 'Bring me some food!' No, we carefully select from the menu just what we want and think we can pay for. Perhaps we say, 'I want the small steak, cooked medium; some French fried potatoes, and spinach. I want black tea, hot, with cream, and orange Jello dessert.' When you go to buy a meal, you are definite."[6]

Rice reminds us about Gideon who prayed for dew on the fleece and dry ground around and got it, then detailed a dry fleece and wet ground and got that, too.

God isn't too busy for itemized details, as this story shows.

Tom was stumped. There did not seem to be a piece of cable in all of Irian Jaya, but he had to have a thirty-five foot piece in order to complete his summer missionary project.

Tom and Barbara Marks knew that classroom instruction was not all they needed for missionary training. They needed to learn to walk by faith, so when mission leaders visiting Prairie Bible Institute told of construction needs, practical Tom heard the call and decided that he would have to do what was needed and trust God to provide for his family for the next school term. During their first year at Prairie they were convinced that God eventually wanted them to serve in Iran, but meanwhile Tom's skills as a first-class electrician and carpenter were needed in many places. So one summer found him in Ecuador, another in Alaska, and another in Irian Jaya.

The missionary children's school of the Christian and Missionary Alliance in Irian Jaya needed someone to set up a power plant. The generator units had been on hand for nearly two years and would serve not only the Alliance, but The Evangelical Alliance Mission, Regions Beyond Missionary Union, The Unevangelized Fields Mission, Baptists, and several little Dutch missionary societies, which all had property needing electricity. The C. & M. A. asked Tom to go. Barbara and little Amber stayed at home in Minnesota.

Tom says, "I was starting to run some distribution lines after I got the generators wired together, and I was running two spans to one side of a particular pole. With the heavy weight of long spans pulling from one side of the pole, it was obvious that I needed a guy wire to pull it back so it would hold up under the stress. I was wondering where we would get the thirty-five-foot piece of cable needed. We went to the largest city, Jayapura, a city of about one hundred thousand people, but there wasn't any technical equipment to speak of, no cable or anything like it. There was some small rope that would soon rot, even if it held up under the weight. The nearest place to get a piece of cable was Australia. It would take several weeks, but I had only a week until time to return to school.

"I was walking along praying, asking God what I should use or how I could get by and get on with the project. The air strip was on one side and the jungle on the other as I walked and prayed. The Lord seemed to impress on me, 'Just look up, look unto Me and I will supply.'

'Yes, Lord,' I said, 'I am looking to You.' And, with head bowed, I continued to pray. 'No,' the Lord impressed upon me, 'look up!' I lifted my head and looked up.

'What's that in those trees?' I wondered. The sun was glinting on something that looked like a piece of cable. Was my mind playing tricks on me? I walked closer. Yes, it was cable. I climbed up and worked for some time to get it unsnarled from the limbs of several trees. It was thirty-eight feet long!"

Tom figured that some G.I.'s in World War II had tossed aside the cable when the trees were small, and when they grew up, they carried it with them. However, a friend with some knowledge of forestry said that such a thing could not happen. Trees don't grow that way: they grow upward from the top and low limbs stay at the same level, or if crowded and starved for sunlight, they may wither and drop off. But the limbs farther up are new limbs. This friend suggested that the cable may have been dropped from a helicopter.

"No," said Tom, "it wasn't in the very tops of the trees, but twelve to fifteen feet up."

So, who knows how it got there? It is obvious who put it there and kept it there until the moment when Tom Marks walked past praying.

Thanking the Lord, Tom added, "Now, Lord, two cable clamps, please!" After all, what good is a cable without clamps? He thought of the pile of old war refuse the missionaries had collected to throw away. As he stood on the edge of the junk pile, Tom thought, "Even if there were any clamps in here, I would never be able to find them." He prayed, 'Lord, open my eyes, and show me the clamps that You're going to give me.

Raising an old truck wheel, he found one clamp. "Good, Lord, now we have only one more to go." There is nothing sacrilegious about such praying. Opening his eyes, he spied the other clamp. The project would go on. It was finished about three days before Tom had to leave.

Tom adds this postscript: "Just to show how unbelieving humanity is, I must also tell you that I thought maybe it was just a coincidence, so I started digging through that junk, looking for a third cable clamp, which I didn't even need. I wasted about an hour and a half of the Lord's time trying to find a clamp that wasn't there."[7]

Conclusion

These three conditions are basic essentials for effective prayer:
- PRAYING IN FAITH
- PRAYING IN THE WILL OF GOD
- PRAYING DEFINITELY.

No matter how much else you may forget from the lessons in this book, memorize these three conditions. Review them frequently. Practice them daily.

Study and Discussion Questions

1. Name several attributes of God (of. Chapter 7) which make faith a logical condition of effective prayer. Explain your choices.

2. Discuss three conditions of effective prayer from the arguments presented in James 1:5-8: 4:2b, 3; 5:13-18.

3. Read Hebrews 11. Then discuss verses 35b-40. How does the condition of faith apply to the people in these verses?

4. Start a Scripture-verse card file (see "Projects" in the back of this book). Begin it with verses under the three categories In this chapter. You could summarize the headings as follows: Faith; Will of God; Definite Praying.

15

PRAYING IN THE HOLY SPIRIT

"And pray in the Spirit — this is the climax of the great Scripture passage on Christian warfare, Ephesians 6:10-20. "And pray in the Spirit on all occasions" (v. 18a), not just when you've reached some mountaintop spiritual experience or an emotional high. "Pray in the Spirit... with all kinds of prayers and requests" (v. 18b). Praying in the Spirit is not some special kind of ecstatic experience. Every kind of prayer from personal petitions to international intercession is to be prayed in the Spirit. It is this which makes prayer effective.

The Apostle Paul moves from the general ("all kinds of prayers and requests") to the particular as he requests intercession for "all the saints," for himself, and specifically for his fearless declaration of the mystery of the Gospel. Judging from the patterns in the New Testament, it appears that praying in the Spirit will not be *primarily* concerned about such matters as personal comfort, material needs, and health, which often dominate our prayer meetings, as important as these necessary considerations are to us. Rather, prayer that is instigated by, directed by, and controlled by the Spirit of God will be concerned with fearless witnessing (Eph. 6:19,20) and with "the Spirit of wisdom and revelation" in order to know God better (Eph. 1:17). It will further focus on heart enlightenment to know the hope of His calling, the "riches of His glorious inheritance in the saints, and His incomparably great power for us who believe" (Eph. 1:18,19).

A believer who is praying in the Spirit will pray that out of God's glorious riches He will strengthen fellow-believers "with power through His Spirit in [their] inner being" (Eph. 3:16).

> *"Having filled us with the desire to pray, the Spirit of supplication next gives us power to pray."*
> —G.H.C. Macgregor

Members of Christ's body praying in the Spirit will uphold one another that each might be rooted and established in love, might grasp experientially the width, length, height, and depth of the love of Christ, and might "be filled to the measure of all the fullness of God" (Eph. 3:18,19). And we won't leave off asking that our brothers and sisters in Christ be filled with the knowledge of God's will "through all spiritual wisdom and understanding" (Col. 1:9).

Of course, such Spiritual praying will include deep intercession for the unsaved (Rom. 10:1: 2 Pet. 3:9). Not that physical and material needs will be overlooked, for Jesus taught us to ask for "our daily bread" (Matt. 6:11) and James encourages the sick person to call for prayer by the elders of the church (Jas. 5: 14-16). Yes, truly, "all kinds of prayers and requests are to be offered 'in the Spirit.'

Jude insisted with equal clarity. "But you, dear friends, build yourselves up in your most holy faith and pray in the Holy Spirit" (v. 20). These are inspired encouragements, yea, commands, for New Testament believers. If we would pray effectively, we must pray in the Holy Spirit.

G.H.C. Macgregor has an excellent little book entitled, *True Praying in the Holy Spirit,* in which he says, "When the Spirit is called the Spirit of supplication, it cannot mean that He prays for Himself, for such a supposition is inconsistent with His absolute deity. Nor can it mean that in His own person He prays for us, for that is the priestly work of Jesus Christ, the only Mediator between God and man. It can only mean that He prays in us, assisting us in prayer, helping our infirmities, so as to make our prayers acceptable and prevailing before God.... The first work of the Spirit as the Spirit of supplication is to fill us with the desire for prayer.... He brings us into and keeps us in a frame of mind in which prayer is not only possible but delightful.... He fills the heart so full of desire that we are driven to prayer for relief... so full of thankfulness that its natural outcome is praise.... Having filled us with the desire to pray, the Spirit of supplication next gives us power to pray. He actually strengthens us in the act of praying."[1]

Who Can Pray in the Holy Spirit?

The Spirit-inspired admonitions to pray in the Spirit were written to born-again believers. Only those who have been born anew by the power of the Holy Spirit can possibly pray in the Spirit. When a person receives the Lord Jesus Christ by simple childlike faith, the Holy Spirit Himself takes up His abode within that new believer (1 Cor. 6:19,20; Rom. 8:9b). What a glorious discovery! Even the babe in Christ has within him the One who motivates prayer, empowers prayer, and makes prayer acceptable to the Father. "Everyone who calls on the name of the Lord will be saved" (Rom. 10:13) and that calling out to God is the first act of effective prayer.

Earlier we considered the Trinitarian dimension of prayer expressed in Dr. Samuel Zwemer's definition, "Prayer is God the Holy Spirit talking to God the Father in the name of God the Son, and the believer's heart is the prayer room."

But are all believers' prayers prayed in the Spirit? Apparently not. Paul was constantly having to deal with Christians who were carnal, worldly, and unspiritual. A believer, although judicially justified through his standing in Christ, may not be walking in the light. He may grieve, even quench, the Spirit within. Paul called the believers at Corinth Infants, incapable of taking strong spiritual meat, worldly, and carnal (fleshly). Yet, surprisingly, this scolding comes in the very same chapter where he asks, "Don't you know that you yourselves are God's temple and that God's Spirit lives in you?" (1 Cor. 3:16).

The lack of harmony between Euodias and Syntyche (Phil. 4:2) is the sort of thing that restricts prayer in the Spirit by the body of Christ on earth. These two women needed to lay aside their differences, each considering the other better than herself, and let the mind of Christ dwell in them (Phil. 2:1-18). Then, and only then, could they rejoice in the Lord and, "by prayer and petition, with thanksgiving," present [their] requests to God (Phil. 4:6; cf. vv. 4-7).

Yes, it is sadly possible for Christians to "grieve the Holy Spirit of God" (Eph. 4:30) and not have freedom to pray effectively. The context of this expression needs to be studied carefully to learn how to avoid it. It indicates the following behavior as that which grieves: sensuality (impurity, lust), deceitful desires, falsehood (lying), stealing, unwholesome talk, bitterness, rage and anger, brawling and slander, and every form of malice. If we read on to chapter 5 we find added to the list: sexual immorality, greed, obscenity, foolish talk or coarse joking. If we do not have victory in any of these areas, let us not wonder why our prayers are not answered. Sins undealt with stymie any striving to pray in the Spirit. Un-Christlike attitudes, motives, desires, thoughts, words, and actions quench the Spirit and render prayer ineffective. "Do not put out the Spirit's fire" (1 Thess. 5:19).

On the other hand, one whose life is bearing the Spirit's fruit of "love, joy, peace, patience, kindness, goodness, faithfulness, gentleness and self-control" (Gal. 5:22,23), can pray in the Holy Spirit without hindrance.

How Can We Pray in the Holy Spirit?

The first step to praying in the Spirit is regeneration, i.e., to be born anew by the Spirit of God. On our part we are born anew by placing faith in Jesus Christ as Savior (John 3:1-18).

Step number two is to yield fully to the Holy Spirit's control. He will exercise this control by His Word as we hide it in our hearts and obey it. He will check the lustful thought, the falsehood, the anger, the critical attitude, the bitterness — all that displeases Him, and will empower us to resist. He will give instead a meek and quiet spirit, will use, all our faculties to bring glory to Jesus' name, and will produce His fruit in our lives.

Corporately, too, the Spirit's control will manifest in the Church definite behavior characteristics. Notice the cause and effects in Ephesians 5:18b-20: "...be filled with the Spirit. Speak to one another with psalms, hymns, and spiritual songs. Sing and make music in your heart to the Lord, always giving thanks to God the Father for everything, in the name of our Lord Jesus Christ." Believers are welded in a fellowship of mutually supportive ministries. The New Testament norm is a group of

Spirit-filled (Spirit-controlled) saints worshipping the Lord and ministering to one another in the Spirit.

So, the Bible's clear answer as to how we can pray in the Spirit is: (1) be born of the Spirit; (2) be filled with the Spirit.

What Will Be the Issue in Life and Service?

I am deeply indebted to Dr. Henry W. Frost for his book *Effective Praying*, especially the fifth chapter, "Prayer in the Holy Spirit."[2] Since that book is now out of print and not available to most readers. I want to pass along Dr. Frost's ideas. He raises the pertinent question, "What will be the issue in life and service if we pray in the Spirit?" He offers six suggestions by way of answer:

"Praying in the Spirit secures for us access to God." Earlier we introduced the concept of a way of access to the throne. We observed the provision of the way of access through the shed blood of Christ. Ephesians 2:18 declares. "For through Him we both have access to the Father by one Spirit." This is the way of access: "through Christ." Notice that it is also "by one Spirit." Dr. Frost's statement regarding the fact that "praying in the Spirit secures for us access to God" complements our earlier observations. What Jesus has purchased for us is secured (obtained) by praying in the Spirit. We avail ourselves of the way of access by prayer in the Spirit. Thus, we can come before the throne of grace with all boldness (Heb. 4:16).

"Praying in the Spirit secures to us the true worship of God." Jesus said, "God is spirit, and His worshippers must worship in spirit and in truth" (John 4:24). Worship includes the act of prayer. "Worship" comes from an old English word meaning "worth-ship." Frost notes that "God's worth is nowhere more clearly set forth as when, in our need and dependence, we make our petitions before Him. Worship, therefore, is both the requisite and determiner of acceptable prayer.

"Praying in the Spirit secures to us the benefits of sonship before God." "Because you are sons, God sent the Spirit of His Son into our hearts, the Spirit who calls out. 'Abba, Father'" (Gal. 4:6); "because those who are led by the Spirit of God are sons of God. For you did not receive a spirit that makes you a slave again to fear, but you received the Spirit of sonship. And by Him we

PRINCIPLES OF EFFECTIVE PRAYER

cry, 'Abba, Father.' The Spirit Himself testifies with our spirit that we are God's children" (Rom. 8:14-16).

Dr. Frost rightly observes that the word "son" in these passages implies more than mere childhood; it includes the legal claims and maturity of an accredited son as Paul teaches in Galatians 4:1-7 and Romans 8:14. "Praying therefore in the Holy Spirit implies that we, as sons, are in a highly developed condition before God, wherein, in the process of prayer, we may know His mind and make our petitions according to His will. This is the case because sonship implies fellowship, and fellowship includes a knowledge of the divine thought and purpose. Such praying as this leads us into large spiritual experiences, and thus into the most ample prayer privileges and enjoyments."

"Praying in the Spirit secures for us God as our environment and sphere." Already we have noticed verses which refer to the Holy Spirit as being in the saint (1 Cor. 3:16) and the saint in the Spirit (Eph. 6:18: Jude 20). Frost's illustration of this is a person as related to the atmosphere: the atmosphere is in the man while the man is in the atmosphere. Another analogy is that of a poker in the fire so hot that the fire gets into the poker. The Holy Spirit in the believer secures for him perfect standing and acceptability before God and gives him life. So also the believer in the Spirit lays hold through prayer of the fullness of life. We enter experientially by faith into all that the Holy Spirit procures for us judicially. "If, therefore, we pray in the Spirit, God the Holy Ghost surrounds and pervades us, and He thus transforms both us and our prayers.

"Praying in the Spirit secures to us subjection to God." This brings us to a re-consideration of those profound and mysterious verses, Romans 8:26,27, "In the same way, the Spirit helps us in our weakness. We do not know what we ought to pray, but the Spirit Himself intercedes for us with groans that words cannot express. And He who searches our hearts knows the mind of the Spirit, because the Spirit intercedes for the saints in accordance with God's will."

Have you noticed how we keep returning to these verses? Whether we discuss the Trinitarian dimension of prayer or praying in the will of God, we are compelled to consider them. And, of course, they are key verses for our present topic. Even when our hearts are right toward God, how many are the infirmities of the flesh and how finite are our minds. Such limitations are bound

> *The Holy Spirit will transform the poorly-expressed prayer into one that is acceptable before the perfect God.*

to restrict the effectiveness of our prayers. At our best we fall far short of the glory of God, which is the objective of all true prayer. But, praise God, the Holy Spirit "helps us in our weakness" and although "we do not know what we ought to pray,... the Spirit Himself [Think of it!] intercedes for us."

Do you sometimes come up against a blank wall in your prayers and have to admit that a situation is so complicated and confusing that you are bewildered as to how you should pray? What should you request? What is right? What is best for all concerned? What will bring glory to God? If you sometimes choke out a sob and cry, "Oh, God, I just don't know!" you are in good company. That is what Paul said, "We do not know." And then there are the times we *think* that we know, but later developments prove how ignorant we were. But is the heart right? That is the crux of the matter. Is our heart-desire for the glory of God at any cost, come what may? Well, God "searches our hearts and knows the mind of the Spirit." He, the Holy Spirit, is not bound by our ignorance and infirmities. His intercession for us is effective because He "intercedes for the saints in accordance with God's will." He will transform the poorly-expressed prayer into one that is acceptable before the perfect God. He is in no way limited to our vocabularies, but through our very groanings reads the desires of hearts which have been brought under subjection. He did it for Paul himself when he prayed three times for that which was not God's will to give, and then He gave Paul the grace to quit asking and to gladly accept that which would better glorify God (2 Cor. 12:7-10).

"Praying in the Spirit secures to us amplification of our intercessions as they are offered unto God." "Now to Him who is able to do immeasurably more than all we ask or imagine, according to His power [the Holy Spirit] that is at work within us, to Him be glory in the church and in Christ Jesus throughout all generations, for ever and ever! Amen" (Eph. 3:20,2 1). The Holy

Spirit lifts our hearts and minds to new planes; He expands our vision, enlarges our horizons, enriches our desires, so that we leave off asking for petty and selfish things. He escorts us into the throne room, presents us to the Father, and fills our hearts, our minds, and our mouths with prayers worthy of the King of kings. (And when our minds and mouths cannot formulate words, He takes the heart-cry and presents it in accordance with the Father's will. Glory!) Frost expresses it like this: "It is the Spirit's longing that we should rise to the majesty of His being and ask things which are commensurate with His measureless ways and works.... It is ever our privilege for these reasons to cast ourselves upon the upward and outward movings of the Holy Ghost, in order that we may be borne away to infinitely high and holy realms of intercession."

It is hoped that the following account will illustrate something of the Holy Spirit's prompting and guidance. However, it should not be imagined that all prayer in the Spirit is as dramatic as this or that only such obvious promptings are to be considered prayer in the Spirit.

Lesette came to my office for counselling two or three times. I don't remember whether I ever suggested that she talk to my wife about some matter; I do know that she had not done so. In fact, they had never met.

One Saturday night I was grading papers at home when I happened to remember Lesette and stopped to pray for her. When I turned to the papers again, there seemed to be a stronger urge to pray. The Lord had been trying to teach me to obey such promptings to pray, but this time it began to take on the dimensions of an undeniable burden.

After a few minutes of prayer, I called to my wife in the kitchen, "Honey, will you do something for me?"

"What do you want me to do?"

"Well, it's not very easy to explain," I replied, "but there's a girl I've counselled a couple of times, and I would appreciate it if you would go to see her. I've been praying for her and I feel that she needs help."

"Where does she live?" Doloris asked.

"I don't know. The girls' dorm. You'll have to inquire."

> *"If you feel that you know, as yet, very little concerning the deep things of prayer and what prayer really is, then, pray for the Spirit of prayer."*
> — O. Hallesby

"What do you want me to say to her? What is her problem?" She probably felt that I wasn't giving her enough information and perhaps that my request was not very reasonable.

"Honey, I know it may sound foolish, but I honestly don't know. I just feel that she needs help, and I can't very well go down to the ladies' dormitory on a Saturday evening to see her, so I want you to go. I don't know what you should say. Just see whether she is in her room and pay her a little visit. Let the Lord
lead you as to what you should say."

Taking off her apron. Doloris shook her head and mumbled, "Well, okay, if that's what you want."

The second door she checked in the dorm had Lesette's name on it. She knocked. Silence. She knocked again A moment later someone called softly, "Come in."

"Oh, are you Mrs. Pike?" Lesette asked Doloris as the door opened.

"Yes. Why do you ask?"

There was a sob before the answer came. "I was just sitting here by the window looking out at the stars and trying to straighten everything out in my mind. I wondered whether there really was a God or not, and if there was, whether He ever really paid any attention to me. It seemed like He never answered my prayers. I looked up into Heaven and said, "God, if You are real, please send Mrs. Pike to help me. That's when you knocked."[3]

Dr. Hallesby said, "The Spirit of prayer throws light upon every phase of our prayer life... not only theoretical light, enlightening our minds, but practical light for our use in praying and for our training in prayer.... Do pray a little each day in a childlike way for the Spirit of prayer.... If you feel that you know, as yet, very little concerning the deep things of prayer and what prayer really is, then pray for the Spirit of prayer."[4]

Macgregor asks, "And after we have been brought to a point where we must pray or die, after we have been brought to a condition of soul which makes it absolutely necessary that we should get to God in prayer, who but the Holy Spirit can help us to pray as we ought? Who but He can fill us with intense desire? Who but He, in the midst of our modern busy life, can still and quiet the soul before God? Who but He can give us the sweet simplicity of childhood as He leads us to the Father's presence? Who but He can give us the boldness which takes no refusal, and obtains the blessing?"[5]

We close this chapter with an ever-timely admonition from S.D. Gordon, "There is One who is a Master Intercessor. He understands praying perfectly. He is the Spirit of prayer.... Let Him teach you."[6]

Study and Discussion Questions

1. Jesus did all things "in the Spirit." List the desires prompted by the Holy Spirit and expressed by our Lord Jesus Christ in John 17.

2. What do each of the following facts about the Holy Spirit imply for our praying?
    a. The Holy Spirit is a **Person**, not a mere force or influence. Rev. 2:7; Acts 13:2; Romans 8:26.27; John 15:26; Eph. 4:30.
    b. The Holy Spirit is **Divine** (i.e. He is **God**). Acts 5:3,4; Heb. 9:14; Psalm 139:7; 1 Cor. 2:10,11; 2 Cor. 3:17.
    c. The Bible (Sword of the Spirit) is inspired (transmitted without contradiction or error) by the Holy Spirit. 2 Pet. 1:21; 2 Sam. 23:2; Acts 3:21b.
    d. The Holy Spirit indwells all believers. Romans 8:9; 1 Cor. 6:19-20.
    e. The Holy Spirit will continually fill the believer who yields to His control. Eph. 5:18.
    f. The Holy Spirit produces fruit in Spirit-filled believers. Gal. 5: 22-26.
    g. The Holy Spirit gives gifts to believers. 1 Cor. 12:4-11.

3. Tell your group about any personal experience you have had which illustrates Romans 8:26,27.

4. Discuss any implications you may see between John 15:26 and praying in Jesus' name (John 14-16). If you don't see any implications, ask your group. Think about and talk about the possible connections.

16

WHY DOES GOD *NOT* ANSWER
OUR PRAYERS?

The title of this chapter is not an expression of curiosity. It is all too often the cry of a soul in anguish.

When I've prayed with deep yearning, when I've pleaded the promises, when I've poured out my petition to God in all humility and faith and nothing happens — why? Doesn't the Lord mean what He says in all those whatever-you-ask promises? Is God's Word really true? What is wrong with my faith? Doesn't God care? Is there some sin in my life of which I am unaware? Why. Lord, why?

Have you endured such soul-searching? If you have tried to maintain a prayer life for very long, you probably are familiar with the agony of ungranted requests. Few saints can claim a one-hundred-percent record of answers to prayer.

Samuel Chadwick tells of praying earnestly and confidently for a sick man. He and others had claimed God's promise and were sure their friend would be restored to health. While they prayed, the man died. Even the saintly Chadwick was overwhelmed with shock and frankly admits that his faith was sorely tried.[1]

Eric Fife says. "At times I wondered if my praying was worthwhile. Sometimes I wondered if those who wrote on prayer were just 'super saints' or if they were silent regarding failure. I wondered if they attempted a sincere but wrong effort to save the reputation of God!"[2]

A missionary-teacher from a Bible school in Africa wrote to me about the preparation of this textbook and said. "I know of no book which I can really use as a textbook on prayer. I guess that I'm too particular, but to me most of them don't get down to the

> *None can offer a panacea for all the problems which Christians face.*

main facts of 'Why God does NOT answer my prayers' and 'How to pray so that God will answer my prayers.'" His deep concern has probably not evolved solely from the need for material to teach but from his own frequent need for an answer.

Unlike the missionary who does not have access to the large selection of Christian books which are available in North America. I have received much help on this aspect of prayer from the following:

> Samuel Chadwick, *The Path of Prayer* (Hodder and Stoughton);
> Eric Fife, *Prayer — Common Sense and the Bible* (Zondervan);
> S.D. Gordon. *Quiet Talks on Prayer* (Baker);
> Harold Lindsell, *When You Pray* (Baker);
> Andrew Murray, *The Prayer Life* (Zondervan);
> John R. Rice, *Prayer — Asking and Receiving* (Sword of the Lord);
> J.O. Sanders, *Prayer Power Unlimited* (Moody).

Yet, none can offer a panacea for all the problems which Christians face. Nor can I. Prayer is a mystery. It does business with omnipotence and infinity; therefore, finite minds find its magnitude too great to comprehend. True, we can research Scripture for clues to the reasons for God's rejection of some of our most urgent requests and find there a treasury of helps. We can even find several clearcut statements which pinpoint certain causes. But there will always be more to learn about prayer, always labyrinths of majesty and mystery in the limitless wisdom of God which elude our limited insights.

We are frequently reminded that there are no unanswered prayers — that God answers with a "yes," a "no," or a "wait awhile," but that He answers every time. Although there is truth in this, it fails to satisfy the grieving soul who cannot understand why his request is not granted. When a believer asks. "Why doesn't God answer my prayer?" he wants to know why he *does not receive* what he asks for. We need to take care that we do not give him a glib answer which causes him to quit asking (at least out loud), but which does nothing to relieve his burden.

On the other hand, we should not assume that our request is ungranted just because we are not aware of an answer. The February 21, 1965, issue of *Power for Living* used fictitious names to tell the *true* story of "Brad," a young serviceman. He was hitch-hiking, and "Lew Masters," a real-estate broker, gave him a ride. Brad led the businessman to Christ. When they parted, the older man gave Brad his business card and urged him, if he was ever in Chicago, to look him up. Five years later, Brad accepted the invitation, only to discover that a few minutes after they had parted, Lew Masters had been killed in an automobile accident.

When Mrs. Masters heard from Brad how her husband had received Christ as his Savior, she said, "I had walked with Christ for many years and had prayed for my husband often. When he was killed, I thought God had not answered my prayers. For five years I've been out of fellowship with God because I thought He'd failed me!"

How limited is our vision and our knowledge!

Yet, not all requests are granted, and there must be reasons for that. John Bisagno declared emphatically, "Answered prayer is not a miracle, it is a law."[3] A law is a foregone conclusion that if certain conditions are met, certain results will follow invariably. Sometimes the law appears to be inoperative. The inconsistency is not with God but with us, with our failure to meet the conditions, perhaps with our lack of comprehension of the conditions of the law.

The preceding chapters call attention to many of the conditions which govern the law of prayer. To violate these conditions will render prayer ineffective. For instance, failure to ask specifically, failure to ask in God's will and for His glory, failure to persist steadfastly — these might be among the most obvious of reasons for ungranted requests.

In addition, let me call your attention to four major categories that must be considered in seeking reasons for denial or delay in receiving answers: sin, self, Satan, and the sovereignty of God.

Sin

A boy on his bicycle took a short cut across an empty parking lot. A dog began chasing him and barking ferociously. The boy pedaled frantically while keeping a wary eye on the dog. So intent was he on escaping that he failed to look up and see the brick wall of a building dead ahead. Instead of escaping, he slammed into the wall and received a brain concussion.

Sometimes we pray like that — frantically, without observing the obstacles. No amount of sincerity, earnestness, emotion, or activity will bring our pleas to the attention of God

> *Disobedience, which is rebellion, takes us off praying ground.*

and free us from our frustration as long as the wall of sin stands between our souls and the just Judge of the universe. One result of sin often overlooked is that it causes God to turn a deaf ear to our prayers. Psalm 66:18-20 states it clearly: "If I had cherished sin in my heart, the Lord would not have listened; but God has surely listened and heard my voice in prayer. Praise be to God, who has not rejected my prayer or withheld His love from me!"

"Then," God's child despairs, "who can pray? No one is perfectly free from sin" (cf. Rom. 3:23; Isa. 53:6; 1 John 1:8). But the Psalmist did not say that no one who commits sin can have prayer answered. If he had, none of us could qualify. He said, "If I had *cherished* sin in my heart..." The King James Version renders it, "If I regard iniquity in my heart...." It may be trite, but there is still truth in the old adage: "You may not be able to stop the birds from flying over your head, but you can prevent them from building nests in your hair." One cause of ungranted requests is a sympathy for sin, a fondness for sin, a refusal to confess and repent of sin. Sin is an abomination to God. If we expect Him to answer prayer while we continue in sin knowingly, we fail miserably to understand the vileness of sin before a holy God.

Here is the principle stated positively in the form of a promise: "Dear friends, if our hearts do not condemn us, we have confidence before God and receive from Him anything we ask, because we obey His commands and do what pleases Him" (1 John 3:21,22).

Some sins which obstruct prayer are specified in Scripture. If you do not find anything here which explains your ineffectiveness in prayer, keep in mind that these are but examples and all sin is vile. The principle remains the same in the age of grace as it was under law: "But your iniquities have separated you from your God; your sins have hidden His face from you, so that He will not hear" (Isa. 59:2). The New Testament reemphasizes it in 1 Peter 3:12: "For the eyes of the Lord are on the righteous and His ears are attentive to their prayer, but the face of the Lord is against those who do evil."

Here are some of the specified sins:

Rebellion (disobedience) — "But if you do not obey the Lord, and if you rebel against His commands, His hand will be against you, as it was against your fathers" (1 Sam. 12:15). In the case of Saul, King of Israel, vs. Agag, King of the Amalekites, Saul proclaimed stoutly, "But I did obey the Lord" (1 Sam. 15:20). However, God pronounced his incomplete obedience to be rebellion and gave His sentence against the compromiser: "For rebellion is like the sin of divination, and arrogance like the evil of idolatry. Because you have rejected the word of the Lord, He has rejected you as king" (1 Sam. 15:23). No amount of whimpering on Saul's part could change God's mind. Disobedience, which is rebellion, takes a person off praying ground.

The reason some people cannot get answers to prayer is that they have never thoroughly repented of and confessed to God and their parents their teenage rebellion in violation of God's command to honor one's father and mother.

The reason some people cannot pray effectively is that they refused to go when God laid His hand on them for service where Christ was not known.

The reason some people do not see their loved ones saved is that they married outside God's will.

"Rebellion" and "disobedience" define the character of sin; God's blessing cannot be claimed by one ho harbors them in his heart.

Lack of faith — "Everything that does not come from faith is sin" (Rom. 14:23b). "But when he asks, he must believe and not doubt, because he who

> *Worry is the opposite of faith. Anxious care stifles prayer.*

doubts is like a wave of the sea, blown and tossed by the wind. That man should not think he will receive anything from the Lord; he is a double-minded man, unstable in all he does" (Jas. 1:6-8). "Consequently, faith comes from hearing the message, and the message is heard through the word of Christ" (Rom. 10:17).

Consistent with Jesus' teaching to ask God for our daily bread are the scriptural injunctions against worrying (cf. Matt. 6:11,25-34; Phil. 4:6). Worry is an insult to God. Prayer honors Him. The two are mutually exclusive. Worry is the opposite of faith. Anxious care stifles prayer.

Because of the limitations of our sinful flesh, we all find that at times we are incapable of strong faith. That, of course, is an understatement, because we are always incapable of faith in ourselves. We must do as the father of the demon-possessed boy did and ask the Lord for help in believing. "Immediately the boy's father exclaimed, 'I do believe; help me overcome my unbelief!'" (Mark 9:24). This is the verse God gave Pastor Moynan to share with the atheist, Leslie Middleton. It set the atheist free, and if we refuse to cast ourselves as simply upon God for faith, we are in danger of becoming bound by practical atheism — for that is what lack of faith is.

We should also use the Word of God to strengthen faith (see Chapter 13).

Wrongs not made right — "Therefore, if you are offering your gift at the altar and there remember that your brother has something against you, leave your gift there in front of the altar. First go and be reconciled to your brother; then come and offer your gift" (Matt. 5:23,24). If you have sinned against someone. God, rather than hear your prayer, promises to hear the offended party's prayer against you (see Exod. 22:22-27).

Slander or gossip shorts out the prayer circuit. Taking unfair advantage or cheating cuts off the power. A misrepresentation on a tax report or an insurance form will come between a person and God until everything possible is done to make restitution.

A young man went to Bible school. In the fall Bible conference he heard a speaker constantly emphasize this sentence: "God will not cover what we refuse to uncover." "But," said the young man to a counsellor, "if I confess to the authorities all I have done,

> *Anyone who agrees with God regarding sin will not take a flippant attitude toward it.*

they will send me to prison." Yet, he knew that he would never have peace as long as he was hiding from the police. Although he had confessed his sins to God and they were under the blood of Christ, he had not paid his debt to society for his crimes. He confessed to law enforcement officials and went to prison, where God gave him a mission field.

Unconfessed sin — Part and parcel with wrongs not made right is unconfessed sin. You have not truly lamented your sin nor repented of it until you have confessed it to God and to any against whom you have personally sinned. It is possible to make restitution for a wrong anonymously, but that will not clear the conscience and give an unclouded atmosphere in the presence of God. "If we confess our sins, He is faithful and just and will forgive us our sins and purify us from all unrighteousness" (1 John 1:9). Study David's confession in Psalm 32, and on your knees read Psalm 51, making it your own prayer while naming your sin. Then, accept the Lord's gracious words, "Neither do I condemn you;... go, now and leave your life of sin" (John 8:11).

I have heard it preached that, since "confess" means merely to "agree with God" about your sin, all that 1 John 1:9 means is that we must agree that we have sinned and it's all taken care of. But anyone who agrees with God regarding sin will not take a flippant attitude which says, "Okay, God, I've sinned; now let's forget about it." To agree with God is to take God's attitude toward sin. God hates sin, refuses to look upon sin, pours out His wrath upon sin. He gave His own dear Son to pay the supreme penalty for sin as our Substitute. If I agree with God about sin, I will detest it, judge it, be done with it, flee from it, and seek my Lord's forgiveness and protection from it.

Marital unfaithfulness — Although Malachi's description of one who unsuccessfully sought God's favor with tears is addressed to Judah, the principle involved is both personal and universal. "You flood the Lord's altar with tears. You weep and wail because He no longer pays attention to your offerings or accepts them with pleasure from your hands. You ask, 'Why?' It is because the Lord is acting as the witness between you and the wife of your youth, because you have broken faith with her, though she is your partner, the wife of your marriage covenant. Has not the Lord made them one? In flesh and spirit they are His. And why one? Because He was seeking godly offspring. So guard yourself in your spirit, and do not break faith with the wife of your youth. 'I hate divorce,' says the Lord God of Israel" (Mal. 2:13-16a). Any course of action that treats the marriage vows lightly jeopardizes effective prayer, whether adultery or divorce. That is not to say that there are no scriptural grounds for divorce, but God says He hates it, and if we agree with Him, we will hate it too.

Although we do our utmost to make restitution, sins cannot be undone. Nor can marriages always be restored. When a divorcee remarries, the first marriage cannot be reconstituted (Deut. 24:1-4). If there is no remarriage to new partners, a broken marriage may possibly be restored in answer to prayer, but there is no guarantee that God will intervene. He hates sin and He hates divorce, and we dare not take them lightly.

A professing Christian girl married an unsaved young man in defiance of God's Word (see 2 Cor. 6:14). Two lovely little girls were born. The marriage ended in divorce and the mother was granted custody of the children. Later, the young man received Christ as his Savior. By this time his former wife was going with another man. The divorced husband prayed fervently that God would cause the romance to break up and his former wife to return to him. Instead, she married her new boy friend. The father did not have opportunity to see his little daughters for years at a time.

Of course, we cannot know all the factors involved, but we must learn that prayer will not set aside all the effects of sin. Even though a sin is forgiven by God, one cannot always escape the consequences. Sinning and then praying that God will not allow the law of cause and effect to operate is like jumping off a tall building and then praying that God will let you down easily. He can, but He probably won't. He can work miracles in answer to prayer, but it usually suits His purposes to honor the laws He has established. Prayer does not negate the law that says. "Do not be deceived: God cannot be mocked. A man reaps what he sows" (Gal. 6:7).

This, of course, applies to immorality resulting in venereal disease and/or the birth of an unwanted child, drunkenness resulting in an automobile accident and its consequences, drug addiction and its effects upon the brain, and many other sins, but we have discussed marital unfaithfulness because Malachi specifically relates it to the withdrawal of God's willingness to hear and answer prayer.

Greed — Covetousness or greed is called idolatry in Ephesians 5:5 and Colossians 3:5. An idolater is a worshipper of a false god. Why should the Lord God grant the request of an idolater? Let him go to his own god: money, possessions, position, job security, advancement, prestige — or whatever name greed goes by. People who trust in uncertain riches have no place to turn when their god fails them. By contrast, those who gladly give God at least His tithe are promised provision and blessing (Mal. 3:8-10). If we are stingy with our possessions and refuse to give generously to the work of the Lord, how can we in prayer claim the promise, "And my God will meet all your needs according to His glorious riches in Christ Jesus" (Phil. 4:19)? That promise was given in a note of thanks to the Philippian church for the generous gift sent to Paul for the Lord's work.

Neglect of God's Word — "If anyone turns a deaf ear to the law, even his prayers are detestable" (Prov. 28:9). Prosperity and success are promised to those who not only read and memorize God's Word, but who "meditate" upon it (Josh. 1:8; Ps. 1:1-3) so that it is digested, is absorbed into the moral fibre and becomes the guiding-principle of life. How can we hope to ask according to God's will (cf. 1 John 5:14,15) if we fail to saturate our minds with His Word?

Before going on to our next major category, may I urge you to cry out with David, "Search me, O God, and know my heart; test me and know my anxious thoughts. See if there is any offensive way in me, and lead me in the way everlasting" (Ps. 139:23,24). There may be some sins which we have put out of mind or have carelessly forgotten which are detrimental to our prayer life.

Self

This second category still involves sin, but it is of sufficient magnitude to warrant special discussion.

> *Refusal to forgive... leaves the good ship Prayer high and dry.*

Laziness, indifference, or self-interest may be the reasons for not asking God for our needs. Whatever the reasons behind the reason, James (4:2) says that the reason we don't have is that we don't ask. Whatever form the self-centeredness takes which keeps us too busy or unconcerned to pray, it can be marked down as the reason we have so little from God to satisfy our real desires. There are two sides to the coin of prayer. One side has this inscription: "Ask and it will be given to you" (Matt. 7:7a). The other side has this one: "You do not have, because you do not ask God" (Jas. 4:2b). Elijah wasn't lazy; he prayed "earnestly" and got what he asked for (Jas. 5:17). Jesus wasn't too busy; He found a solitary place in the wee hours and talked to His Father. Laziness and busy-ness eliminate importunity in prayer (cf. Luke 11:5-10; 18:1-8).

Pride and hypocrisy are in view in Matthew 6:5 as causes for unanswered prayer. According to this verse the hypocrites, who pray to be seen of men, have all the reward they will ever get. Self is contrary to the spirit of true prayer. If you do more praying in the presence of others than alone, perhaps a motive-check would be in order.

Did you know that a *squabble with your wife* can send your prayer life into a tailspin and wreck your hopes of any answer? It violates the principle of asking in agreement (cf. Matt. 18:19) and is mentioned especially as a hindrance to prayer in 1 Peter 3:1-7. *Unsubmissiveness* on the wife's part or *failure of the husband to honor his wife as the weaker vessel or to take his rightful role as spiritual leader* will preclude effective prayer. A husband and wife who have determined to have a daily ministry of prayer together will find that unrepentant anger rides their backs when prayer time comes. One or the other has to go. Anger and intercession cannot coexist.

Now, here is one that takes all the wind out of the sails of prayer — *an unforgiving spirit.* Matthew 6:14,15 indicates that a refusal to forgive disqualifies us for God's forgiveness, and that leaves the Good Ship Prayer high and dry.

Matthew 6:7 puts the *formality of empty (vain) repetition* in the camp of the heathen, not the Christian prayer warrior. Harold Lindsell tells of a woman with a doctor's degree who was dissatisfied with the prayer life of her four children. When her counsellor inquired about her personal prayer life, she admitted that all it involved was the nightly repetition of the prayer she learned in childhood, "Now I lay me down to sleep...."[4] Such formality as this or the liturgical repetition of the Lord's Prayer on Sunday morning in church may make one feel pious or may soothe the conscience somewhat, but it is of no value in moving men for God through prayer. The deadness of formality is too often substituted for living faith.

No wonder God doesn't sit up and take notice when we pray. Of the ten who were cleansed of leprosy, only one returned to say, "Thank You" (Luke 17:11-19), and I imagine the percentage hasn't improved much in our day. Instead of complaining about unanswered prayer, we would do well to pour out our hearts In *praise and thanksgiving* for all the answers the Lord has given — and all the provisions and blessings He has given which we never really asked for at all. An *unthankful spirit* is contrary to the New Testament spirit of prayer. Faith thrives on humility, but unthankfulness on pride.

Satan

The archenemy of Christ and Christians hates prayer. He knows its power and fears it. Since whole chapters have been given to the subject of prayer warfare, we shall not re-develop it here, but we need frequently to be reminded that a very real hindrance to effective prayer is *Satan himself along with his demons*. Daniel 10 (studied in the warfare chapters) is no fairy tale.

When my mother went home to Florida from her visit with us in Alberta, I expected to hear from her very soon regarding her flight and safe arrival, but a letter did not arrive until three weeks later. I looked at the postmark and found it had been delayed en route somewhere. Daniel's answer to prayer was delayed en route, too. The answer originated in Heaven three weeks before Daniel received it. He was entirely unaware that it had even been sent. There was no sign during that time that God had heard.

> *We don't understand all that God is doing. Nor do we have to.*

Usually, we cannot see behind the scenes, but, because we believe God's Word to be true, we know that Satan and his hosts of evil ones are constantly seeking to stop us from receiving God's answer. Let us put on the whole armor of God, take our position of authority in the heavenlies in Christ at the Father's right hand, plead the blood of Christ, bind the enemy, and pray in the Spirit with importunity until the answer is received.

Sovereignty of God

If we have met the conditions of prayer sincerely and still have not received the answer to our request, we must acknowledge God's sovereignty. The part of faith is humbly and joyfully to accept God's decision in the matter whether we understand it or not. He will give grace commensurate with the burdens He allows us to bear. All our logic may scream against it, but when God says "No" or when He allows a delay in the answer, it is because His ways are not our ways nor His thoughts our thoughts. All things do work together "for good to those who love Him, who have been called according to His purpose" (Rom. 8:28). But the greater good is "to be conformed to the likeness of His Son" (from Rom. 8:29), and God alone knows what people, circumstances, suffering, disappointments, and events to allow us to experience in order to bring us into conformity to the likeness of His Son.

Sometimes we can catch a glimpse of God's purposes. At other times we must walk entirely by faith.

What about that friend who lingers on with cancer week after week in the hospital bed? God has not yet seen fit to heal him or to take him Home.

What of the young couple who looked forward so eagerly and prayerfully to the birth of their baby only to receive from God a severely retarded mongoloid child with a serious heart problem? The keen disappointment, the difficulty of childcare, the neglect of the other children in the family, the anguish of not knowing how to pray — these, compounded by the well-intentioned advice of friends who don't really understand, cause weeping and crying out to God in the night hours. Yet, after some years of anguish the parents find much for which to thank God, especially in the area of their own lives and attitudes.

A husband and father in the prime of life and much-used on the mission field is stricken with a dread, undiagnosed disease. People in many lands pray earnestly. He dies.

No, we don't understand all that God is doing. Nor do we have to. Whether we walk in well-lit paths or through dark valleys, we can place our hand in His confidently. If He does not grant our requests for life and health for a loved one, for relief from a burden, or for the provision of some felt need, it is because He is working out something better for us.

"But, I can't see why! I just can't understand," someone cries. That is where faith comes in, for faith is "being...certain of what we do not see" (Heb. 11:1). Oh, that eleventh chapter of Hebrews is so helpful. Whereas it lists many who received blessings in answer to prayer, it also tells of those who "were tortured," who "faced jeers and flogging," who "were chained and put in prison," who "were stoned" and "sawed in two," who "were put to death by the sword," who "went about in sheepskins and goatskins," who were "destitute, persecuted, and mistreated." And it says, "the world was not worthy of them." Verses 39 and 40 form the capstone of this great chapter on faith and give one of the most important answers to the question of unanswered prayer: "These were all commended for their faith, *yet none of them received what had been promised.* God had planned something better for us so that only together with us would they be made perfect" (italics mine).

God has a plan of the ages. Each of us fits into His design. We cannot see what the finished product will look like. It is as though we are looking on the back side of a tapestry. Someday, when we see the completed work, we will stand in awe at the marvellous wisdom of our mighty God who works all things after the counsel of His will.

Herod had James put to death by the sword. That's recorded in Acts 12:2. Peter was rescued from prison and impending death by an angel sent from God. That's only five verses later. Why was one spared and the other taken? God has not condescended to satisfy our curiosity about it. Surely the Church prayed fervently for Peter and God answered their prayers, but should we assume that prayer was not made for James? Hardly.

When all has been said on the subject, we must come back to the fact that there is a certain amount of mystery about ungranted requests because God has no obligation to explain His workings to us. If prayer is true, it is subjected to His will and He has the final word on the subject.

Think of the three spiritual giants, Moses, Elijah, and Paul. Great prayer warriors all! Yet, God denied Moses' prayer to enter Canaan (Deut. 3:23-25), Elijah's prayer to die (1 Kings 19:4), and Paul's prayer for deliverance from his thorn in the flesh (2 Cor. 12:8,9). God did not allow David to build God's house, although it was the great desire of his life (1 Chron. 22:8). The demoniac who was delivered prayed to go with Jesus, but his request was refused (Luke 8:38).

God never refuses without a reason, but often we are not in a position to see the reason. Therefore, it is always fitting for us to subject ourselves to His will and never insist on having our own way. Let us remember the children of Israel in their wilderness wanderings, of whom it is written, "So He gave them what they asked for, but sent a wasting disease upon them," (Ps. 106:15). Also, remember that God gave the Israelites a king as they requested, but what sufferings and sorrows resulted! God gave Hezekiah fifteen more years to live, but he and the nation would have benefitted by his going when the Lord first called him Home.

Dr. Chadwick reminds us that "no" is not God's last word.[5] Moses stood on the Mount of Transfiguration with Christ in the land of Canaan — to which he had been denied entrance in this life. Elijah went to Heaven in God's time, rather than when death was requested, in a far more wonderful manner than by death. God's answers are much more glorious

> "Keep on praying, you will learn that the delay in the answer to prayer is one of the most precious means of grace that God can bestow on you."
> — J.A. Stuckle

than our requests.

Sometimes answers that seem to be denied are actually delayed in the sovereignty of God. We feel sure that we are praying in God's will and we have asked Him to search our hearts and cleanse us from any sin, yet the answer does not come. Concerning such delays, Rev. Elmer V. Thompson, in his "Worldteam Intercessors" prayer letter (August, 1980), has some very helpful insights. First, he quotes from an article in "Beacon Intercessor" (May and June, 1980) by Mr. J.A. Stuckle of LaCross, Washington, as follows:

One of the greatest drawbacks to the life of prayer is the fact that the answer does not come as speedily as we expect. We are discouraged by the thoughts: "Perhaps I do not pray aright," and so we do not persevere in prayer. This was a lesson that our Lord taught often and urgently. If we consider the matter, we can see that there may be a reason for the delay, and the waiting may bring a blessing to our souls. Our desire must grow deeper and stronger, and we must ask with our whole heart. God put us into the practising school of persevering prayer that our weak faith may be strengthened. Do believe that there is a great blessing in the delayed answer to prayer.

Christians, listen to this warning. Be not impatient or discouraged if the answer does not come. "Continue in prayer." "Pray without ceasing." You will find it an unspeakable blessing to do so. You will ask whether your prayer is really in accordance with the will of God, and the Word of God. You will inquire if it is in the right spirit and in the name of Christ. Keep on praying, you will learn that the delay in the answer to prayer is one of the most precious means of grace that God can bestow on you. You will learn too that those who have persevered often and long before God, in pleading His promises, are those who have had the greatest power with God in prayer.[6]

Then Mr. Thompson calls our attention to the fact that the answers to some prayers in the Bible (with which God was in full accord) were delayed for years. Then he adds some convictions which God has given him relative to His reasons for delaying prayer answers.

> We need to remember first of all that the favorable divine response to a good portion of our petitions involves time. True, God is not limited to time, but He commonly uses time in connection with His spiritual dealings with people.
>
> For instance, George Muller prayed constantly for an unsaved friend for 50 years and died without seeing that prayer answered; but the man was saved a year after George Muller died. The Holy Spirit used the changing circumstances of time to convince that man of his spiritual need. The spiritual lesson for us in this is that George Muller continued to be a co-laborer with God all through the long struggle of leading that needy soul to a voluntary acceptance of God's provision. I feel certain that delayed answers strongly invite this sort of prayer participation with God.
>
> Let us look at delayed prayer answers from another standpoint. Requests in relation to other believers or even ourselves, sometimes require spiritual growth before the answer becomes pertinent.
>
> How often we also ask for blessings for others or ourselves beyond the level of our spiritual comprehension. For example, we ask God to make a Christian worker of a son or daughter. Again we pray, "Fill my friend with Thy Spirit, O Lord." Such petitions are often inspired of God and accepted before God. However, since these prayers are commonly beyond or contrary to the

aspirations of the person for whom the petition is made, a period of spiritual dealing by God must precede the actual answer of the prayer. Believers who lay hold of God and see such prayers fully answered, usually watch before God and wait some time before their prayers are answered. The first major lesson I learned regarding prayer related to a deeper personal interest which I presented before the Lord almost daily for perhaps two years. It is now clear to me that God never intended to say "yes" to that request. However, in tenderness toward me He waited in responding to my insistent petition until I was big enough spiritually to accept His "no."

Can we wait — trustingly wait — for delayed prayer answers? Can we as trustingly accept God's "no" in regard to something we really desire?

These factors relative to delayed prayer answers teach us the importance of continuing in prayer about matters concerning which we have sensed concern until God supplies the answer or shows that a particular petition is not His will.

May God enable each of us to ponder and learn the lessons He would teach us about delayed prayer answers.[6]

Chadwick quotes E.B. Browning's poem to close his book, and I'll close this chapter with it too.

"Unanswered yet! The prayers your lips have pleaded
    In agony of heart these many years?
Does faith begin to fail? Is hope departing?
    And think you all in vain those falling tears?
Say not, the Father hath not heard your prayer,
    You shall have your desire — sometime — somewhere.

"Unanswered yet! Though when you first presented

This one petition at the Father's Throne
It seemed you could not wait the time of asking,
So urgent was the heart to make it known;
Though years have passed since then, do not despair,
The Lord will answer you — sometime — somewhere.

"Unanswered yet! Nay, do not say ungranted,
Perhaps your work is not wholly done.
The work began when first your prayer was uttered,
And God will finish what He has begun.
If you will keep the incense burning there,
His glory you shall see — sometime — somewhere.

"Unanswered yet! Faith cannot be unanswered;
Her feet are firmly planted on the Rock;
Amid the wildest storms she stands undaunted,
Nor quails before the loudest thunder shock.
She knows Omnipotence has heard her prayer,
And cries, 'It shall be done —
              sometime — somewhere.'"

E.B. Browning[7]

Study and Discussion Questions

1. Discuss any prayer requests you have given to God but for which you have not yet received an answer. Discuss all the possible reasons you can think of why you have not. Then pray together about them.

2. Tell your group about any time when God has **delayed** an answer to your prayer. Discuss possible reasons why it was delayed.

3. When should a believer **persist** in prayer (cf. Luke 18), and when should he take it to the Lord and leave it there"? That is, when should he keep on until the answer comes, and when should he stop praying for it and start thanking God in faith? (This is a tough question. Don't be satisfied with anyone's pat answer. Glib answers won't do. Dig in and try to find clues in God's Word. If still not satisfied, keep the question in mind as you continue your personal Bible reading. Be patient. The teaching of the Holy Spirit isn't dumped on us all in one load!)

4. Discuss delayed answers to prayer and delayed fulfillment of prophecies in the Bible.

5. Discuss Paul's thorn in the flesh (2 Cor. 12:1-10).

17

PRAYING FOR THE LOST

"Please pray for my unsaved husband."

"Pray for my father; he doesn't know the Lord."

Quite often, one of the first impulses the Holy Spirit puts in the heart of a new believer is a burden to pray for unsaved loved ones.

Listen to Peter Deyneka, Founder of the Slavic Gospel Association: "I shall never forget experiences I had in White Russia some years ago, when I visited my home and family for the first time after I had been saved. My mother professed to have religion but did not know Christ as her personal Savior. Because of this, I met great opposition and persecution right in my own home. My mother insisted that in two weeks I would stop following the Lord and preaching the Gospel. She wanted me to go back into the type of life I formerly lived. I told her that since Christ had saved me, I belonged to Him and no one could ever make me turn back to the sinful life I had lived. I was a new creature in Christ and had passed from death unto life, a new life in Him. 'Therefore if any man be in Christ, he is a new creature: old things are passed away; behold, all things are become new' (2 Cor. 5:17).

"For nearly a year I had to endure suffering for the Gospel's sake in my home. The more I prayed for my mother, the more disturbed she got. This showed me that the Holy Spirit was working in her heart. So I kept on praying. When I returned to the United States, my mother was still unsaved. However, I continued praying for her salvation for several years more. Humanly speaking, it looked as if she would never turn to Christ as her Savior. It seemed impossible. But my hope was in Christ. I am happy to say that

PRINCIPLES OF EFFECTIVE PRAYER

when I returned home to White Russia again after many years of much prayer, my mother met me with open arms, even before I got to the house and cried out, 'Peter, I am giving my heart to Christ now.' There while we were greeting one another, she broke down and wept for joy because she had now accepted Christ as her Savior. Thank God, my mother was saved. If you have an unsaved father, mother, children, relatives or friends whom you want to see come to Christ, keep on praying in spite of any suffering or persecution. Be faithful in prayer."[1]

> *Prayer for the lost and witnessing are not mutually exclusive; they are complementary.*

A False Teaching by Evangelicals

There is a theory that is gaining all too much popularity among evangelical Christians which goes like this: "We are not to pray for the lost; we are to witness to the lost and pray for the one who witnesses." This is a mixture of error and truth. Apparently, it is a recent innovation. I find no mention of it in any of scores of great classical books on prayer which I have read. But I have come across it in one recent book and in an article in one of the finest Christian magazines. Hopefully, It will be short-lived. It deserves to die.

The purpose of such teaching may be to offset a tendency to request prayer for the unsaved person and expect God to save him without our witnessing to him. But prayer for the lost and witnessing are not mutually exclusive; they are complementary.

The actual result of such teaching is to dissuade Christians from praying for their unsaved loved ones. How pathetic!

The argument is based on silence and at least implies that since the New Testament does not tell us to do it that we are not supposed to do it. This is unacceptable logic. We do a lot of things which God blesses which are not specifically commanded in the New Testament. We conduct Sunday schools, morning and evening services, and midweek prayer meetings; we build church buildings, Bible colleges, and seminaries; we utilize mission boards, radios, and airplanes to proclaim the Gospel. Suppose we stopped doing everything that the New Testament does not command. Such a suggestion is nonsense. Yet, some Christian people will believe that we should not pray for the lost because a seminary professor said that it is not stated in Scripture that we should.

> *"The... Devil ... laughs at our toil, mocks at our wisdom, but trembles when we pray."*
> —Samuel Chadwick

As for the absurd claim that Paul prayed only for the saved, never for the lost, how can such a broad assertion be made unless one has access to records of *every* prayer the apostle ever prayed?

If the purpose is to encourage witnessing, that is fine, but let us not take a humanistic approach to it; let us not become overbalanced and fall into the Devil's trap of discouraging intercession and avoiding prayer warfare on behalf of lost souls. The Devil is not in the soul-saving business; Jesus is. That is the warfare. Let's be careful to use the effective weapon, the Sword of the Spirit, and the effective method of prayer for the lost. Let's not aid the enemy by teaching Christians to eliminate either. Satan will do anything to obstruct the salvation of lost souls.

The one concern of the Devil is to keep Christians from praying. He fears nothing from prayerless studies, prayerless work and prayerless religion. He laughs at our toil, mocks at our wisdom, but trembles when we pray, said Samuel Chadwick.

What the New Testament Teaches

Now, let's see what the New Testament *does* teach. The Apostle Paul, under the inspiration of the Holy Spirit, said, "Brothers, my heart's desire and PRAYER TO GOD for the *Israelites* is THAT THEY MAY BE SAVED" (Rom. 10:1, caps mine). By what strange exegesis can it be said that Paul never prayed for the lost? Eternity alone will reveal how many Israelites have been saved in answer to the prayers of the apostle to the *Gentiles*.

First Timothy 2:1-8 may not be a "command" to pray for the lost, but it is certainly an urgent admonition to pray for *everyone* (including the lost) and focuses especially on the lost as those whom God wants saved. Read this passage for the obvious sense of it:

> I urge, then, first of all, that requests, prayers, intercession and thanksgiving be made for EVERYONE — for kings and all those in authority, that we may live peaceful and quiet lives in all godliness and holiness. This is good, and pleases God our Savior, who wants ALL MEN TO BE SAVED and to come to a knowledge of the truth. For there is one God and one Mediator between God and men, the man Christ Jesus, who gave Himself as a ransom for ALL MEN — the testimony given in its proper time.... I want men everywhere to lift up holy hands in prayer, without anger or disputing (caps mine).

This in no way legislates against our witnessing to the lost. A.B. Simpson captured the correct scriptural balance when he wrote, "Put in my heart the woe, put in my feet the go." It is not a case of either-or, but of both praying and witnessing.

The Lord Jesus taught His disciples to pray, "Your will be done on earth as it is in Heaven" (Matt. 6:10), and the Holy Spirit through the Apostle Peter declared God's will as "not wanting anyone to perish, but everyone to come to repentance" (2 Pet. 3:9b). Are we not to pray for those for whom Christ died?

The Old Testament gives us an excellent illustration of the burden of intercession needed for sinners. Too few of us have entered into the depth of identification in intercession which Moses demonstrated when he said to God, "Oh, what a great sin these people have committed! They have made themselves gods of gold. But now, please forgive their sin — but if not, then blot me out of the book You have written" (Exod. 32:31,32).

Paul entered the same depths of intercessory identification in Romans 9:2-4a, "I have great sorrow and unceasing anguish in my heart. For I could wish that I myself were cursed and cut off from Christ for the sake of my brothers, those of my own race, the people of Israel."

The Question of Free Will

Praying for lost friends and loved ones is sometimes the most difficult activity in which a Christian can participate. Satan will fight with every scheme at his command to discourage us and defeat us.

Added to that is the staggering truth that every person has a will of his own which God will not violate. God made man in His own image; one aspect of that image of God which lifts man above all other creatures of earth is volition or will. Although man's will, like all other aspects of his being, has been sadly marred by sin, it has not been eradicated. God, in His wisdom and sovereignty, gave each of us a will and He will always honor our decisions. We can choose Heaven or Hell, God or the Devil. For God to force anyone to be saved would be to dishonor His own sovereignty and to reduce that person to an automaton, a robot. God created persons. The will is essential to *personality*, to *personhood*. For God to override that will would be to depersonalize His creature. He won't do it. It is not God's will to deny His own sovereign act of giving man a will, so there is no need for us to pray for Him to do it.

Have I contradicted myself? I think not.

Are our hands tied because the lost person for whom we are concerned has a will of his own? No! Must we *merely* witness to him and leave him on his own to decide, without the Holy Spirit's influence on his heart, what he will do with Jesus? No! Must we pray *only* for the one who witnesses that he might be persuasive and skillful in presenting the Gospel? No!

There is a supernatural element in winning the lost. In fact, Jesus said categorically, "No one can come to Me unless the Father who sent Me draws him" (John 6:44a). Salvation is the work of God from beginning to eternity. It is a miracle. You and I haven't the personal power to perform miracles. God has. And He has condescended to use that saving power at our request. He has assured us that it is His will that all men be saved (2 Pet. 3:9b), and 1 John 5:14,15 is applicable when it says, "This is the assurance we have in approaching God: that if we ask anything according to His will, He hears us. And if we know that He hears us — whatever we ask — we know that we have what we asked of Him.

This supernatural element is not some added benefit, some aid to the personal worker and preacher. It is the means of the soul's salvation. The Word of God is the Sword of the *Spirit*, not primarily of the human witness. The Holy Spirit uses that Sword in the hand and the mouth of the faithful witness and in the heart of the lost person in answer to prayer for the witness and for the sinner.

Philip and the Ethiopian eunuch (Acts 8) beautifully illustrate the Spirit's preparation of the soul to be saved as well as preparation of the witness.

Paul E. Billheimer defends prayer for the lost with this shocking statement: *"God will not go over the head of His Church even to save a soul without her cooperation, if she will not intercede, the Holy Spirit, by His own choice, cannot do His office work of convicting and persuading"* (italics Billheimer's).[2]

The witness of Stephen probably influenced the thoughts of Saul of Tarsus, but Saul was not saved without the supernatural manifestation of Jesus Christ. And Stephen prayed for Saul and his other murderers as he was dying the martyrs death. How many other Christians prayed for that great enemy of the early Church is not recorded.

Perhaps Paul the Apostle remembered his Damascus Road conversion as he penned these words: "The weapons we fight with are not the weapons of the world. On the contrary, they have divine power to demolish strongholds. We demolish arguments and ever pretension that sets itself up against the knowledge of God, and *we take captive every thought to make it obedient to Christ*" (2 Cor. 10:4.5: italics mine).

Concerning these verses, Billheimer asks, "Was Paul ignoring the free moral agency or full moral responsibility of men when he wrote these words?... Was he remembering what the Celestial Voice said about the pain of kicking against the goad? Was he thinking about how his own heart's desire was instantly changed by the powerful illumination of the Holy Spirit into a desire to obey Christ? Was this the inspiration for his faith that these same weapons, which changed him from a rebel into a willing 'captive' of Christ, were just as effective in his hands 'to capture rebels and bring them back to God'?... By means of these weapons he changes them from rebellion to voluntary cooperation. Their free will is not violated. They become willing 'captives' of Christ. If such weapons were available to Paul, are they not also available to the Church to whom Christ gave authority over all the power of the enemy?"[3]

"And even if our Gospel is veiled, it is veiled to those who are perishing. The god of this age has blinded the minds of unbelievers, so that they cannot see the light of the Gospel of the glory of Christ, who is the image of God" (2 Cor. 4:3,4). Satan is making his bid for souls; he is doing all within his power to influence them against God; he is blinding their eyes so that they cannot see the light when it shines upon them through our Gospel witness. And make no mistake about it, Satan has no scruples about violating people's wills. Pray against that vile deceiver and, in the authority that is yours in Christ, remove the veil in order that the light of the Gospel might shine into sin-darkened souls. Such intercession does *not violate* men's wills; it *frees* them. It is Satan who has enslaved them; it is our duty to use authoritative prayer to set them free.

Jesus' Upper Room Discourse is not a variety of unrelated strands of thought. Rather, *Christ's second coming, the promise of the Holy Spirit, prayer in Jesus' name, and the abiding of the branches in the vine* are skillfully interwoven topics which make a tapestry of rare beauty. Six times the Lord encourages us to ask in His name and promises that if we remain in Him and His words remain in us, we may ask whatever we wish, and it will be given us (John 15:7). In the same discourse, He says of the coming Paraclete, the Holy Spirit, "When He comes, He will convict the world of guilt in regard to sin and righteousness and judgment; in regard to sin, because men do not believe in Me; in regard to righteousness, because I am going to the Father, where you can see Me no longer; and in regard to judgment, because the prince of this world now stands condemned" (John 16:8-11).

What could be more obviously in keeping with asking in Jesus' name than praying for the souls for whom He died, prayer for the convicting power of the Holy Spirit to accompany our witness?

Some Answers To Prayer for Lost Souls
Georgia

One Sunday afternoon at about two o'clock I went into a Sunday school room of the church where I was pastor to spend some time in prayer for the evening service. As I prayed, a strong compulsion came into my heart to pray for a person to be saved in the service. Furthermore, I felt that the prayer should not be merely that *some* person would be saved, but that there was a particular person for whom that request should be made. Yet, admittedly, I did not know who the person was. I tried to dismiss the impression as the working of my imagination, but I could not. My head reasoned; If God desired that I pray for a particular person to be saved, would He not identify the person? My heart simply said, "Pray."

"Who is it, Lord?" I asked. No voice came in answer, no handwriting on the wall, no vision. Yet the compulsion remained unabated — not a dark, depressive cloud, but a convincing conviction.

I prayed for first one and then another unsaved person in the community but with the feeling that those prayers were not given by the Spirit, and the compulsion did not dissipate. The voice within was as clear as an audible voice would have been; "No, I have one particular soul for you to intercede for, one that I want to save in the service tonight."

It was incredible. Nothing like this had ever happened to me before. I was not given to dreams or visions or voices and did not expect any now. Nor did I have any except that persistent inner conviction. I thought that perhaps I had been working too hard and my imagination was working overtime, so I went for a walk. By the time I returned from my rather lengthy stroll the inner conviction was stronger than ever.

And so I prayed something like this, as well as I remember, "Lord, I believe there is one particular unsaved soul which You want to bring to

> *It is Satan who has enslaved them; it is our duty to use authoritative prayer to set them free.*

Yourself in tonight's service. I don't know who it is. I don't have any idea whether it is a man or a woman. But, whoever it is, wherever he or she may be, save this soul tonight. Bring him or her under deep conviction...." I don't remember now all that I said. I probably prayed against Satan, resisted him in Jesus' name, asked the Lord to remove the veil Satan had put on the eyes of the unidentified person so the light of the Gospel could shine in. But as much as I have forgotten the exact words, I don't think I'll ever forget that afternoon.

When the time came for some men to meet with me for prayer the hour before the evening service, I wondered whether I should tell them about the strange burden. Would they think I was a bit queer, that I had gone off the deep end? But I soon found myself blurting it out. No, they did not react negatively.

"Lord, You know who this person is You've laid on our pastor's heart. Save him tonight, Lord." Their prayers were in this vein.

Getting up from my knees, I walked down the hall to the sanctuary.

As I walked through the doorway near the platform, a man and a little girl two to three years old came through the main entrance at the other end of the room. He looked around as though uncertain whether to proceed.

"Good evening, I'm Wentworth Pike, the pastor," I greeted him and extended my hand.

"Can I join your church?" he asked with no introduction. All over his face was written "Troubled Soul," I had never seen him before.

"Well, I'm not sure that joining the church is what you need," I replied. "Let's sit over here for a few minutes and get acquainted until time for the service to begin."

"I don't know what it is I need," he exclaimed, "but I've got to get right with God."

As the people were arriving for the service, the conversation continued and the visitor's need for salvation came into sharper focus.

When it was time for the service to begin, I encouraged him to listen carefully to the message, which would present the plan of salvation, and to come forward when the invitation was given to receive the Lord Jesus Christ as Savior.

He responded immediately to the invitation. After personal counselling and prayer, he stood before the congregation, smiling through his tears, and, at my request, told this fascinating story.

"About two o'clock this afternoon a strange thing happened. My wife was away visiting relatives, and my little girl and I were at home alone. I was reading the Sunday comics to her when the strangest feeling came over me. I just knew that I had to get right with God. I put the paper down and said. Come on, Honey, let's go for a ride."

"I didn't know where to go for help. The only place I could think of was a little church out in the country where I went a few times when I was a boy. When we got there, the grass in the yard was knee high and there were boards on the windows. I didn't know what else to do or where to go, so I just sat on the steps while my little girl played in the cemetery where the grass wasn't so high. After a while a man came down the road and I asked him whether there would be a service there tonight. 'No,' he said, 'that church has been closed for ten years.'

"So we just got back in the car and drove around, but I couldn't get rid of the feeling that I had to get right with God. As I drove back into town, I came down this street (I never had driven through this part of town before) and noticed the sign out in front of the church. Somehow, I just knew that this was the place where I was going to find the answer. When I came in, the pastor talked to me and showed me from the Bible that what I needed was to be saved. His sermon made it all so plain, so I received Jesus as my Savior and that awful feeling I had all afternoon is gone."

I glanced around at the men who had prayed with me. Some were grinning from ear to ear, while others were wiping tears from their eyes.

Saskatchewan

Many years later, I was travelling with a quartet and a pianist in extension ministry for Prairie Bible Institute. One Saturday we were with Pastor Peter Dyck in Wymark. Saskatchewan. We had been on quite a busy schedule going from church to church, and I had found very little time to pray. Saturday afternoon, everything was quiet at the church except for the quartet practicing, so I found a vacant Sunday school room in the basement and spent a while in prayer. As I prayed, I recognized that same compulsion to pray for a particular unsaved soul. But I did not know anyone in that area except the pastor and his family. However, the burden persisted. After a while, I went over to the parsonage and asked the pastor and his son to come pray with me. We stopped upstairs in the church and got the quartet and the pianist.

The eight of us went into a Sunday school room, and I told them the story of the man and the little girl. It had been years since that experience, but I explained that I had a similar compulsion that day. We prayed for the soul whom God wanted to save while we were in Wymark.

I am a teacher, not an evangelist, although I believe we should all be evangelizing. Most of the people who attended the services held by our Bible Institute team were believers. Saturday evening in a strong Christian community hardly seemed like the time and place to expect anything unusual.

The church was packed that night. Everyone was friendly and talked freely about the things of the Lord. I did not meet anyone who gave the impression of being unsaved. No one responded to the invitation to acknowledge Christ as Savior.

Back in the room at the farm home where I was staying, I knelt by the bed and asked the Lord what had gone wrong. I had been so sure that He had laid it on my heart to pray for one particular person to be saved while our team was in Wymark. Had I been foolhardy in voicing that conviction to the others? Was it just the enthusiasm of the flesh? But the Lord gave peace. I was confident that the prayer burden had come from Him, although I could not understand the apparent outcome.

The next morning as we drove to Swift Current for a service, I asked, "Where will we go tonight?"

"Wymark," came the reply.

"Wymark? But we just left Wymark! Oh, that's right, I remember now. We are to go to a different church in that same vicinity."

"Yes, our instructions say that it is just four miles from the church where we were last night."

Suddenly, I remembered the request I had shared the day before for a soul to be saved "while we are in Wymark "— not necessarily on Saturday night!

At supper time Sunday evening we were all seated at the table in Pastor Peter's home in Wymark when the phone rang. Pastor Dyck was calling. Here is the story he told.

A few minutes earlier, a young man had called from Swift Current.

"Is there going to be a service at your church tonight?" he asked.

"No," replied Pastor Dyck. "The Prairie Bible Institute team is going to be over at the other church, and we are going over there tonight to hear them again."

"Oh," sighed the man with noticeable disappointment in his voice.

"Why? Is there something I can do to help you?" asked the pastor.

"I wanted to come to your church tonight and get saved."

"Well, I'll be happy to lead you to Christ. Just come on out now and I'll show you from God's Word how to be saved and will pray with you. Do you know where I live? I'm right beside the church."

"Yes, sir. I know where you live, but I can't do it that way. I know how to be saved, but I want to do it publicly. You see, I was raised in Wymark. Everybody in that community knows how I turned my back on Christ when I was a teenager. I didn't do that secretly, and I can't accept Him secretly now. I feel like I ought to walk down the aisle and let everybody know what I'm doing."

"Fine," responded the pastor. "Just come on out and meet me at my house and you can go to church with us. Meanwhile, I'll call Mr. Pike, the speaker from Prairie, and ask him to be sure to give you an opportunity to make a public profession of faith in Christ."

And that's the way it happened. The man, about 30 years old, and his uncle, who had prayed for him for years, walked down the aisle together, and in the prayer room the matter was settled.

Space does not permit all the details of more accounts of souls saved in answer to prayer. I'll just give you a quick glance into the experience of one more, because we must not leave the impression that we should wait for some spectacular leading before we pray for the unsaved.

> *On the ground of redemption through the shed blood of Jesus Christ, let us claim and take for God in Jesus' name that which is His purchased possession.*

Pennsylvania

Mrs. Davidson asked my wife and me to pray for her unsaved husband. We did — for about two years. Mr. Davidson, in his sixties, was affable, but could turn the conversation from the things of God to baseball more adeptly than anyone I had ever known. Occasionally, when I persisted, he would tell me that he had been a drunkard but had quit drinking ten years earlier and had held a good job and provided a good home for his wife ever since. He even acknowledged, "And God helped me. Yes, He helped me a lot." I could not get him any closer than that to admitting that he was a sinner in need of a Savior.

Gradually, Mr. Davidson began coming to church, not regularly, but we were encouraged to keep praying. One Sunday morning, as people were leaving the service, I noticed Mr. Davidson standing to one side, dabbing at his eyes with a handkerchief. After a few moments, when no one else was around, he came over, shook my hand, and said, "Preacher, will you say a prayer for me?"

"Certainly, Mr. Davidson, what...?" But he was gone.

I greeted others, but soon was able to look out the door and see Mr. Davidson standing on the porch, off to one side, wiping his eyes with the handkerchief.

"Mr. Davidson," I said, laying a hand on his shoulder, "you asked me to pray *for* you. Wouldn't you like for me to pray *with* you?"

"Oh, would you?" he asked.

We went back into the nearly empty sanctuary where we were joined by Paul Pyle, the Youth for Christ Director for Chester

County, and Mr. Manley, an octogenarian prayer warrior, who had often prayed for Mr. Davidson.

It was a desire to take communion with his wife that had made him tearful. As I had read 1 Corinthians 11:27-30 before serving communion, he had been stricken with the conviction that he could not partake worthily because he was not a true Christian.

> *Let us take our place of authority in Christ at the right hand of the Father and use it against the Enemy.*

We prayed. He received the Lord Jesus. By that time my wife and another lady had accompanied Mrs. Davidson back into the church. They were sitting at the back, praying. I motioned for them to join us, and Mrs. Davidson fell into her husband's arms, sobbing.

"Paul," I said, "will you please serve the communion?" And we partook of the Lord's supper with the newborn babe in Christ and his dear wife, who believed in praying for the lost.[5]

Conclusion

When Jesus said, "And I will do WHATEVER you ask in My name, so that the Son may bring glory to the Father" (John 14:13), are we to read it, "Whatever you ask except the Spirit's wooing and winning of lost souls for whom I died"? Nonsense!

Jesus prayed for me before I was saved, before I was even born (John 17:20), and so my wife and I prayed for our children and grandchildren before their birth — that they should be saved at an early age.

Jesus also prayed for the sinners who crucified Him.

Fifty-two American hostages were held by Moslem fanatics in Iran for 444 days. Thousands of people were praying for their release. When the great day arrived, there were celebrations with bells, bands, and banners. What of the millions who are held captive by Satan? Will we intercede as fervently for their release? The angels of Heaven rejoice over one sinner who repents. But the ministry of reconciliation is committed to us, not angels.

Let us take our place of authority in Christ at the right hand of the Father and use it against the enemy. Let us ask for the Holy Spirit's direction in such prayer warfare.

On the ground of redemption through the shed blood of Jesus

Christ, let us claim and take for God in Jesus' name that which is His purchased possession.

> *We prepare the soil by intercessory prayer and plant the seed by witnessing.*

An anonymous writer in the *Alliance Witness* (later called *Alliance Life*) wrote, "We should claim the tearing down of all the works of Satan, such as false doctrine, unbelief, communistic teaching and hatred which the enemy may have built up in their thinking, and that their very thoughts shall be brought into captivity to the obedience of Christ.

"In the authority of the name of the Lord Jesus claim their deliverance from the power and persuasion of the Evil One and from the love of the world and the lusts of the flesh. We should pray also for the quickening of their conscience, and that God might grant them repentance and hearing ears and believing hearts as they hear or read the Word of God. Pray that God's will and purposes be accomplished in and through them." (This excellent article is available in tract form, entitled "How I Learned to Pray for the Lost," from Back to the Bible Broadcast, Lincoln, Nebraska, or Winnipeg, Manitoba.)

Pray, also, that God will manipulate circumstances so as to cause lost souls to become sick of sin and have a deep hunger for satisfaction in Christ. That is not a violation of the will. It is a liberating of the will.

Someone has said that "It takes two to grow a potato, God and man." The ministry of reconciliation also involves miracle (God's part) and mandate (man's part). God will do His part in cooperation with our believing prayer. We prepare the soil by intercessory prayer and plant the seed by witnessing.

Study and Discussion Questions

1. Discuss prayer-backed witnessing to the unsaved. (a) Why is prayer needed for the person who witnesses? (b) Why is prayer needed for the unsaved? (c) Why is it not enough to pray only?

2. Discuss the case history of someone who was saved in answer to prayer. It may be someone of your own acquaintance or someone you have read about.

3. Since God says that it is not His will that any should perish, but that all should come to repentance (2 Pet. 3:9b), why do so many remain in a lost condition? Discuss it from the standpoint of: (a) the sinners' knowledge and will; (b) Satan's activity; (c) Christians' neglect.

4. If a Christian prays that the Holy Spirit might bring an unsaved loved one to the point of repentance and salvation at any cost, what are some specific things which He might do which would not violate the sinner's will?

18

PRAYER FOR FELLOW BELIEVERS

Far be it from me
that I should sin against the Lord
by failing to pray for you
(1 Sam. 12:23a).

We have mentioned the profound duty and privilege of believers to pray for one another, but let's give more in-depth consideration to this subject.

Recorded prayers in the Gospels show Jesus' concern for the spiritual edification of His followers. Those in the epistles, too, dwell on the spiritual experiences of the believers in the churches to which they were written. Besides these prayer samples, there are numerous admonitions for brothers in Christ to intercede for each other. What a privilege...what a ministry...what a responsibility!

Spontaneity as opposed to formality in prayer has been stressed so much in evangelical circles that we have gone to the other extreme. Our prayers have degenerated into materialistic requests with very little spiritual content or concern for the glory of God. We have given so little attention to the words of our prayers that they are ineffective because they are nonspecific: "Lord, bless the pastor and the Sunday school teachers, and bless the missionaries."

If we do get specific, we zero in on health, transportation, shelter, employment, and other "practical" concerns of daily life. Not that God is indifferent toward your need for a better car or the missionary's need for an airplane, but the New Testament prayers had a different emphasis. God may even answer our prayer for a parking space near the store where we are going to pick up Sunday school supplies.

◄ But if we *limit* our praying to conversation with God about the things that come along (even during the hectic pace

Without God's glory as the focal point, all of the things we pray about lose their essential quality of permanence, and we become spiritually disoriented.

which we glibly call "Christian service") and we never set aside blocks of time to seek the mind of Christ regarding our supplications, we may never rise much above the parking-space mentality. Such limited vision should cause us to blush with shame.

What sort of requests do we find in New Testament prayers? Requests such as —

—the unity of the body of Christ,

—a knowledge of God's will in all spiritual wisdom and understanding,

—strengthening by God's Spirit in the inner man.

—love abounding more and more in knowledge and depth of insight,

—power to grasp the width, length, height, and depth of the love of Christ.

—filling to the measure of all the fullness of God,

—grace,

— peace,

—open doors of opportunity to proclaim the Gospel, and

—boldness to enter those doors.

We are assuming that believers do pray for one another. Certainly, many do. Prayer is the very breath of the Body. Without it, the Church would soon expire, but that cannot happen because Jesus said that Hell itself cannot prevail against it. The question, then, is not *whether* to pray for fellow-believers, but how to do so. A survey of Jesus' prayer for believers and some of Paul's prayers should enlighten us.

Jesus' High-Priestly Prayer

John 17 is the Holy of Holies of the New Testament. It is our High Priest's intimate intercession. It is truly the *Lord's* prayer, every word of it the Savior's personal petition.

The first stanza of this prayer-poem centers in the glory of God. May this be the conscious, consuming passion of our hearts whenever we approach the throne of grace. As our Savior drew near to the cross, His one burden was for the glory of His Father. Everything else was subservient to that.

Here alone is the true focus of our lives. When we align all of our motives and purposes with God's glory, every detail of life acquires proper perspective. Without this focal point, all of the things we pray about lose their essential quality of permanence and we become spiritually disoriented. Keep His glory ever before you as you pray. If what you ask for sharpens your vision of His glory, it is worth the time and effort it costs to pray fervently.

The second stanza reveals a very disarming camaraderie between Jesus and His Father. On the one hand, it is not a formal, ritualistic invocation; on the other hand, it is not the common grocery-list variety by which we so often order benefits from Heaven. Rather, this is Jesus' conversation with His Father.

Development of such prayer-companionship with God will strengthen us and will help us to clarify our motives and be more specific in our requests. God seeks such fellowship with His redeemed ones. The better we get to know Him in prayer, the more we will enjoy His presence. It is important that we understand this companionable approach to God so that we do not mistake it for the irreverent attitude which treats the transcendent God as our equal. Although Jesus is one with the Father, His prayer is never lacking in reverence.

Verse 11b is Jesus' specific request for the believers spiritual protection. Verse 15 clarifies it as protection from the Evil One. The point of the petition is "so that they may be one as We are one." The genuine unity of believers always holds a high priority in the New Testament. Divisions which range from personality conflicts to church splits give ample evidence of the need today for our praying as Jesus prayed.

Jesus wants us joyful — full of joy — His own joy.

This chapter reveals the heart of our Lord, and it is reasonable to assume that His continuing intercession for us (cf. Heb. 7:25; Rom.

PRINCIPLES OF EFFECTIVE PRAYER

8:34) expresses the same desire. When we enter into His purpose in our praying, His petition becomes our plea, and there is no more powerful force in God's universe!

Peter's cry, "Lord, save me!" in Matthew 14:30 is legitimate prayer, but it is kindergarten by comparison with the university level of John 17. Let us pray that we might be permitted to grasp the significance of Jesus' words.

The New Testament strongly stresses the unity of the body of Christ. In Ephesians 4:3 we are admonished to "make every effort to keep the unity of the Spirit through the bond of peace." The magnificent passage on Christ's humility in Philippians 2:5-11 is given in order to encourage the Church to be "one in spirit and purpose" (v. 2).

Jesus prayed, therefore, for protection from any wiles of the enemy which would create disunity among His followers. How often do we hear such a prayer in our local assembly?

Then, Jesus asked that His disciples "may have the full measure of My joy within them" (v. 13). Joy! Jesus wants us joyful — full of joy — His own joy. Our joy and God's glory are parts of the same package.

In a park in Singapore a sun dial has this inscription printed respectively on its four sides: (1) What Thou (2) Seekest (3) Is A (4) Shadow. How pitifully true of all seeking for happiness outside Christ. Seekers for fun or fulfillment find that these are shifting shadows without substance, whether sought in drugs or drink, sex or science, advancement or affluence, religion or riches.

The joy of the Lord alone makes life worth living. Place joy as a high priority on your prayer list for each member of the body of Christ.

I prayed this morning for such joy for my wife and children and for my co-workers. Walking across the campus on my way to my office, I saw a young lady from another department of the Bible school. I do not know her well, but I lifted my heart in silent

> *Jesus prayed for you and me — believers today.*

prayer that she might have the full measure of Christ's joy within her today. And I believe it will be granted. If I could give each of these a paid vacation in Hawaii, it would be of far less value than that which is within my reach for them.

Guess who else is experiencing real joy today!

In verses 14-19 our Lord requests the sanctification of believers while they are in the midst of a world that will hate them as it hated Him. The footnote in the *New International Version* defines the Greek word translated "sanctify" as "set apart for sacred use" or "make holy." Let us not limit our praying to the physical protection of loved ones, but let us be as diligent in praying for their protection from the Evil One (v. 15). As the temple vessels of old were set apart for holy purposes, so let us pray that our sons and daughters, our Sunday school class members, and all our Christian acquaintances be set apart. Then we will be praying as Jesus prayed.

"I pray also for those who will believe in Me through their message, Jesus continued in verse 20. That includes you and me today! Again, the point of the request was for the unity of believers (vv. 2 1-23). This is our effective testimony to the world. Let us love one another, bear one another's burdens, and seek each other's welfare. No organizational union can produce such unity.

Believers are never independent. We are spiritually *inter*dependent, just as the members of one's body are physically interdependent. Facing the cross, Jesus' consuming desire was that His Church should manifest to the world the love of God through this genuine unity (vv. 24-26). Ought we to limit our prayers to anything less?

Paul's Prayers

The Apostle Paul's prayers were effective. So will ours be if we follow his example. Concentrate on just one of his prayers for several days at a time; personalize it — i.e., pray its requests for particular fellow-believers of your acquaintance. Try praying it for your wife or husband, for your pastor, for friends, and for those to whom you are not naturally attracted. Then move on to another of Paul's prayers.

Notice the emphasis on *thanksgiving* for the believers — all of them, even those who disappointed the apostle in many ways. Was he flattering them as a means of diplomacy? Was this merely good psychology to gain a receptive hearing? No, his sincerity, his transparent honesty, comes through so strongly that any thought of flattery is ruled out. Take your Bible and read the following passages to get the feel of Paul's genuine appreciation for fellow-members of the family of God: Romans 1:8; 1 Corinthians 1:4; 2 Corinthians 1:11; Ephesians 1:15-16; Philippians 1:3-8; Colossians 1:3-5; 1 Thessalonians 1:2-3; 2 Thessalonians 1:3.

All the riches of earth do not compare with the wealth we have in our blood-bought relationship with a brother or sister in Christ. Thank God regularly for him or her and do nothing to spoil the bond of love between you. If we practice this, we will see rifts healed, splits avoided, and unity strengthened. If we spend time on our knees thanking God for our brother, enumerating qualities for which we are grateful, we shall not easily engage in idle gossip about him. The attitude of gratitude is a healthy habit.

Particular points for thanksgiving in the apostle's prayers were: their enduring faith in Christ and their manifest love for the saints (Rom. 1:8; Eph. 1:15-16; Col. 1:3-4). A special reason for thanks regarding Philippian believers was their partnership in his ministry through giving (Phil. 1:3-5; 4:10-20). Even in the carnal, worldly church at Corinth, Paul found cause for genuine thanksgiving; "I always thank God for you because of His grace given you in Christ Jesus" (1 Cor. 1:4). Here is an enriching prayer to pray for any Christian, no matter how weak or disappointing he may be. If you cannot find something in his behavior for which to give thanks, express your appreciation for what Jesus has done for him — God's grace given him in Christ Jesus. That is something to be excited about.

One of the most difficult things in life, however, is the giving of generous, genuine thanks for some fellow-Christians. When we have been wounded by false reports, nothing but the grace of God can enable us to do it. Let us seek God for such grace to give thanks for specifics both privately and publicly. The very practice will put feet to our prayer for unity and will add a new dimension to our Christian experience.

True spiritual perception (insight into the real nature of things) was high on Paul's prayer list for believers. There is no record of his ever praying for exemption from suffering, but how often he asks for knowledge, understanding, wisdom, enlightenment of "the eyes of your heart." If we are sincere in our desire to learn effective prayer from such a seasoned prayer warrior, we will meditate much on Ephesians 1:17ff; 3:17-19; Philippians 1:9-11; and Colossians 1:9-10; and we will use the Sword of the Spirit in our own praying.

Another oft-repeated request had to do with an inner strengthening by the Spirit of God. He refers to it in Ephesians 1:19-21; 3:17-18; Colossians 1:11 (cf. Col. 1:29; 2 Thess. 2:16-17). When we see a brother or sister falter in the Christian walk, may God help us to refrain from criticism and remember to intercede for this inner empowerment. That is the supernatural power which it took to raise Jesus from the dead (Eph. 1:19-21). By it Jesus was exalted to the right hand of the Father far above all Satanic and demonic power. By it we were raised from spiritual death, and in Christ we, too, are far above the enemy (Eph. 2:1-6). The knowledge of our identification with Christ not only in death, burial, and resurrection, but also in exaltation to the position of authority over the enemy is a great need in the Church today. This knowledge and this power are inseparable. The power is available in Christ, but without the knowledge Christians cannot appropriate it. They are constantly intertwined in Paul's prayers for the saints.

The power is the power of love. As Jesus stressed love in John 17, so Paul does in Ephesians 3:17-19; Colossians 1:4, 8; 1 Thessalonians 1:3.

This missionary, who was all-out for Christ in his own life and service, was never satisfied with halfway measures. What he requested he asked for in full; "filled to the measure of all the fullness of God" (Eph. 3:19), "filled with the fruit of righteousness" (Phil. 1:11), "asking God to fill you with the knowledge of His will through all spiritual wisdom and understanding" (Col. 1:9).

As always with Paul, doctrine and practice went hand-in-hand, and the deeply spiritual subjects for prayer were not theoretical, but were intensely practical. The purpose of his prayer for the Colossian believers to be filled "with the knowledge of His will through all spiritual wisdom and understanding" was "in order that you may live a life worthy of the Lord and may please Him in every way; bearing fruit in every good work, growing in the knowledge of God, being strengthened with all power according to His glorious might so that you may have great endurance and patience, and joyfully giving thanks to the Father, who has qualified you to share in the inheritance of the saints in the kingdom of light" (Col. 1:9-12).

We have merely glimpsed the possibilities of meaningful intercession for believers in this chapter. May it serve as an appetizer to create within you a desire for deeper study. All that the New Testament teaches regarding Christian truth and practice is subject matter for prayer.

Study and Discussion Questions

1. Discuss the motto: "Prayer is not a duty; it is a privilege." What good thing is it trying to teach us? What is wrong with it? Show in the following examples that **"duty"** and **"privilege"** are not conflicting terms, that one does not rule out the other:

   a. Parents' care for their children;

   b. Christian service;

   c. A Christian husband's love for his wife and her submission to him as to the Lord.

   d. Prayer.

2. Discuss the deep spiritual quality of any of Paul's prayers in the New Testament.

3. From Jesus' High Priestly prayer discuss Jesus' own prayer requests for believers, John 17.

4. Pray a New Testament prayer for a friend (a believer). Personalize it by using your friend's name and by using personal pronouns — I, he, she, my, etc. Now, pray the same prayer in the same way for a believer who irritates you, one you don't consider a close friend. (If you keep on praying like this, you'll have **more** friends and fewer people you don't care for!)

THE INTERNATIONAL IMPACT
OF INTERCESSION

Is it possible, with all of the international intrigue and political ploys of the demonic forces which seek to influence governments, that humble Christians can turn the tide of events by simple prayer? If the Bible has a direct and forthright interpretation, then honest exegesis can render no other meaning from 1 Timothy 2:1-8.

Praying for Nations

Paul E. Billheimer, in *Destined for the Throne*, amplifies this startling truth; *"....by virtue of her organic relationship with Christ, the Supreme Sovereign, she [the Church], not Satan, holds the balance of power in human affairs."*[1]

"If it were not for the Church," adds Biliheimer. "Satan would already have turned this earth into hell. The fact that it has been preserved from total devastation in spite of him, proves that at least a remnant of the Church is effactually functioning and already has entered upon her rulership in union with her Lord. She is even now, by virtue of the scheme of prayer and faith, engaged in 'on-the-job' training for her place as co-sovereign with Christ over the entire universe following Satan's final destruction."[2]

An Example

In ancient Babylon, the captive Israelite, Daniel, held tenaciously to a philosophy of life which recognized the sovereignty of God in the affairs of men and nations and which acknowledged prayer as the *modus operandi* by which God brings to pass His will.

> *"The United Nations is not the final court of appeal in the affairs of nations."*
> —J.O. Sanders

After a night of prayer with his three friends. Daniel said, "Praise be to the name of God for ever and ever;... He changes times and seasons; He sets up kings and deposes them" (Dan. 2:20-21a).

In the face of King Darius' decree, which carried a penalty of being thrown to the lions if anyone prayed to any god or man other than the king, Daniel continued to get down on his knees three times a day to pray to God (Dan. 6:10). Heathen kings praised the God of Heaven as they observed His answers to Daniel's prayers.

When he realized that the time for the fulfillment of Jeremiah's prophecy was near, Daniel did not sit and wait for it to happen but "turned to the Lord God and pleaded with him in prayer and petition, in fasting, and in sackcloth and ashes" (Dan. 9:3). The prayer which follows is one of the greatest examples to be found for the study of the theological basis of prayer, confession of national sin, and petition for God's intervention in international affairs.

In the New Testament, James uses an Old Testament example to prove that what was possible in another dispensation is possible now: "Elijah was a man just like us. He prayed earnestly that it would not rain, and it did not rain on the land for three-and-a-half years. Again he prayed, and the heavens gave rain, and the earth produced its crops" (Jas. 5:17-18). The economy and politics of the nation were controlled by Elijah's prayers.

It is difficult for us to admit to ourselves that men like Daniel and Elijah were not super men endowed with fantastic power, but men of faith and prayer. To admit that reveals something of our own potential through the same avenue.

J. Oswald Sanders declares, "The United Nations is not the final court of appeal in the affairs of nations. The Church could dominate politics from her prayer room if this priority were observed."[3]

The Tools

How can God's people become such nation-swaying intercessors? We can diligently study our Bibles for examples and principles of prayer warfare. Concurrently, we can follow world events through the news media and in missionary periodicals. Then,

> *The disciplined student of prayer will become enlightened concerning national and world needs in order to pray intelligently.*

instead of complaining and criticizing, we can pray. Finally, we can avail ourselves of some of the excellent informative helps offered by mission societies and organizations which are devoted to the ministry of national and international intercession.

One of the finest tools available is the book, *Operation World,* by Patrick Johnstone and Jason Mandryk.[4] Its former subtitle, "A Handbook for World Intercession," is accurate. Information is presented for every country of the world, which has been gleaned from significant evangelical missions, the names and addresses of which are listed, and from major statistical sources. The book is packed with concisely summarized facts regarding each nation's area, population, peoples, economy, politics, religion, and specific prayer targets. The newest edition also includes major answers to global prayer which have been realized over the 1990s. The beautiful family edition - *Window on the World,* a desktop prayer calendar and map are also available to aid global intercession. These were all updated and released for the year 2001, and can be obtained from a Christian bookstore or the contact information in the back of this book.[5]

The "Intercessors for America Newsletter,"[6] published monthly, focuses prayer on moral and spiritual problems in the United States, as well as some international concerns. It presents a very sane, balanced evangelical viewpoint on current issues and an excellent editorial in each issue by some leading Christian national personage.

It would be impossible to list here all the organizations and materials which are dedicated to prayer for the nations. In addition to regular denominational and interdenominational mission boards, there are those that are dedicated to specialized work, such as literature, radio, or translation. The list of organizations' addresses in *Operation World* may be used to obtain ample material for prayer targets around the world.

The disciplined student of prayer will become enlightened

concerning national and world needs in order to pray intelligently. He will take careful aim at specific targets — perhaps a national referendum, an act of Parliament or Congress, legislative action regarding abortion, or God's intervention in the rule of a murderous dictator.

More things are wrought by prayer
Than this world dreams of. Wherefore,
let thy voice
Rise like a fountain for me night and day.
For what are men better than sheep
or goats
That nourish a blind life within the brain,
If, knowing God; they lift not hands
of prayer
Both for themselves and those who call
them friend?
For so the whole round earth is
every way
Bound by gold chains about the feet
of God.[7]

—Alfred Lord Tennyson

"I looked for a man among them who would build up the wall and stand before Me in the gap on behalf of the land so I would not have to destroy it, but I found none" (Ezek. 22:30).

"If My people, who are called by My name, will humble themselves and pray and seek My face and turn from their wicked ways, then will I hear from Heaven and will forgive their sin and will heal their land" (2 Chron. 7:14).

> "...so real is the power which the Lord gives His people to exercise in Heaven and earth, that the number of the labourers and the measure of the harvest do actually depend upon their prayer."
> —Andrew Murray

Praying for Missionaries

To become an effective world-changer, become a prayer partner with missionaries whose work you can follow with intense interest and intelligent intercession. Correspond with them personally. Support them financially to whatever sacrificial extent it is possible. Invite them to your home when they are on furlough. Pray for them according to a regular schedule: daily, weekly, etc. Include their needs in family devotions, personal devotions, and special times of prayer. Share their requests with others in your prayer group. (Suggestion: Review the section on family devotions in Chapter 4: PRAYING TOGETHER.)

> Then He [Jesus] said to His disciples,
> "The harvest is plentiful but the
> workers are few. Ask the Lord of the harvest,
> therefore, to send out workers
> into His harvest field"
> (Matt. 9:37,38).

"The Lord frequently taught His disciples that they must pray, and *how*; but seldom *what* to pray," said Andrew Murray. "This He left to their sense of need, and the leading of the Spirit. But here we have one thing He expressly enjoins them to remember; in view of the plenteous harvest, and the need of reapers, they must cry to the Lord of the harvest to send forth laborers...

"Prayer is no form or show. The Lord Jesus was Himself the truth; everything He spoke was the deepest truth. It was when (see v. 36) 'He saw the multitude, and was moved with compassion on them, because they were scattered abroad, as sheep having no shepherd,' that He called on the disciples to call for laborers to be sent among them. He did so because He really believed that their prayer was needed and would help....

"So real is the power which the Lord gives His people to exercise in Heaven and earth, that the number of the labourers and the measure of the harvest do actually depend upon their prayer."[8]

If you acquire a world view and pray for the nations, your heart will surely echo the cry of the Lord Jesus for soul-winners to be sent. Jesus gave many invitations to pray, many admonitions to pray, many promises to answer prayer, much instruction about prayer, but only one specific request for which He asked us (yea, commanded us) to pray: "Ask the Lord of the harvest, therefore, to send out workers into His harvest field." Yet, how many prayer meetings are held, without once hearing anyone ask the Lord to send out new missionaries from our congregations and our families? Millions live and die without once hearing the name of Jesus, but our prayer time is consumed with material and physical concerns! If we pray as Jesus commanded, we will put feet to our prayers. We will step forward and ask God where and how He can best use us in His harvest field. Not one of us has an inconsequential role.

What about praying for the needs of cross-cultural missionaries? Although they face many physical, cultural, linguistic, and family problems unknown to folks at home, Steve Read is correct when he says, "Missionaries are normal, growing Christians and have all [the] same needs in their lives as all of us. It is important that we pray for the new van which may be needed, ...but our intercession must primarily be for their spiritual growth, strength, and maturity. The bulk of our prayer for our missionaries should be that they too learn Christ's humility, that they have the compassion which causes them to weep over their Jerusalem, that they find grace daily to be totally dependent on the Father. As these attitudes become more and more real in their lives, their ministry will become that much more effective."[9]

All that was said in Chapter 18 regarding prayer for fellow believers is applicable to prayer for missionaries. But, in addition, we must keep in mind that missionaries are often more severely opposed by Satan and his demonic forces. This is especially the case when a missionary enters new territory with the Gospel. When Satan has long held unchallenged sway in an area, he will not withdraw without a fight. The evangelist-missionary needs the faithful and fervent support of prayer partners who understand prayer warfare, those who will staunchly resist Satan and claim territory for Christ.

The apostle to the Gentiles recognized his constant need for the prayer support of Christians in the battle against the enemy of souls.

I urge you, brothers, by our Lord Jesus Christ

and by the love of the Spirit, to join me in my struggle by praying to God for me. Pray that I may be rescued from the unbelievers in Judea and that my service in Jerusalem may be acceptable to the saints there...(Rom. 15:30,31).

We were under great pressures far beyond our ability to endure, so that we despaired even of life... He has delivered us from such a deadly peril, and He will deliver us. On Him we have set our hope that He will continue to deliver us, as you help us by your prayers. Then many will give thanks on our behalf for the gracious favor granted us in answer to the prayers of many (2 Cor. 1:8-11).

Pray also for me, that whenever I open my mouth, words may be given me so that I will fearlessly make known the mystery of the Gospel, for which I am an ambassador in chains. Pray that I may declare it fearlessly, as I should (Eph. 6:19,20).

I know that through your prayers and the help given by the Spirit of Jesus Christ, what has happened to me will turn out for my deliverance (Phil. 1:19).

And pray for us, too, that God may open a door for our message, so that we may proclaim the mystery of Christ, for which I am in chains. Pray that I may proclaim it clearly as I should (Col. 4:3,4).

Finally, brothers, pray for us that the message of the Lord may spread rapidly and be honored, just as it was with you. And pray that we may be delivered from wicked and evil men, for not everyone has faith (2 Thess. 3:1,2).

These requests should be priority items in our prayers for Christian workers today, especially for cross-cultural missionaries and national Christian leaders.

Those who leave their homelands to take the Gospel to the

unreached also need prayer for special adjustments and difficulties. Some of these needs will be indicated in prayer letters and mission bulletins, but often the most crucial concerns cannot be publicized.

> *Discipline your missionary prayer ministry so that it is not dependent on "exciting" stories.*

Matters related to governmental and political policies should not be put into duplicated letters lest they fall into the wrong hands. Some things, if written, could cause the missionary's expulsion from the country. To pray intelligently, we must, as much as possible, keep abreast of the political situation where the missionary is serving. Then, the Holy Spirit will give discernment to "read between the lines" of letters and news reports. During furlough invite the missionary to your home and let him know that you are sincerely concerned not just about glowing reports, but also about trials and difficulties.

Sometimes the oppression of the enemy in a variety of forms wears down the missionary emotionally, mentally, and spiritually, but he does not feel free to share such problems openly. If a long period passes without a letter from your missionary, do not assume that all is well. The adage, "No news is good news," is not Scripture and is often not correct. Missionaries know that North American Christians crave sensational reports, and when the attack of Satan is sore and results are less than "exciting," it is difficult for them to know what to include in a letter. Consider the absence of news to be a cry for help, or at least discipline your missionary prayer ministry so that it is not dependent on "exciting" stories.

Some very real needs which may not get into a prayer letter are these: loneliness, personality conflicts and petty differences between missionaries, personal temptations and spiritual struggles, friction between mission society and national church, personal discouragement or even depression, rebellion of missionaries' children.

Single missionaries may be especially affected by loneliness. Temptation to enter an unwise marriage is not unheard of. Couples, too, who are in isolated places with no companionship with other Christians or with those of similar cultural background may feel very much alone. In Alaska the social withdrawal which sometimes results is called "cabin fever."

Many anxieties can afflict missionaries, robbing them of joy and effectiveness. We can bear these burdens with them in prayer even when we do not know the details. God knows. Whether they are anxieties related to family, finances, the local church, political unrest, safety, or problems in the lives of converts, they may not make the pages of the prayer letter, but they constitute real prayer needs.

Since travelling in West Africa, I have felt a new urgency to pray for missonaries' safety on the roads. Friends in several other areas of the world also mention erratic driving habits.

Prevalence of diseases, such as malaria, typhoid, hepatitis, or Lassa fever, may characterize an area. These, combined with few hospital facilities and poor sanitation, create health hazards few of us ever consider at home.

Have you realized that missionaries have moral temptations? They do. In fact, they might be special targets of Satan's darts. Isolation may compound such enticements to wrong doing.

Sexual immorality has ruined more than one missionary's ministry, whether we care to admit it or not. A head-in-the-sand attitude toward such temptations will not help. Prayer will.

A real estate agent wanted to misrepresent the amount actually paid by a missionary for a piece of property. To report a lower amount to the government would save the missionary several thousands of dollars in taxes. The argument was "everybody does it." It was an accepted custom in that country. The missionary needed the money but refused the offer to misrepresent the sale. He paid the higher taxes. As a result, the real estate agent became favorably impressed with the gospel.

Financial pressures can take an inordinate amount of time and attention where inflation has skyrocketed prices beyond anything imaginable in North America. And the missionary cannot increase his income by moonlighting. When I visited Ghana, I found that each month a couple went to the neighboring country of Togo to buy the month's supply of groceries for the several missionary families of the Sudan Interior Mission in Accra. The exorbitant prices in Ghana put even necessities out of reach.

Missionaries' children need special prayer, as do the parents, regarding health, education, separation, and spiritual commitment. What happens to the children can make or break the parents' effectiveness in service.

One last word about this important sphere of prayer ministry: pray for the students and staff members of institutions of higher learning where missions courses receive the priority given to them in the New Testament. Most evangelical missionaries come from these schools.

Among the many helpful tracts and booklets on this subject are the following, to which I am indebted:

1. *How to Pray for Me,* SIM Int., Cedar Grove, NJ 07009, U.S.A.; 10 Huntingdale Blvd., Scarborough, Ontario M1W 2S5.
2. *How to Pray for Missionaries,* The Overcomer Literature Trust, 3 Munster Road, Parkstone, Poole, Dorset BH14 9PS, England.
3. *Lord, Bless Charles,* Sarah Gudschinsky, Wycliffe Bible Translators, Inc., P.O. Box 1960, Santa Ana, California 92702; Box 3068, Station B, Calgary, Alberta T2M 4L6.
4. *Prayer, Strategic in Missions,* J. Oswald Sanders, Overseas Missionary Fellowship, 404 5. Church St., Robesonia, PA 19551; 1058 Avenue Road, Toronto, Ontario M5N 2C6.
5. *Praying for Missionaries,* Moody Press, Chicago.
6. *Why and How to Pray for Missionaries,* Will Bruce, Overseas Missionary Fellowship (addresses with #4, above).

Study and Discussion Questions

1. Discuss 1 TImothy 2:1-8 in the light of Matthew 28:18-20. How do Paul's instructions relate to the Great Commission? Or to Matthew 9:37,38?

2. Discuss people in history (the Bible or elsewhere) who have influenced nations by prayer.

3. Prepare a report on a nation of your choice. Share it with your group and pray intelligently and specifically for it. (Use an encyclopedia and/or **Operation World** as well as National Geographic, missionary prayer letters, and any helps you can.)

4. Prepare a report about a missionary or a mission of your choice. Share it. Pray for specific needs.

5. Share with your group your plan for praying for missions and missionaries. If you don't have a plan, ask the group for help in starting one.

20

KNOWING GOD INTIMATELY

"Now this is eternal life;
that they may know You,
the only true God,
and Jesus Christ
whom You have sent."
—Jesus speaking in John 17:3

"And what is the chief and the best and the most glorious thing that a man needs every day, and can do every day? Nothing less than to seek and to know, and to love and to praise this glorious God."[1]

—Andrew Murray

This is what the Lord says: Let not the wise man boast of his wisdom or the strong man boast of his strength or the rich man boast of his riches, but let him who boasts boast about this; that he understands and knows Me, that I am the Lord, who exercises kindness, justice and righteousness on earth, for in these I delight, declares the Lord (Jer 9:23,24).

"Communion with God discovers the excellence of His character, and by beholding Him the soul is transformed, Holiness is conformity to Christ, and this is secured by a growing intimacy with Him."[2]

—D.M. McIntyre

"My heart says of You, 'Seek His face!'
Your face, Lord, I will seek.
Do not hide Your face from me..."
—King David in Psalm 27:8,9a

"That God can be known by the soul in tender personal
experience while remaining aloof from the curious eyes of reason
constitutes a paradox best described as
Darkness to the intellect
But sunshine to the heart."[3]
—Frederick W. Faber

"...growing in the knowledge of God."
—The Apostle Paul in Colossians 1:10

*"Men who know
their God are before
anything else men
who pray..."*
—J.I. Packer

"We cannot read the biographies or
come within the orbit of great men and
women of God, who so obviously enjoy intimacy with Him, without
wistfully desiring to share such an experience."[4]
—J. Oswald Sanders

"Enoch walked with God" (Gen 5:24).

"In God's school the students receive private tutoring. God...
adapts His teaching to the need of the individual student, and He
Himself undertakes to train each in His own class."[5]
—T.S. Rendall

"The man who says. 'I know Him,'
but does not do what He commands is a liar,
and the truth is not in him."
—John the Beloved, 1 John 2:4

"Men who know their God are before anything else men who
pray, and the first point where their zeal and energy for God's
glory come to expression is in their prayers."[6]
—J. I. Packer

The testimonies of those who have found the secret of God's presence where He communes with them as Friend with friend are too numerous to ignore. The

> *Each member of the Trinity is a Divine Person, and, for that reason, is capable of knowing and being known.*

names also are impressive. Can we believe them that there is such an intimate walk with God? YES! Is such a glorious relationship possible for us? YES! Let's examine three vital questions which can only point as signposts for further study and prayer.

Is It Possible to Know God Intimately?

John White says. "We confuse intimacy with its counterfeit, familiarity. Intimacy is what we want but familiarity is all we achieve. Intimacy is dangerous, a knowing and a being known deeply and profoundly."[7]

A young man said to me. "I didn't agree with something you said in the Bible study."

"Fine." I replied. "I appreciate your frankness so we can discuss it. What was it you disagreed with?"

"Well, you mentioned 'knowing God.' I don't think that's right. We can't *know* God! We can know *about* God — things about Him — but we can't *know* God. We *know* persons. Those are two different kinds of knowledge: knowing *about* and *knowing*. I don't think it's right to talk about knowing God."

Now, that is the kind of student a teacher really enjoys, one who thinks and reacts instead of immediately accepting everything the teacher or the textbook says. It would have been better yet had he voiced his objection in the Bible study so there could have been interaction and the learning process would have been enhanced for us all.

Interestingly enough, I agreed with some of his statements. Let's look at what he said.

"We can't know God." There is a very real sense in which he was correct. We'll look at it in more detail in a minute.

"We can know about God." Yes, to some extent, that is true. At least, we can know truth which God has revealed about Himself.

"We know persons." The implication was that God does not have personality and therefore is unknowable. But each member of the

> *"Proud man must not equal himself to God, nor cut God as short as his own line."*
> —Stephen Charnock

Trinity is a Divine Person and for that very reason is capable of knowing and being known. So his conclusion that we can *only* know *about* God but cannot *know* Him is incorrect.

Now, let's go back to the first two statements: "We can't know God. We can know about God."

One thing we know as a fact about God (but do not understand) is that He is infinite, that is, without limits, boundless. Everything about God is infinite: His holiness, His love, His power, His wisdom, His justice, His mercy. You name it and, if it is true of God, it is infinite. Does His justice limit His mercy? No, His infinite justice is perfectly compatible with His infinite mercy in Christ's atonement. The prefix "omni-" before such words as "potence," "presence." and "science" suggests that God's power, presence and knowledge are infinite.

Even God's creation appears to finite men to have spatial infinity. If there is any outer limit on space, telescopes haven't been built large enough to find it yet. Of course, everything within this inconceivably vast expanse of created matter has some kind of description or definition which indicates its limits: weight, size, shape, volume, mass or whatever. Yet it would be ridiculous for any human to say, "I know the universe," or "I know creation," or "I know science." Obviously, no one can objectively observe with telescope or microscope, let alone understand, more than a tiny fraction of what there is to be known in the universe.

If man's finite mind cannot comprehend every *finite* thing, how vastly unknowable is the *infinite* Creator. If anything is beyond comprehension, God is.

Charnock said of God, "As He can do what is above the skill of man to perform, so He understands what is above the skill of man to discover: shall man measure God by his scantiness? Proud man must not equal himself to God, nor cut God as short as his own line."[8]

Again he stated, "God knows Himself, and [He] only knows Himself. This is the first and original knowledge, wherein He excels all creatures. No man doth exactly know himself; much less doth he understand... the nature and perfections of God; for what proportion can there be between a finite faculty and an infinite object?"[9]

> *To know God intimately is possible.*

Packer agrees: "'Your thoughts of God are too human,' said Luther to Erasmus. 'This is where most of us go astray. Our thoughts of God are not great enough: we fail to reckon with the reality of His limitless wisdom and power....We think of God as too much like we are. Put this mistake right, says God; learn to acknowledge the full majesty of your incomparable God and Savior.'"[10]

The young man who disagreed with statements about knowing God appears so far to be in scholarly company!

Does not the Apostle Paul, under the Spirit's inspiration, also confirm that God is incomprehensible when he says, "No one knows the thoughts of God except the Spirit of God" (1 Cor. 2:11)?

While we cannot know God comprehensively, we can know what He reveals about Himself. Tozer reminds us, "The gravest question before the Church is always God Himself, and the most portentous fact about any man is not what he at a given time may say or do, but what he in his deep heart conceives God to be like. We tend by a secret law of the soul to move toward our mental image of God."[11] With these thoughts he introduces a delightful devotional study of the attributes of God and their meaning in the Christian life. An attribute he defines simply as "something true about God." While a person may have an intellectual grasp of the attributes of God and still not know Him with spiritual perception, it is not true that he can know Him spiritually without cognitive knowledge about Him. Such subjective knowledge might be of a false god, an imaginary god. It is important that we know that God is holy, true, omnipresent, omniscient, omnipotent, a God of love, goodness and mercy, as well as justice. A person may know God intimately without being able to define the terms but not without believing that He is this kind of God.

To know God intimately is possible, as attested by those quoted in the introduction to this chapter and many others. It is a craving which God delights to satisfy, for He initiated it. The Bible teaches this not only in precept but by numerous examples.

Abraham was one such example. "'For I know [Abraham].' The

word *know* in Hebrew can be translated 'chose' or 'made... my friend.' In saying He knows Abraham, God is saying, 'I chose Abraham to be My friend.'"[12] Then White reminds us that we are called Jesus' friends (cf. John 15:15). This involves what he terms, "a sharing and a taking counsel with God on matters of importance to Him."[13] In *Drawing Near to God* he gives us ten instructive studies of some who knew God intimately. One of the most enlightening chapters concerns Hannah, so let no woman think that only men of the Bible knew this intimacy with Deity.

Why Should We Know God Intimately?

There is always the temptation to the Christian to want to appear spiritual and to think of himself as a spiritual person. It takes little thought to see looming through this the ugly head of that monster *self*. To know God intimately is not in order to attain a higher rung on the ladder of piety than one's fellow-believers. Such ego-pampering is given the death knell in Galatians 2:20, Romans 6, and the many passages which teach our identification with Christ in His crucifixion. The desire to be known as a "great prayer warrior" falls into the same category.

The desire for intimacy with God may have the same psychological appeal for some that experiencing a "high" on drugs or psychedelic music has for others. It may be thought that an other-worldly sensation is involved. But the Almighty Lord God, Maker of Heaven and earth, does not reveal Himself to the seeker of cheap thrills. Of course, we are emotional beings and an ever-increasing intimacy with God will be evidenced in such areas as peace, comfort and joy, but let all who are of a mystic bent beware of looking for spine-tingling thrills and goose bumps. Hypnotic trance is not prerequisite for getting to know God better.

Job's knowledge of God increased tremendously through his trials. They brought him to this conclusion: 'My ears had heard of You but now my eyes have seen You. Therefore I despise myself and repent in dust and ashes" (Job 42:5,6).

What should be our motive in seeking to know God intimately? I see but one answer in Scripture: the glory of God. The "praise of His glory" (Eph. 1:6,12,14). That's all. That's everything! (See John 17:1-

5; Eph. 1:3-14.)

The reason for this pursuit, its goal, is not in me. What a liberating realization! It has nothing to do with my feelings or my reputation. This being true, my personal fellowship with the Lord can be as genuine and precious through times of the "discipline of darkness,"[14] [15] as during mountaintop experiences. It can be as constant when I feel rejected as when everyone is saying nice things about me.

Only as we know God can we worship Him to the praise of His glory. The more intimate the knowledge, the more intelligent the worship, the more in accord with His true character. It is significant that the one man in history, aside from our Lord Jesus Christ, who has given us the finest examples of worship is David, whom God described as "a man after My own heart."

Only as we know God intimately can there be the Christ-like growth in our lives which He desires to effect in us. The significance of growth in the knowledge of God for a life worthy of the Lord is very clear in Colossians 1:9,10, "We have not stopped praying for you and asking God to fill you with the knowledge of His will through all spiritual wisdom and understanding. And we pray this in order that you may live a life worthy of the Lord and may please Him in every way: bearing fruit in every good work, growing in the knowledge of God."

Only through prayer-intimacy can we glorify Him through effectually employing our authoritative partnership with Christ at the right hand of the Father (cf. Chapter 10).

Only as we know God personally on an intimate basis can our personal testimony carry weight with a skeptical world. The Holy Spirit blesses His own Word through our witness as the unsaved observe in us the reality of the knowledge of God which we profess.

How Can We Know God Intimately?

On June 16, 1948, a busy pastor in Chicago wrote a paragraph which I hope is as valid today as it was a generation ago. Dr. A.W. Tozer's book, *Pursuit of God* continues to bless hearts now as it did then, and he prefaced it with these words:

In this hour of all-but-universal darkness one

cheering gleam appears: within the fold of conservative Christianity there are to be found increasing numbers of persons whose religious lives are marked by a growing hunger after God Himself. They are eager for spiritual realities and will not be put off with words, nor will they be content with correct "interpretations" of truth. They are athirst for God, and they will not be satisfied till they have drunk deep at the Fountain of Living Water.[16]

Such books whet our appetites for reality in our relationship to God Himself. Yet, we do not get to know God intimately by merely reading the books of those who do. They cannot satisfy the appetite nor slake the thirst which they arouse.

Where do we go after we have read the books and studied the course on prayer? The Apostle Paul would answer, "I want to know Christ... [Therefore] I press on toward the goal to win the prize for which God has called me heavenward in Christ Jesus" (Phil. 3: l0a, 14). Here are some suggestions for beginning or continuing this pursuit of an intimate knowledge of God:

1. *Be sure of your own personal salvation.*
Make certain that your new birth, your birth into God's family, is a settled fact. Intimate knowledge begins with personal relationship. You can find such assurance by applying the following Scripture portions by faith to your own life: Romans 3:23; 6:23; 10:9,10; John 1:12; 3:16-18, 36; 1 John 5:13.

2. *Thoroughly integrate the study of the Bible with prayer.*
Read God's Word with a prayerful attitude, expecting Him to reveal Himself to you. Listen with the ears of your heart as you perceive with the eyes of your mind.

Read comprehensively. Read the Bible through regularly on a definite plan. At times, read New Testament epistles through a-book-at-a-sitting. In the Old Testament the Minor Prophets may be read the same way. Longer books may profitably be read several chapters at a time. Do not skip books which are difficult to understand. Even when there is much which we do not comprehend, we assimilate truths about God s character. As you read, you will frequently find passages which you may incorporate into your prayers (cf. Chapter 13).

Study intensively also. Ask your pastor or Bible teacher for help if you need it in selecting study helps. Join a good Bible class. Take Bible correspondence courses or enroll in a Bible college (many do even in middle life). But even if you are a Bible college or seminary graduate, do not grow lazy in your personal Bible study. As you study verse-by-verse, even phrase-by-phrase, pray that God will illuminate the Word to you so that you will see Him revealed in it.

Memorize, meditate, and obey. Someone has pointed out that every time you expose your mind to the Word of God you come in contact with God Himself. Saturate your mind with it so much that it will come naturally to talk things over with the Author. He will remind you of biblical principles and specific verses to apply to every situation in life and thus He will converse with you throughout the day.

"Oh, how I love Your law! I meditate on it all day long" (Ps. 119:97).

"Obedience is the test of love and it is rewarded by deepening intimacy."[17]

3. *Develop intimacy with God the Father by cultivating your acquaintance with His Son.*

"No one has ever seen God, but God the only Son, who is at the Father's side, has made Him known" (John 1:18).

"Jesus answered, 'I am the way and the truth and the life. No one comes to the Father except through Me' " (John 14:6).

"Anyone who has seen Me has seen the Father" (John 14:9).

Make an intensive study of the Gospels. Memorize many verses with the words of Christ in them. Use them in prayer. Study the passages which deal with the Person and work of Christ, such as the priestly ministry of Christ in the Book of Hebrews. Make a topical study of the Doctrine of Christ (Christology) with the help of a topical study Bible or a book of Bible doctrine.

Think often of what it means to pray in Jesus' name and use His authority for effective prayer.

4. *Ask God to reveal Himself to you through His great creation* as He did to people in Bible times. Then, take time to let Him do it! It will take will power as well as practice in observation and meditation to develop the spiritual insight of David (Psalms 8,19,121) or of Paul (Rom. 1:20). It is doubtful if God would have appealed to Job as He did in chapters 38-41 if Job had never spent time contemplating the evidences of God Himself in His handiwork.

5. *Interpret all circumstances and happenings prayerfully in the light of God's revelation of Himself in Scripture.*

Only by the habit of continual prayer is it possible to discern God's hand in and through all the trials and exigencies of life. Without the prayer habit we are more prone to "push the panic button." But God stands ready to teach us His ways and help us to a deeper knowledge of Himself in health and illness, in prosperity and poverty, in joy and sorrow, in love and rejection, in loneliness and interpersonal relationships, in anything and everything. Never have lovers found such comfort and strength in each other's presence as we will find In His. Sometimes we will not understand, but we will know the One who is weaving the circumstance into His plan for our life.

Romans 8:28 never becomes trite, but rather constantly more precious to the believer, "And we know that in all things God works for the good of those who love Him, who have been called according to His purpose."

6. *Make wise use of your time* (cf. Chapter 3).

Remember the 96 quarter-hours in a day, the moments and hours which can be salvaged for prayer — that last hour of sleep in the morning, the occasional noon hour, the hour spent reading the newspaper or watching T.V. Lorne Sanny of the Navigators wrote an excellent booklet, *How to Spend a Day in Prayer.* If you ever get a whole day in which to cultivate intimacy with God, you'll have to plan for it. It will never just happen. Hire a baby-sitter if need be. Take along a Bible, a notebook and a hymn book.

Ask God at the beginning of each day to remind you throughout the day to use your moments for fellowship with Him. The more you do it the easier it becomes, like any other habit. Withdraw often into the secret place of the heart.

"True intimacy with anyone, most of all God," wrote Graham Scroggie, "is not a thing that can be assumed at will; it is the outcome alone of dwelling 'in the secret place of the Most High and abiding under the shadow of Shaddai.'"[18] (Shaddai: the All-Bountiful One.)

I keep asking
that the God of our Lord Jesus Christ,
the glorious Father,
may give you the Spirit of wisdom and revelation,
so that you may know Him better.

(Ephesians 1:17; italics added)

"It is of no advantage for man to know much
unless
he lives according to what he knows."[19]

Study   and   Discussion   Questions

1. How would you answer someone who says, "We cannot **know** God"?

2. How do you know that God is a Person — a Person whom you can know personally?

3. Consider Job 42:5,6. What did Job mean? Why had he come to this conclusion?

4. Is anything hindering you from knowing God Intimately? What things are hindering you? Do you really want to know Him better? What are you willing to do about it?

5. Tell about someone you know (or someone whose biography you have read) who evidently knows God intimately. Discuss ways this intimate knowledge was developed.

6. Ask yourself, "How can I **know** God?" Not merely, 'How can I know about God?" And not, 'How can I have an acquaintance with God?" Nor even, "How can I be saved from hell?" But, "How can I really know Him?" Phil. 3:10.

TEN TEACHING HINTS

1. *Be selective.* The chapters in this book may be used by home Bible study groups and Sunday school classes as well as larger and more formal classes in Bible colleges and seminaries. Select those ideas from this list and elsewhere which meet the needs of your group.

2. *Use variety.* Frequent change of teaching methods generates interest. However, mere variety for its own sake is not spiritually productive. For each lesson use the method or combination of methods which will best accomplish your aim for that particular lesson.

3. *Involve students.* I have found that a workshop atmosphere is more effective and more appreciated for this study than the constant use of the lecture method.

    a. The Study and Discussion Questions after each lesson can be used frequently in class or small groups.
    b. Use classwork. Prepare mimeographed guide questions for topical Bible studies (such as: a study of the Tabernacle and New Testament priestly ministry, a study of prayer warfare passages, etc.) or for detailed expository studies of great prayers of the Bible and other pertinent passages. Guide your students in digging out truth for themselves.
    c. Use hymn books, mimeographed sheets, or an overhead projector to teach a prayer hymn and lead your group in a discussion of the concepts it includes.

d. Use neighbor nudging," a technique in which group members study together in pairs. One member of the team of two looks up the Scripture portions indicated on a mimeographed sheet or on the chalkboard: his neighbor takes notes as they discuss the verses and questions together. You may have the whole class working on the same material or have small groups working on related topics. Follow with a time of sharing.

4. *Motivate discussion.* If your group has more than ten members, you will do well to have several groups of 6-8 members. Appoint a leader for each group. (See: Ten Proven Helps for Leading a Small Group Discussion.) I usually have 60-70 students each year in my Bible school course on "Principles of Effective Prayer," so I form about 9 groups. Several groups can meet in the same large room, but I still have to use several available rooms. In a home Bible study, put groups in your living room, kitchen, rec room, or out on the patio if weather permits.

5. *Give assignments.* To maintain a workshop atmosphere will require preparation by participants as well as by the teacher. It is worthwhile to let the group know this at the first meeting so you can have a group which is interested enough in the study to put some effort into it. However, be careful not to overload them. For instance, no group should be assigned a written lesson involving all eight Study and Discussion Questions which follow Lesson 1. If you ask your group to answer three or four of them, allow each individual to decide which ones to answer. This will give more variety in the discussion because members will choose to answer different questions. Often, only one question will be enough for one assignment.

6. *Invite speakers.* If you know someone whose prayer ministry is blessed of the Lord, invite him or her to share with your group. Don't limit your choices to professional Christian workers. Whether your prospective guest is a mechanic or

missionary, a painter or a pastor, be sure you get a person whose prayer life has God's blessing. Or use an occasional tape recording from the series on prayer by Rev. Dick Sipley available from Canadian Revival Fellowship, Box 584, Regina, Sask., Canada S4P 3A3.

7. *Be creative.* I like to start each prayer class by projecting an overhead transparency on which I have printed a choice Scripture verse, a brief quotation from some author who has dealt well with the day's topic, and a prayer chorus or verse of a hymn. This is on the screen while the class is arriving and getting settled. Then we open the class by singing the song, and someone leads in prayer. If you like this idea, use it. Or think and pray for some ideas to make your class interesting and perhaps a bit different. Don't be afraid to give a well-prepared lecture occasionally.

8. *Avoid intellectualism.* Effectiveness in prayer is unrelated to scholarship. However, I don't want students in my class who want credits without work, so I require assignments and projects and give points in each of these categories. For a grade, I average the assignment points and the project points. But I prefer not to use tests in this course. It works out that slow students can earn A's as well as bright students. You see, I know some non-scholarly people who have learned deep and wonderful secrets of prayer. People can pray well who can't take tests well.

9. *Read widely.* There are literally scores of good books on prayer, some classics that are out of print, and some current publications. You will find many of them quoted in this textbook. Refer to: NOTES. Some are general books on prayer which deal with a variety of prayer topics. Others are written on specific topics such as intercession, prayer warfare, the authority of the believer, the Lord's Prayer, the High Priestly Prayer, or Jesus' prayer habits and teachings. And don't overlook biographies, especially missionary biographies,

which are often rich in principles of prayer and answers to prayer. If you have a wealth of such reading experiences, you will be able to draw on it to teach with spontaneity and enthusiasm.

10. *Share personally.* Tell your class what God has done for you. Focus on Him so it won't come across as boasting. Don't hesitate to admit your struggles. Encourage your group members to share, also.

TEN PROVEN HELPS FOR LEADING A SMALL-GROUP DISCUSSION

Having asked God's blessing on your discussion...

1. Do not lecture. Your job is to *motivate* and *guide discussion*.

2. Promote *discussion*, not merely question and answer.

3. Prepare. Think out questions ahead of time which will promote discussion. Such questions cannot be answered with a "Yes" or "No," because these answers do not lead anywhere. Use questions which ask for the sharing of opinions. Here is the difference:

    > *Non*-discussion question: Do you like Dr. Zwemer's definition of prayer?
    >
    > *Discussion* question: Why is Dr. Zwemer's definition of prayer a humbling thought?

4. Here are some good key words and phrases to use in preparing discussion questions: How? Why? Who? What? When? Where? Your opinion? The reason for? What do you think about this? If you were in this situation?

5. In addition to questions given in the text and your own prepared questions, ask spontaneous questions which grow out of the discussion. This requires careful listening.

6. Do not ask too many questions. If the discussion is lively and on target, let it go without interrupting to ask questions.

7. Motivate quiet members to enter the discussion by calling them by name and asking them questions about which you are sure they will have some opinions. Caution: Do not embarrass them with questions they may not be able to answer.

8. Control the discussion by politely preventing one or two from monopolizing it. Instead of scolding those who tend to lecture or allowing it to continue, just say, "Thank you, Bill, for your opinion. Mary, what is your idea on this matter?" Or, "I would also like to hear John's opinion." Or, ask a specific question of a quiet member.

9. Keep the discussion on the subject by saying, "That is an interesting observation. Now, what are your thoughts about...?" and repeat or re-phrase the question you want discussed.

10. Allow time for conversational prayer (Chapter 4). Don't feel that you have to discuss every point in the lesson or every question in the STUDY AND DISCUSSION QUESTIONS. It is more important to put into practice the principles of prayer you are learning.

PROJECTS

The following are suggested projects. I require students to do five projects for an "A" grade. I grant 40 points for a fully satisfactory project, which gives a maximum of 200 points for the five projects. Each daily assignment receives a score of 10 for a fully satisfactory answer, making a total of 200 for 20 lessons. The project scores and assignment scores are added and divided by four for the final grade.

1. A *book report* on 100 pages read from a book on the *general topic* of prayer. This type of book will contain chapters on such topics as: the meaning of prayer, how to pray, hindrances to prayer, waiting on God, praying in the Spirit, intercession, prayer warfare, praying for missionaries, claiming the promises, praying in Jesus' name (any general collection of prayer topics).

2. A *book report* on 100 pages read from a book on some *specific prayer topic*. It may be a book on any one of these topics: Jesus' prayer habits, the authority of the believer, conversational prayer, the Lord's prayer, John 17, prayers of the Apostle Paul, the ministry of intercession (any prayer topic to which the entire book is devoted).

3. A *book report* on 100 pages read from a *biography* of a great prayer warrior.

Form for book reports:
Upper left: category of the book (general, specific, biography).
Upper right: name and address of the student.
Name of author and title of book.
Number of pages read.
Report of 500-1000 words. In the first two categories focus on principles taught. For a biography summarize the person's life story as it regards his prayer life. Anything quoted should be in quotation marks and have a footnote to identify the source. Evaluate the book as to its strong and/or weak points.

4. A *card-file of prayer verses.* Make a card file of 100 3" by 5" cards of *choice* Scripture verses and passages which relate to prayer. Use any helps you wish, but do not confine yourself to copying just any verses on prayer which you find in a concordance or topical index. *Choose* verses which you might later memorize or which will be readily available to you if you are called upon to speak in a Bible study or to a prayer meeting, verses which are rich in meaning: principles, promises, injunctions to pray, etc. In using a concordance, check these words: pray, prayer, praying, ask, petition, supplication, intercession, thanks, confess. Use the following form:

PETITION	**Matthew 7:7**

Ask, and it shall be given you;
    seek, and ye shall find;
        knock, and it shall be opened unto you.

Use the version of your choice. Here are some good categories in which to arrange your verse cards, but use any categories you wish. At the beginning of each category put a tab on the card indicating the category like this:

Adoration

Admonitions to pray
Adoration
Answers to prayer
Benedictions
Communion
Conditions of prayer
Confession
Contrition
Definiteness in prayer
Faith
Fasting and prayer
Forgiveness in relation
     to prayer
Hindrances to prayer

Holy Spirit & prayer
Humility
Importunity
Imprecation
Intercession
Intensity
Jesus' name
Jesus' prayers
Jesus' teachings
Missions
"No" answers
Praise
Promises
Public prayers

Purpose in prayer
Requests
Revival praying
Secret prayer
Seeking
Thanksgiving
Time for prayer
Unity in prayer
Universality of
     prayer
Warfare
Will of God
Worship

5. *Essay.* Write a research paper of about 2000 words on the prayer topic of your choice. Use any helps you wish (concordance, word-study books, commentaries, books on prayer, periodicals, etc.). Use standard footnotes and bibliography. Footnotes may appear at the bottom of each page or at the end of the essay.

Suggested topics:

Great Answers to Prayer in the Bible

Jesus' Personal Prayer Habits

Great Intercessory Prayers in the Bible

John 17

The Disciples' Prayer ("The Lord's Prayer")

The Prayer Ministry of the Apostle Paul

The High Priestly Ministry of Jesus

The Prayer Life of the Early Church

Conditions of Successful Prayer

Thanksgiving in Prayer

Praise

United Prayer

Private Prayer

A character study of any person in the Bible in relation to his/ her prayer life: Abraham, Jacob, Moses. Samuel, Hannah, David, Solomon, Hezekiah, Elijah, Elisha, Ezra. Nehemiah, etc.

A study of prayer in any particular book of the Bible (such as James)

A sermon based on some prayer topic (such as those above or those suggested for the card-file)...expository, topical, or textual...based on careful exegesis and written in good homiletical style

6. *Original project.* If you have an idea for a project you would like to work on, write a description of it and tell how many hours you expect to spend on it. Submit this to your teacher or group leader for approval.

NOTES

— 1 —

1. Watchman Nee, *Let Us Pray* (New York: Christian Fellowship Publishers, Inc.,1977), p.1.
2. Samuel Chadwick, *God Listens* (Westchester: Good News Pub., 1973), pp. 10,12.
3. Elmer V. Thompson, "Prayer in Four Words," tract (Coral Gables: Worldteam).
4. Thompson.
5. Helen Roseveare, M.D., story told at Prairie Bible Institute's World Mission Conference, used by permission.
6. R. Earl Allen, *Prayers That Changed History* (Nashville: Broadman, 1977), p.16.
7. Thompson.
8. Wayne R. Spear, *The Theology of Prayer* (Grand Rapids: Baker, 1979), p. 7.
9. An Unknown Christian, *The Kneeling Christian* (Grand Rapids: Zondervan, 1945), p. 53.
10. Rosalind Rinker, *Prayer: Conversing with God* (Grand Rapids: Zondervan, 1959), n.p.
11. Alhaji A.I. Umaru Sanda [Imam] , Nigerian Air Force Training Command, Kaduna, "The Fast of Ramadan," *New Nigerian*, 5 Aug., 1977.
12. George Sweeting, "Harnessing Your Prayer Power," *Moody Monthly*, Vol. 75, No. 7, Mar., 1975, p. 51.

13. J.O. Sanders, *Prayer Power Unlimited* (Chicago: Moody, 1977), p.11.
14. William M. Runyan, "Lord I Have Shut the Door." Copyright by Hope Publishing Co. Used by permission.
15. Nee, p.11.

— 2 —

1. F.J. Huegel, *Successful Praying* (Minneapolis: Dimension Books, Bethany Fellowship, Inc., 1959), p. 14.
2. Huegel, p. 15.
3. S.D. Gordon, *Quiet Talks on Prayer* (Grand Rapids: Baker, 1980), p. 129.
4. O. Hallesby, *Prayer* (Minneapolis: Augsburg, 1959), p. 37.

— 3 —

1. Gordon, pp. 12, 13.
2. Andrew Murray, *With Christ in the School of Prayer* (Old Tappan: Fleming H. Revell, 1953), p. 26.
3. Hallesby, p. 89.
4. Ralph Spaulding Cushman, "The Secret," *Masterpieces of Religious Verse*, ed. James Dalton Morrison (New York: Harper and Brothers, 1948), No. 1338.
5. Dick Eastman, *No Easy Road* (Grand Rapids: Baker, 1971), p. 124.
6. Gordon, p. 151.
7. Gordon, p. 226.
8. E.M. Bounds, *Power Through Prayer* (Grand Rapids: Zondervan, 1962), p. 24.
9. Andrew Murray, *The Secret of Adoration* (Fort Washington: Christian Literature Crusade, 1979), p. 27.

— 4 —

1. J. Edwin Orr, *Prayer, Its Deeper Dimensions* (London: Marshall, Morgan and Scott, 1963), p. 21; quoted in J.O. Sanders, *Prayer Power Unlimited*, p. 133.

2. Sanders, p. 133.
3. Watchman Nee, *The Prayer Power of the Church* (New York: Christian Fellowship Publishers, Inc., 1973), pp. 18, 22, 23.
4. Andrew Murray, *The Ministry of Intercession* (New York: Fleming H. Revell 1898), p.13.
5. Gordon, p. 130.
6. Sanders, p. 133.
7. Evelyn Christenson, *What Happens When Women Pray?* (Wheaton: Victor Books, Scripture Publications, 1976), pp. 38-51.
8. Rinker, p.23.
9. Rinker, p.19.

— 5 —

1. G.T. Manley, "God, Names of" ed. J.D. Douglas, *The New Bible Dictionary* (Grand Rapids: Wm. B. Eerdmans, 1962), p. 478.
2. Spear, p. 18.
3. Spear, p. 23.
4. Doris Salter, *Talks on the Prayer Life* (Brooklyn: Bible Christian Union), p. 38.
5. Spear, p. 25.
6. Spear, p. 25.
7. Spear, p. 28.
8. C.F. Keil and F. Delitzsch, *Biblical Commentary on the Old Testament:* Psalms, 3 (Grand Rapids:Wm B. Eerdmans, 1952), p. 26.
9. Sam Walter Foss, "The Prayer of Cyrus Brown" In *Stars to Steer By*, ed. Louis Untermeyer (New York: Harcourt Brace, 1941), pp. 301, 302. Quoted in *If You Haven't Got a Prayer,* Stephen M. Crotts (Downers Grove: Inter-Varsity, 1978), pp. 16, 17.
10. Ralph A. Herring, *The Cycle of Prayer* (Wheaton: Tyndale House, 1966), p. 55.
11. Herring, pp. 55-56.
12. Phil Keller, *A Layman Looks at the Lords Prayer* (Chicago: Moody, 1976), p.11.

—6—

1. Sanders, p. 9.
2. Keller, p. 45.
3. Sanders, p. 10.
4. Sanders, p. 11.
5. Charles R. Eerdman, *The Gospel of John* (Philadelphia: Westminister, 1944), p. 47.
6. Wentworth Pike, *Worldwide Journeys in Prayer* (unpublished book manuscript), n.p.
7. Norene Bond, "Our Prayer by the Red Sea," *Africa Now* (Scarborough: Sudan Interior Mission, May-June, 1976), p. 15. (Used by permission.)
8. Eugene Myers Harrison, *Giants of the Missionary Trail* (Chicago: Scripture Press, 1954), p. 26.
9. A.B. Simpson, "My Trust," *Hymns of the Christian Life* (Harrisburg: Christian Publications), p. 451.
10. Pike, n.p.

—7—

1. *Webster's New World Dictionary* , College Edition (Toronto: Nelson, Foster, & Scott Ltd.,1960.)
2. A.W. Tozer, *The Knowledge of the Holy* (New York: Harper and Brothers, 1961), p. 9.
3. Tozer, p. 80.

—8—

1. A. J. Pollock, *The Tabernacle's Typical Teaching* (London: The Central Bible Truth Depot), p. 91.
2. Keil and Delitzsch, *Pentateuch*, 2, 399.
3. Murray, *With Christ*, Preface.
4. Bounds, p. 26.
5. Gordon, p. 18.
6. Bounds, p. 27.

— 9 —

1. Sanders, p. 56.
2. Eerdman, p. 128.
3. Albert Barnes, *Barnes' Notes on the New Testament* (Grand Rapids: Kregel, 1978), p. 334.
4. Everett F. Harrison, "John," *The Wycliffe Bible Commentary*, ed. Charles F. Pfeiffer & Everett F. Harrison (Chicago: Moody, 1962), p. 1105.
5. Samuel Chadwick, *The Path of Prayer* (London: Hodder and Stoughton, 1975), p. 38.
6. Sanders, p. 57.
7. Murray, *With Christ*, pp. 133, 134.
8. Philip R. Newell, Foreword: James W. Thirtle, *In Jesus' Name, Amen!* (Leesburg: The Great Commission Prayer League, 1977), pp. 7, 8.
9. James W. Thirtle, *In Jesus' Name Amen!* p. 24.
10. Thirtle, p. 24.
11. Thirtle, p. 42.
12. Torrey, *The Power of Prayer* (Grand Rapids: Zondervan, 1924), p. 98.
13. Torrey, p. 100.
14. Chadwick, *Path*, p. 52.

— 10 —

1. Theodore H. Epp, *Praying with Authority* (Lincoln: Back to the Bible, 1965), p. 68.
2. Epp, pp. 72,73.
3. J. A. MacMillan, "The Authority of the Believer," pamphlet (Harrisburg: Christian Publications, Inc., n.d.) pp. 5, 6.
4. R. C. H. Lenski, *The Interpretation of John's Gospel* (Columbus: The Wartburg Press, 1942) p. 1041.

— 11 —

1. T.S. Rendall, "The Battle is the Lord's!" *The Prairie Overcomer,* 53, No. 6 (June, 1980), 344.

2. Rendall, p. 344.
3. H.A. Ironside, *Expository Notes on the Prophet Isaiah* (Neptune: Loizeaux Brothers, 1952), p. 146.
4. Keil and Delitzsch, *Isaiah*. 1, 433, 434.
5. Gordon, p. 36.
6. Gordon, p. 37.
7. Gordon, p. 120.
8. Gordon, p. 28.
9. Theodore H. Epp, *How to Resist Satan* (Lincoln: Back to the Bible, 1958), pp. 26, 27.
10. Epp, *How to Resist Satan*, p. 28.
11. Epp, *How to Resist Satan*, p. 30.
12. Epp, *How to Resist Satan*, pp. 31, 32.
13. F. J. Perryman, " *Whom Resist"* (Leesburg: Great Commision Prayer League, 1979), p. 46.
14. Jessie Penn-Lewis, *The Spiritual Warfare* (Fort Washington: Christian Literature Crusade), p. 6.
15. Penn-Lewis, p. 15.
16. A. Sims, ed., *Prayer Warfare* (Grand Rapids: Zondervan), p. 20.
17. Sanders, p. 127.
18. F.J. Huegel, *The Mystery of Iniquity* (Minneapolis: Bethany Fellowship, 1968), p. 115.

— 12 —

1. Epp. *Praying with Authority*, p. 81.
2. Penn-Lewis, p. 6.
3. Huegel, *Successful Praying*, p. 62.
4. Mrs. Howard Taylor, *Behind the Ranges* (London: Lutterworth Press and the China Inland Mission, n.d.), p. 90.
5. Taylor, p. 91.
6. Sims, p. 14.
7. Epp, *Praying with Authority*, p. 85.
8. Oswald Chambers, *If Ye Shall Ask...*(London Marshall, Morgan & Scott, 1958), p. 17.
9. "Triumph," *The World Book Encyclopedia* (1974), 19, 365.
10. Sims, p. 18.

— 13 —

1. Sanders, p. 62.
2. Pike (unpub. mss.), n.p.
3. Andrew Murray, *Waiting on God* (London: Oliphants, 1961), pp. 7, 8.
4. Gordon, p. 162.
5. Jerome Hines, "The Voice Within," *Guideposts*, May, 1967. (Used by permission of Christian Arts, Inc. of which Hines is President.)
6. Gordon, p. 33.

— 14 —

1. Sanders, pp. 69, 70.
2. Johnstone, Patrick and Jason Mandryk, *Operation World* 6th Edition, Paternoster Publishing: Carlisle, UK, 2001.
3. Sanders, pp. 71-73.
4. Don Bjork, "Prayers God Doesn't Want to Answer," *Harvest Today* (Coral Gables, Fla.: Worldteam, April-June, 1977).
5. Pike (unpub. mss.) n.p.
6. John R. Rice, pp. 141, 142.
7. Pike (unpub. mss.), n.p.

— 15 —

1. G. H. C. MacGregor, *True Praying in the Spirit* (Leesburg: Great Commission Prayer League, 1978), pp. 14, 15.
2. Henry W. Frost, *Effective Praying* (New York: Harper & Brothers, 1925), pp. 71-86.
3. Pike (unpub. mss.), n.p.
4. Hallesby, pp. 98, 99.
5. Macgregor, p. 33.
6. Gordon, p. 153.

— 16 —

1. Chadwick, *The Path of Prayer*, p. 89.
2. Eric Fife, *Prayer – Common Sense and the Bible* (Grand Rapids: Zondervan, 1976), p. 9.
3. John Bisagno, *The Power of Positive Praying* (Grand Rapids: Zondervan, 1965), p. 10.
4. Harold Lindsell, *When You Pray* (Grand Rapids: Baker, 1969), p. 130.
5. Chadwick, *The Path of Prayer*, p. 94.
6. Elmer V. Thompson, "Worldteam Intercessors" prayer letter (Coral Gables: Worldteam, 1980).
7. Chadwick, *The Path of Prayer*, pp. 94, 95.

— 17 —

1. Peter Deyneka, *Much Prayer – Much Power!* (Grand Rapids: Zondervan, 1958), pp. 24, 25.
2. Paul E. Billheimer, *Destined for the Throne* (Fort Washington: Christian Literature Crusade, 1975), p. 65.
3. Billheimer, p. 67.
4. Pike (unpub. mss.), n.p.
5. Pike (unpub. mss.), n.p.

— 18 —
No notes
— 19 —

1. Billheimer, p. 62.
2. Billheimer, p. 62.
3. J.O. Sanders, "Prayer: Strategic in Missions," tract (Overseas Missionary Fellowship: see list at end of Chapter 19.)
4. Johnstone, n.p.
5. OM Canada, 212 West St., Port Colborne, ON L3K 4E3, Canada; Gabriel Resources, PO Box 1047, Waynesboro, GA 30830 USA, Tel: 706-554-1594, Fax: 706-554-7444, Email: gabriel@omlit.om.org
6. Intercessors for America, P.O. Box D, Elyria, Ohio 44035, U.S.A.
7. Alfred, Lord Tennyson, "Morte d' Arthur." in *The Encyclopedia*

of Religious Quotations, ed. & comp. Frank S. Mead (Westwood: Revell, 1965), p. 348.

8. Murray, *With Christ*, pp. 52, 53.
9. Steve Read, "Action News" (P.O. Box 2068, Lynwood, WA 98036), Spring, 1981.

— 20 —

1. Andrew Murray, *The Secret of Adoration* (Fort Washington: Christian Literature Crusade, 1979), p. 18.
2. D.M. M'Intyre, *The Hidden Life of Prayer* (Minneapolis: Dimension Books, 1971), p. 79.
3. A.W. Tozer, *The Knowledge of the Holy* (New York: Harper & Brothers, 1961), p. 18.
4. J. Oswald Sanders, *Enjoying Intimacy with God* (Chicago: Moody Press, 1980), p. 11.
5. T.S. Rendall, *In God's School* (Three Hills: Prairie Press, 1971), p. 123.
6. J.I. Packer, *Knowing God* (Toronto: Hodder and Stoughton, 1973), p. 26.
7. John White, *Drawing Near to God* (Downers Grove: Inter-Varsity , 1977), p. 100.
8. Stephen Charnock, *Discourses upon the Existence and Attributes of God* (1853; rpt. Grand Rapids: Baker, 1979) I, 407.
9. Charnock, p. 414.
10. Packer, p. 94.
11. Tozer, p. 9.
12. White, p. 16.
13. White, p. 17.
14. Rendall, pp. 155-164.
15. Sanders, *Intimacy*, pp. 110, 111.
16. A.W. Tozer, *Pursuit of God* (Harrisburg: Christian Publications, 1948), p. 7.
17. Sanders, *Intimacy*, p. 102.
18. W. Graham Scroggie, *Method in Prayer* (London: Pickering and Inglis, Rev. Ed., 1955), p. 84.
19. Jo Petty, Comp., *Wings of Silver* (Norwalk: C.R. Gibson, 1967), p. 78.

Other fantastic titles available from Gabriel Publishing!

Gabriel
Publishing

Contact us for details on any of these books -
PO Box 1047, 129 Mobilization Dr., Waynesboro, GA 30830
Tel.: (706) 554-1594   Fax: (706) 554-7444
E-mail: gabriel@omlit.om.org

Coming soon... *Worldwide Journeys in Prayer*
by Wentworth Pike!
ISBN: 1-884543-66-9

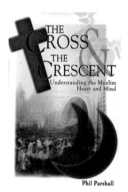

The Cross & The Crescent
Understanding the Muslim Heart and Mind
Phil Parshall

ISBN: 1-884543-68-5
Living as a missionary among Muslims, Phil Parshall understands the Muslim heart and mind. In this very personal book, he looks at what Muslims believe and how their beliefs affect - and don't affect their behavior. He compares and contrasts Muslim and Christian views on the nature of God, sacred Scriptures, worship, sin and holiness, mysticism, Jesus and Muhammed, human suffering and the afterlife.

101 Ways to Change Your World
Geoff Tunnicliffe
ISBN: 1-884543-47-2

Geoff Tunnicliffe has compiled an invaluable collection of ways to change the world in his newly revised *101 Ways to Change Your World*. In addition to 101 practical ways to put faith into action, Tunnicliffe has also included statistics and resources for individuals desiring to make a difference in God's World.

Street Boy
Fletch Brown
ISBN: 1-884543-64-2

Jaime Jorka, a street boy in the Philippines, lays a challenge before the missionary whose wallet he has stolen - and discovers for himself what Jesus can do. This true-to-life story reveals the plight of street children worldwide and shows that they too can be won to Christ. "The lot of the street children of the world is a guilty secret that needs to be exposed and addressed. This book does it admirably." - Stuart Briscoe

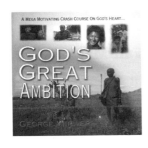

God's Great Ambition
Dan & Dave Davidson & George Verwer
ISBN: 1-884543-69-3

This unique collection of quotes and Scriptures has been designed to motivate thousands of people into action in world missions. George Verwer and the Davidsons are well-known for their ministries of mission mobilization as speakers and writers. Prepare to be blasted out of your comfort zone by this spiritual dynamite!

Operation World
21st Century Edition
Patrick Johnstone & Jason Mandryk
ISBN: 1-85078-357-8

The definitive prayer handbook for the church is now available in its 21st Century Edition containing 80% new material! Packed with informative and inspiring fuel for prayer about every country in the world, *Operation World* is essential reading for anyone who wants to make a difference! Over 2,000,000 in print!

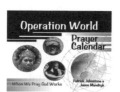

Operation World Prayer Calendar
ISBN: 1-884543-59-6

Containing clear graphics and useful geographic, cultural, economic and political statistics on 122 countries of the world, the *Operation World Prayer Calendar* is a fantastic tool to help you pray intelligently for the world. Pray for each country for three days and see how God works!

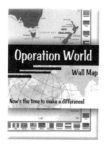

Operation World Wall Map
Laminated or Folded

This beautiful, full-color wall map is a great way to locate the countries each day that you are praying for and build a global picture. Not only an excellent resource for schools, churches and offices but a valuable tool for the home.

Youth & Missions
Leading the Way
Paul Borthwick
ISBN: 1-884543-49-9
1-884543-37-5

In *Youth and Missions*, noted author and missions professor Paul Borthwick has created a practical handbook filled with principles, guidelines and examples of how to help young people grow in their understanding of the world and their role in it. He effectively addresses the great need for younger men and women to rise to the challenge of leadership in the growing leadership vacuum in his book *Leading the Way*.

Dr. Thomas Hale's Tales of Nepal

Living Stones of the Himalayas
(1-884543-35-9)
Don't Let the Goats Eat the Loquat Trees
(1-884543-36-7)
On the Far Side of Liglig Mountain
(1-884543-34-0)

These fascinating accounts of the true-life stories of doctors Tom and Cynthia Hale share everyday and incredible experiences of life with the beguiling character and personalities of the Nepalese people. In sharing these experiences the reader is truly transported to a most enchanting land.